THE CONDUCT OF LIFE

By Ralph Waldo Emerson

A Philosophical Reading

Edited and Introduced by
H. G. Callaway

University Press of America,® Inc.
Lanham · Boulder · New York · Toronto · Oxford

Copyright © 2006 by
University Press of America,® Inc.
4501 Forbes Boulevard
Suite 200
Lanham, Maryland 20706
UPA Acquisitions Department (301) 459-3366

PO Box 317
Oxford
OX2 9RU, UK

Library of Congress Control Number: 2005938643
ISBN-13: 978-0-7618-3410-6 (clothbound : alk. paper)
ISBN-10: 0-7618-3410-9 (clothbound : alk. paper)
ISBN-13: 978-0-7618-3411-3 (paperback : alk. paper)
ISBN-10: 0-7618-3411-7 (paperback : alk. paper)

The Religion which is afraid of science dishonors God and commits suicide.

Ralph Waldo Emerson in his Journal, 4 March 1831

What point of morals, of manners, of economy, of philosophy, of religion, of taste, of the conduct of life, has he not settled? What mystery has he not signified his knowledge of? What office, or function, or district of man's work, has he not remembered? What king has he not taught state, as Talma taught Napoleon? What maiden has not found him finer than her delicacy? What lover has he not outloved? What sage has he not outseen? What gentleman has he not instructed in the rudeness of his behavior?

Ralph Waldo Emerson in *Representative Men*, "Shakespeare, or the Poet" (1850)

Work is victory.

Ralph Waldo Emerson in *The Conduct of Life*, "Worship" (1860)

TABLE OF CONTENTS

FOREWORD

The present edition of Ralph Waldo Emerson's book, *The Conduct of Life*, closely follows the original 1860 edition. This volume is primarily intended to present Emerson's work in a readable and understandable form. The chief difference of the present volume, beyond the annotations and the provision of a chronology, a bibliography, and an index, is that Emerson's nineteenth-century spellings have been modernized throughout. This volume is intended as a reading and study edition, and the modernization of the prose spellings, together with the notes, index, and bibliography will assist students and the educated public in a deeper reading of Emerson as a contribution to American and to world philosophy.

Emerson can be read as literature, and his methods are literary in character. He is a chief figure of the New England Renaissance of the mid-nineteenth century. Yet the academic compartmentalization of Emerson as a figure of American literature has often prevented or inhibited the appreciation of his contributions on philosophical topics of general interest. Thus, the present volume emphasizes Emerson's philosophy: freedom and fate; creativity and established culture; faith, experience, and evidence; the individual, God, and the world; unity and dualism; moral law, grace, and compensation; wealth, success, and dissipation, etc. My premise is that we need to look back at Emerson as philosopher, especially at his mature work, to better appreciate his distinctive outlook and to better understand his position in relation to prior and subsequent philosophy.

As much as Emerson's philosophy is centered in his conception of self-reliance, it is also marked by universalism and pantheistic idealism, and centered in the confluence of diverse philosophical and social-political traditions. Part of understanding Emerson, then, requires our establishing elements of the broader context of his work. We should be able to trace his intellectual heritage through its general Platonic, Idealist, and pantheistic background and through the social, religious, and even political influences which formed the individualism of the Reformation, of the English Civil Wars of the 1640's and the American Revolution, and of the Unitarian turn away from Calvinism. We need to understand Emerson's emphasis on each and on all; and understanding Emerson as individualist and as universalist may help us better understand the similar combination we find in the career of American history.

Often Emerson was not greatly concerned to define with precision his relation to the doctrines and tendencies of prior thought. We find instead frequent listings of thinkers and actors in history, evoked to emphasize a particular point. Yet we know, too, that Emerson was a deeply learned and well-read scholar. Thus, to understand Emerson's philosophy in greater depth, we need to see, on occasion, where he agrees, differs, or criticizes a Plotinus, or Böhme, a Kant, Schelling, or Goethe, a Bacon, Calvin, Cromwell, Burke, Voltaire, or Webster. We need to understand something of his relation to prior traditions, to his contemporaries, a Coleridge, Carlyle, or Channing, and also something of his substantial relation to the subsequent pragmatist tradition, especially C. S. Peirce, William James and John Dewey. The present volume is intended to help in the contextualization of our contemporary understanding of Emerson's philosophical contributions, innovations, and subsequent influence.

The text has been worked over fully anew, the most important of Emerson's corrections to the 1860 edition are included. Beyond tracing ideas and connections of interest in the footnotes, definitions for words and concepts from Emerson's impressive vocabulary are supplied, which the student or general reader may otherwise be inclined to pass over too lightly. In exploring Emerson's references and authors, I have often found that some brief suggestions from various articles in the *Encyclopedia Britannica* proved a useful starting place, and these notes have sometimes survived, as amended or elaborated in the annotations, usually by reformulation or abbreviated or as combined with other materials. The same work proved useful in hunting for Emerson's readings and the connected background literature, as detailed in the Bibliography, and this provided a check on the annotations. With some few exceptions, definitions have been adapted or checked against the *Merriam Webster Collegiate Dictionary*, tenth edition, cross-checked and amended on the basis of similar sources. Notes to the text by Emerson are identified as such, and all others are by the editor. Cross-reference between annotated names is provided for by the Index.

INTRODUCTION

Emerson on Creativity in Thought and Action

The opening essay of Emerson's 1860 book, *The Conduct of Life*,[1] posed, in that fateful year of threatening Civil War and disunion, the philosophical problem of human freedom and fate. The essay "Fate" is followed in the present book by a series of essays on related themes, including: "Power," "Wealth," "Culture," "Worship," "Beauty" and "Illusions." The central question of the volume is, "How shall I live?" Appreciating both our freedom and its limits, we understand the vitality of power to acquire what wealth is needed to scale the corrections and heights of culture and worship, find beauty in life and human society, wary still of the illusions. Overall, the book is a call for creative solutions. Yet the nation, in the year of Abraham Lincoln's election, seemed fated to war or disunion in spite of all its dedication to freedom.

1. Fate, Thought, and Freedom

The opening essay elaborates the preliminary point that "in our first steps to gain our wishes, we come upon immovable limitations." That there are limitations to the fulfillment of our wishes and desires, no one doubts. Yet, these *are* limitations to existing powers to fulfill our wishes and desires. Where we find limitations to power, then we find power, too. "If we must accept Fate," Emerson says, "we are not less compelled to affirm liberty, the significance of the individual, the grandeur of duty, the power of character." Limitation also has its limits.

"Every spirit makes its house," he says, affirming freedom and power, though "afterwards the house confines the spirit." So, we need on occasion to get out of or transcend that self-fabricated house and explore the larger world and its potentialities. Emerson recognizes that every solution brings new problems. The essay "Fate" is, overall, a forceful affirmation of human freedom, though it dwells on all those elements of life which bring us to doubt and hesitate. Emerson's aim is to find a practical balance.[2]

"We have to consider two things: power and circumstance." What power we will have depends partly on recognizing the circumstances which confine and define it. "The Circumstance is Nature. Nature is, what you may do. There is much you may not. We have two things, the circumstance, and the life. Once we thought, positive power was all. Now we learn, that negative power, or circumstance, is half." Or, in more personal terms, "A man's power is hooped in by a necessity, which, by many experiments, he touches on every side, until he learns its arc." The extent of our freedom is both a philosophical and an experimental question, and since we ever lack omniscience and omnipotence, the experiments can never completely cease. "Fate, then, is a name for facts not yet passed under the fire of thought; for causes which are unpenetrated." Though thought penetrates or dissolves the impact of fate as non-comprehended circumstances, circumstances both old and new continue adamantly to limit the sphere of freedom. We never achieve complete power or freedom in our growth: there are always things we can do and others we cannot.

A key to Emerson's solution to the problems of fate and freedom is found at the end of the poem, "Fate," which prefaces the essay. "The foresight that awaits," he says there, restating the prior conclusion suggested in the poem, "Is the same Genius that creates." The poem links freedom to the human power of creative thought, which allows us to understand lawful regularity, foresee events, and sometimes exercise control of them. The conclusion of the essay is summarized in the opening poem:

> Delicate omens traced in air
> To the lone bard true witness bare;
> Birds with auguries on their wings
> Chanted undeceiving things
> Him to beckon, him to warn;
> Well might then the poet scorn
> To learn of scribe or courier
> Hints writ in vaster character;
> And on his mind, at dawn of day,
> Soft shadows of the evening lay.
> For the prevision is allied
> Unto the thing so signified;
> Or say, the foresight that awaits
> Is the same Genius that creates.

The poem is not the argument, nor is it the inquiry on fate and freedom. The poem summarizes and illuminates the inquiry. It may plausibly be thought to illuminate the point that our inquiries are central in the practical problems of freedom and fate.

The perspective is complex: "even thought itself is not above Fate: that too must act according to eternal laws, and all that is willful and fantastic in it is in opposition to its fundamental essence." Thus, Emerson turns in degree from his musing cultivation of romantic insights into nature to "learn of scribe or courier," to his study, for "previsions." There he looks to find "Hints writ in vaster character." There is a strong anti-nominalist theme in Emerson's philosophy. Creative thought requires more disciplined method, though Emerson remains a "poet-philosopher," and something of the secularized preacher, in his exposition and in his rhetoric. He never departs from his conviction of the value of an artful style, immersed in genuine piety and religious rhetoric, yet he insists that there are truths to be discovered. The aim of avoiding the merely fantastic requires observance of "eternal laws of thought." These, too, structure that "soul which animates Nature;" and "all successful men" are "causationists," believing "there was not a weak or a cracked link in the chain that joins the first and last of things."

"Intellect annuls Fate," says Emerson, partly as we may suppose, by breaking down heretofore unpenetrated circumstance into a collection of laws, regularities, and facts. "So far as a man thinks, he is free." Yet this freedom is always limited however much it may expand. No genuine intellect ignores confining realities, including the need of preparation and study. "Just as much intellect as you add, so much organic power. He who sees through the design, presides over it, and must will that which must be. We sit and rule, and, though we sleep, our dream will come to pass. Our thought, though it were only an hour old, affirms an oldest necessity, not to be separated from thought, and not to be separated from will." Clinging to our insights, our will and character are molded by the reality uncovered. "Of two men, each obeying his own thought, he whose thought is deepest will be the strongest character." Thought makes for freedom and power but also for character: a person who is equal to and can better remake and withstand confining circumstance.

"There are times, indeed," wrote philosopher John Dewey in 1903, "when one is inclined to regard Emerson's whole work as a hymn to intelligence, a paean to the all-creating, all-disturbing power of thought;" Dewey recognized the "final word of Emerson's philosophy," "the identity of Being, unqualified and immutable, with Character."[3] By thoughtfully building character, we acquire needed powers to control circumstances. For character is disposition to act and an integration of knowledge and emotion manifested in disciplined will.

Emerson argues as follows: "But insight is not will, nor is affection will. Perception is cold, and goodness dies in wishes; as Voltaire said, 'tis the misfortune of worthy people that they are cowards.'" Affection must be modified by thought and insight: "There must be a fusion of these two to generate the energy of will. There can be no driving force, except through the conversion of the man into his will, making him the will, and the will him." Yet this conversion is open to anyone who can set aside the miscellany of activity to focus on a purpose. "This is Emerson's revelation:" said philosopher William James also in 1903: "The point of any pen can be an epitome of reality; the commonest person's act, if genuinely actuated, can lay hold of eternity."[4]

Ralph Waldo Emerson (1803-1882) exercised a formative influence on American society and culture as the central figure of the nineteenth-century New England renaissance. He was born in Boston, the son and grandson of Unitarian ministers, and he trained for the same profession. Educated at the Harvard Divinity School, he was ordained and became a Boston pastor. But he left the ministry, because he felt himself unable, in good conscience, to administer the Lord's Supper. He wrote, lectured and traveled widely both in the United States and Europe, and in later years he ventured as far as Egypt. His success as a writer was phenomenal both in the U.S. and in Great Britain. He made his living by delivering public lectures and by writing.

2. Departures from Transcendentalism?

Though Emerson used it himself, "transcendentalism" is in some ways a misleading term for his philosophy. It better characterizes his early thought. Certainly, Emerson sought to transcend some things in American society. He was aware, too, of transcending his own prior views—going beyond them. We do well to translate the Latin-derived word, back into more vernacular Anglo-Saxon terms to appreciate what persists through the turns and developments of Emerson's thought. To "transcend" means, to "overcome," and we should ask about what Emerson sought to overcome. Moral purpose is central in Emerson's philosophy.

The word "Transcendentalism" is borrowed from Kant, indirectly as inspired by Coleridge.[5] Emerson was never properly a Kantian. What the word meant to Emerson, when he used it, was a commitment to Idealism. Emerson was both an "Idealist" and a self-defined "transcendentalist" in

1841, at the time he published his first series of *Essays*. He says so clearly in the following passage from "The Transcendentalist:"

> What is popularly called Transcendentalism among us, is Idealism; Idealism as it appears in 1842. As thinkers, mankind have ever divided into two sects, Materialists and Idealists; the first class founding on experience, the second on consciousness; the first class beginning to think from the data of the senses, the second class perceive that the senses are not final, and say, the senses give us representations of things, but what are the things themselves, they cannot tell. The materialist insists on facts, on history, on the force of circumstances, and the animal wants of man; the idealist on the power of Thought and of Will, on inspiration, on miracle, on individual culture. These two modes of thinking are both natural, but the idealist contends that his way of thinking is in higher nature. He concedes all that the other affirms, admits the impressions of sense, admits their coherency, their use and beauty, and then asks the materialist for his grounds of assurance that things are as his senses represent them. But I, he says, affirm facts not affected by the illusions of sense, facts which are of the same nature as the faculty which reports them, and not liable to doubt; facts which in their first appearance to us assume a native superiority to material facts, degrading these into a language by which the first are to be spoken; facts which it only needs a retirement from the senses to discern. Every materialist will be an idealist; but an idealist can never go backward to be a materialist.[6]

Fundamentally, Emerson's transcendentalism is set in opposition to "materialism" and the empiricist's emphasis on experience and sense perception. If we are now inclined to agree that "the senses are not final," then I think the most we will want to say in our contemporary empiricisms is that sense experience requires some interpretation. This is far from claiming that the senses cannot tell us about "the things themselves," though it does allow for occasional recognition of the "illusions of sense." If, in some tension with the quotation above, we equally accept no indubitable deliverances of reason and emphasize the possible delusions of interpretation, then in what ways should we continue to find Emerson's philosophy and his "transcending" of sensual materialism of interest?

We have room to think that Emerson overcame his own transcendentalism, though he retained the moral urgency of his dedication to overcome the moral materialism in which he saw the nation captured, say, a "nation conceived in liberty" to use Lincoln's phrase, but maintaining and cultivating pernicious financial interests and investments in human slavery. Though "the materialist insists on facts, on history, on the force of circumstances, and the animal wants of man," as Emerson saw the matter in 1842, he too came to emphasize these things, notably in his essay "Fate," addressing the "conduct of life." He admits yet seeks to counter-balance this emphasis on circumstance.

Part of the contemporary and systematic interest of the present book, then, is to understand how Emerson seeks to combine his later emphasis on circumstance while preserving his contrary early stress, so far as possible, "on the power of Thought and of Will, on inspiration, on miracle, on individual culture." Emerson gives us many a thread to follow in his development, and we need to understand in more concrete terms what he sought to overcome. In his "Lecture on the Times," from 1841, Emerson's social-intellectual aims stand out. He challenges a conservative establishment, that moneyed conservatism which says:

> 'I will hold fast; and to whom I will, will I give; and whom I will, will I exclude and starve:' so says Conservatism; and all the children of men attack the colossus in their youth, and all, or all but a few, bow before it when they are old. A necessity not yet commanded, a negative imposed on the will of man by his condition a deficiency in his force, is the foundation on which it rests. Let this side be fairly stated. Meantime, on the other part, arises Reform, and offers the sentiment of Love as an overmatch to this material might. I wish to consider well this affirmative side, which has a loftier port and reason than heretofore, which encroaches on the other every day, puts it out of countenance, out of reason, and out of temper, and leaves it nothing but silence and possession.[7]

Has the prospect of reform only "love" to offer as a weapon in opposition to this "material might?" While Emerson never wavers on the value of love, he also mentions "reason" here, and the Emersonian philosophy of transcendentalism takes a particular slant in understanding the term. "Reason," in a tradition following Coleridge,[8] is contrasted with the philosophy of common-sense and the empiricist-realist common-sense "understanding," a term strongly related to the Lockean tradition established by the American Revolution. Emerson's view is that the Revolution had devolved into a materialistic and conservative establishment oriented chiefly to gaining and preserving wealth. This conservatism was blocking the road to reform needed to avoid the catastrophe to come after mid-century. If we come to "bow before" the colossus of wealth and social influence, then we lack sufficient force to oppose this defining circumstance of our problems. Emersonian "reason" is to overcome our common-sense understanding, where it is compromised and where it preserves problems along with established positions and advantage.

Continuing the passage above from 1841, Emerson promises a discussion of the contemporary conflict between "aristocracy" and "transcendentalism:"

The fact of aristocracy, with its two weapons of wealth and manners, is as commanding a feature of the nineteenth century, and the American republic, as of old Rome, or modern England. The reason and influence of wealth, the aspect of philosophy and religion, and the tendencies which have acquired the name of Transcendentalism in Old and New England; the aspect of poetry, as the exponent and interpretation of these things; the fuller development and the freer play of Character as a social and political agent;—these and other related topics will in turn come to be considered.[9]

To some people, if poetry, literature, revitalized religion, love, and even Emersonian reason sufficed to overcome such an established order and its material incentives, that would be a miracle. But we need not suppose something supernatural. Viewed more naturalistically, what is required is more like a turn of conviction, a moral and cultural conversion, and shifts in public opinion, which finally draw needed political and social consequences and act on them. Human beings organize and re-organize themselves not by material incentives alone.

It is not that Emerson thought reform does without incentives. In his "Address on the Emancipation of the Negroes in the British West Indies" (1844), he notes that "in 1791, three hundred thousand persons in Britain pledged themselves to abstain from all articles of Island produce. The planters were obliged to give way; and in 1807, on the twenty-fifth March, the bill passed and the slave trade was abolished."[10] Great Britain had been aroused to action and reform once the horrid facts of the slave trade became generally known. But the result did not come about without public action and economic pressures.

Emerson included a significant practical orientation in his moral idealism. Still, from a more philosophical perspective, there is good reason to look into what became of Emerson's more mystical, metaphysical, and epistemic doctrines in the progression of thought which brought him to write "Fate" and *The Conduct of Life*. That Emerson persisted and developed in his moral idealism is beyond doubt. But what became of the typical philosophical doctrines of transcendentalism in the time between *Nature* and the first series of *Essays* in the early 1840s and the publication of *The Conduct of Life* in 1860? The words "transcendental" and "transcendentalism" are not to be found in the present work. There are certainly hints along the way of a more naturalistic and pragmatic, esoteric doctrine which yet speaks Emerson's distinctive religious language. "The soul which animates Nature," he says in "Behavior," in the present work, "is not less significantly published in the figure, movement, and gesture of animated bodies, than in its last vehicle of articulate speech."[11] The moral idealist is an astute literary observer of manners and comportment; and the emphasis on intuition arising directly from nature is balanced by good efforts to interpret human society. Early on, Emerson looked more to the natural surroundings, since a reorientation and adaptation of traditional European thought was needed in the new American environment. Later, Emerson is more concerned with culture and cultures in comparison—partly from the requirements of confirming his comparative evaluations of culture.

Though Emerson is not a technical philosopher or a philosopher of the sort which the twentieth century has often taught us to expect, one basic tendency of his thought is toward an idealist metaphysics in which soul and intuition, or inspiration, are central. The new American experiment needed every idea within its reach. Taking a practical and democratic, yet poetic interest in all of nature and in individuals of every walk of life, Emerson stresses the potentiality for genius and creativity in each person. It is a source of creative insight within, which yet speaks to us from Nature's inspirations, and which Emerson identified as Divine. Emerson was concerned with nature and with the observation of natural phenomena. However, he was not centrally concerned, in his more poetic moods, to test his insights and interpretations by reference to predictions or systematic collection of observations, since according to Transcendentalism, all facts and perception require interpretation. Moreover, such interpretation is not dictated to us by either fact or perception. This reasoning is the basis for any rationalism which fails to find the sources of our ideas of perfection, or beauty, or lawful necessity in sense experience. Yet we find in *The Conduct of Life* that Emerson's more youthful idealism has come down to earth and come to grapple with circumstances.

Emerson's transcendentalism is an idealist pantheism—though not without a more naturalistic and humanistic tendency. We often find in his work praise for Plato as well as the German Idealists. He says in "The Transcendentalist," not leaving any doubt concerning his early idealism, that "Mind is the only reality of which men and all other natures are better or worse reflectors."[12]

This early rationalistic idealism is tempered in the essay "Worship" in the present book: "The religion which is to guide and fulfill the present and coming ages," says Emerson "whatever else it be, must be intellectual. The scientific mind must have a faith which is science." Such a "scientific" religion or faith in science would surely not be content with poetic inspiration, thought to emanate directly from the World-Soul, as a basis for belief. Yet the point stands in some conflict with the philosophical underpinnings of transcendentalism: the self-sufficiency of "reason" in contrast with the scientific and common-sense understanding. If we once see the insufficiency of pure "reason" in isolation from the common-sense understanding and empirical study, then there is no other source from which to hope to correct the delusions of reason or faith, or of common sense, except that we rely on growing experience. Relying on experience, in contrast to a self-sufficient "reason," we still have room for an evolving higher criticism of accepted beliefs and values.

"If one would study his own time," writes Emerson in the opening of "Fate," "it must be by this method of taking up in turn each of the leading topics which belong to our scheme of human life, and, by firmly stating all that is agreeable to experience on one, and doing the same justice to the opposing facts in the others, the true limitations will appear." Not intuition or inspiration is called for here, but "method" and reliance on "experience." This is needed in order that "Any excess of emphasis, on one part, would be corrected, and a just balance would be made." Facing the threat of civil war, an understanding of American society could not plausibly be based on unaided inspiration or intuition. Still Emerson's method is in fact more literary than it is scientific. He consults the recorded wisdom of ages gone by and seeks reconciliation. Insight and inspiration survive, in the later views, as a faithfulness to the perspective at which we arrive. He writes as follows in the essay "Worship:"

> There is a principle which is the basis of things, which all speech aims to say, and all action to evolve, a simple, quiet, undescribed, undescribable presence, dwelling very peacefully in us, our rightful lord: we are not to do, but to let do; not to work, but to be worked upon; and to this homage there is a consent of all thoughtful and just men in all ages and conditions. To this sentiment belong vast and sudden enlargements of power.[13]

Though the point is expressed in Emerson's religious language, this "presence" is what we would otherwise understand as the inner source of our hypotheses and interpretations, including those which arise as we attempt to reconcile conflicting positions or themes in tension and contradiction. To understand a problem we need to arrive at an organizing idea, proposed solution, or hypothesis; and we need this organizing idea actually to organize the material under study. It is "the rightful lord" of the material to be organized, of the intellectual problem which is addressed. It cannot be something which we merely impose on the material. As Emerson puts the matter, "we are not to do, but to let do." The idea comes to us, and it must actually fit the need. We must consent to our own insight, and this is the root and basis of Emerson's method. It is only if we regard such insight, the solution or resolution or organizing idea at which we arrive as infallible and not open to revision in light of new problems, or new elements of former problems, that we fall into a kind of rationalism or *a priori* method which feels itself secure in disregarding appeal to experience. Emerson, in contrast, teaches intellectual honesty, in the light of evolving experience, as the basic religious and intellectual value.

There is also always moral purpose to the intellectual task at hand. Emerson complains in the essay "Beauty," below, against science lacking such purpose: "Science in England, in America, is jealous of theory, hates the name of love and moral purpose. There's a revenge for this inhumanity." The revenge is in the defects of the products and in the peccant narrowness of the developed persons following such practice. Yet, though moral purpose is needed, such moral purpose is not regarded as unchanging or rigidly set. "Religion or worship," says Emerson, "is the attitude of those who see this unity, intimacy, and sincerity; who see that, against all appearances, the nature of things works for truth and right forever." The human mind is part of the world, we might say, and however this works, "it works for truth and right." We should aim for and act in the confidence of this aim. Emerson reflects the Enlightenment values of his Unitarian predecessors, but he goes further:

> We say, the old forms of religion decay, and that a skepticism devastates the community. I do not think it can be cured or stayed by any modification of theologic creeds, much less by theologic discipline. The cure for false theology is mother-wit. Forget your books and traditions, and obey your moral perceptions at this hour.[14]

Your moral perceptions "at this hour" may not be the same as those at which you later arrive, but to get from point A to point B, you must start where you stand. We cannot do without our moral purpose any more than we can do without intellectual virtues. This combination of moral and intellectual virtues defines Emerson's relation to religious tradition. "Let us have nothing now which is not its own evidence," he says; since "there is surely enough for the heart and imagination in the religion itself. Let us not be pestered with assertions and half-truths, with emotions and snuffle."

3. Faith and Divine Providence

Along with his emphasis on intellectual and moral virtues and practice, Emerson also has a more nearly orthodox and traditional side to his religious thought which arises most directly from his early essay on "Compensation." The doctrine of compensation is a doctrine of balances and acceptance of life, and a doctrine of cosmic justice, not unconnected with what any Pastor or Rabbi might tell you about the experience of loss and recovery, fall and re-birth, and related themes. Emerson preaches a religion of hope, acceptable in many ways to his more traditionally religious countrymen. But in the present book, this teaching takes a realistic turn to acknowledge and emphasize the terrors and harshness of life. He writes much to this effect in "Fate:"

> Providence has a wild, rough, incalculable road to its end, and it is of no use to try to whitewash its huge, mixed instrumentalities, or to dress up that terrific benefactor in a clean shirt and white neck cloth of a student in divinity.[15]

Truculence in the course of Providence is part of the traditional theme of the problem of evil. If God is all-good and all-powerful, and creator of the world, then why is there so much pain, suffering and evil in this world—so much ferocity, cruelty and savagery? Emerson does not deny the evidence of evil in the world upon which the argument rests. Nor does he deny the traditional assumptions about the power and goodness of Divinity. For Emerson, the world as it is "is best,"—so far. Evil, pain and suffering in this world are among the instrumentalities of the Divine Providence, the means employed to bring about what is needed and wanted and better. But expense of means to arrive at an end is a proof of circumstance, constraint, and even "fate." That "mind is the only reality" is no longer clearly true. At least it is not mind as unqualified will or willfulness, unconstrained by law. Providence itself must go to some expense of means to reach its ends, and if even Divine Providence is constrained by expense of means to deal with circumstances, we are certainly in no better position. Emerson can only plead, in the face of this problem, that an expense of means to deal with circumstance belongs to the divine "eternal laws" of the world itself. That is substantially his view.

Still, Emerson writes: "Fate involves the melioration. No statement of the Universe can have any soundness, which does not admit its ascending effort. The direction of the whole, and of the parts, is toward benefit, and in proportion to the health." Essentially, this is a doctrine of cosmic progress, and it functions in Emerson's thought to encourage our efforts in the right directions. He does not see this message of melioration and the need of ameliorative efforts as inconsistent with recognizing the facts as they are:

> I see not why we should give ourselves such sanctified airs. If the Divine Providence has hid from men neither disease, nor deformity, nor corrupt society, but has stated itself out in passions, in war, in trade, in the love of power and pleasure, in hunger and need, in tyrannies, literatures, and arts,—let us not be so nice that we cannot write these facts down coarsely as they stand, or doubt but there is a counter-statement as ponderous, which we can arrive at, and which, being put, will make all square. The solar system has no anxiety about its reputation, and the credit of truth and honesty is as safe; nor have I any fear that a skeptical bias can be given by leaning hard on the

sides of fate, of practical power, or of trade, which the doctrine of Faith cannot down-weigh.[16]

Subsequent philosophy in America has taken a clue from Emerson's emphasis on the need for ameliorative efforts, even where the faith in an all-powerful intelligence in the world, or the inevitability of moral progress, has not been upheld. Later meliorism, in contrast with optimism, bases hope not in the inevitability of moral progress and improvements but instead in the possibility of improvements. There is also much attention to empirical conditions and methods which allow us to track and project tendencies and propensities of action and activity based, in part, on our commonalities of ethics, affinity, tradition and ethnicities. Recognizing our problems, as Emerson recommends, we may see the need for improvements and sometimes discover the means—even for those lacking faith in an all-powerful intelligence to see to and guarantee final outcomes. Propensity to self-correction and moral compensation exist in any living culture—much as they exist in any healthy psyche.

4. Culture, Worship and Illusions

Can we reasonably expect that all our efforts and projects in life, or human life itself, will always turn out for the best in the end, or in the long-run? Though expressing his faith in religious and pious terms, Emerson always allows that we are subject to illusions and errors of belief. Can we, then, be sure of Emerson's own optimistic faith in the human capability to overcome the stings of circumstance and the limitations of fate? Though intent on advancing his own distinctive views of the matter, Emerson leaves possibilities of doubt. In the final essay of the book, he writes of a kingdom of illusions:

> In this kingdom of illusions we grope eagerly for stays and foundations. There is none but a strict and faithful dealing at home, and a severe barring out of all duplicity or illusion there. Whatever games are played with us, we must play no games with ourselves, but deal in our privacy with the last honesty and truth. I look upon the simple and childish virtues of veracity and honesty as the root of all that is sublime in character. Speak as you think, be what you are, pay your debts of all kinds. I prefer to be owned as sound and solvent, and my word as good as my bond, and to be what cannot be skipped, or dissipated, or undermined, to all the *éclat*[17] in the universe. This reality is the foundation of friendship, religion, poetry, and art. At the top or at the bottom of all illusions, I set the cheat which still leads us to work and live for appearances, in spite of our conviction, in all sane hours, that it is what we really are that avails with friends, with strangers, and with fate or fortune.[18]

How are we to avoid or escape this kingdom of illusions? Might we be sometimes condemned, in spite of all our progress, to fail to escape the essential constraints and limitations of circumstance? What are the proper and appropriate foundations of our efforts and inquiries? How do we know what we can accomplish and what we cannot?

Emerson says that there are no better foundations than intellectual honesty: "A strict and faithful dealing at home, and a severe barring out of all duplicity or illusion there." This simple honesty opens up the power in nature and in mankind by which we think, discover, progress, correct our errors and even change our desires and aims. It is the source of creativity in thought and action.[19] It puts us in the best position, too, to benefit from and appreciate the contributions of others. "This reality is the foundation of friendship, religion, poetry, and art," says Emerson. We are set on the pursuit of culture, by means of which we may fine-tune or revise our success, put our wealth and growing power to the best uses, find reverence for life, and better appreciate its beauty. There is little guarantee for ambition in this approach to life, but we stand to make the best use of the opportunities actually encountered.

5. Double Consciousness

It is worth examining Emerson, early and late, on the notion of "double consciousness," since this idea enters with great significance into the method which he expounds in *The Conduct of Life*. To see the full force of the later doctrine, however, we must first understand something of his early thoughts on the topic. In "The Transcendentalist," Emerson complains of a "double consciousness" which appears as a typical romantic dilemma. The problem is to understand how one might escape this double consciousness, and it is a source of no little frustration and doubt:

> Much of our reading, much of our labor, seems mere waiting: it was not that we were born for. Any other could do it as well, or better. So little skill enters into these works, so little do they mix with the divine life, that it really signifies little what we do, whether we turn a grindstone, or ride, or run, or make fortunes, or govern the state. The worst feature of this double consciousness is, that the two lives, of the understanding and of the soul, which we lead, really show very little relation to each other, never meet and measure each other: one prevails now, all buzz and din; and the other prevails then, all infinitude and paradise; and, with the progress of life, the two discover no greater disposition to reconcile themselves.[20]

On the one hand is a consciousness of "the divine life," of "infinitude and paradise." This is the source of inspiration from within or from without. The trouble is that it seems to have no significant relationship to every-day life, the common-sense understanding, and the work-a-day life—"all buzz and din." This "double consciousness" is a confession of dualism. The life of the soul seems to have no significant relation to what we do in the world. Our work is "not what we were born for," says Emerson, and, implicitly, one may wonder, from this perspective, why we are born to it at all

The doctrine is very different in Emerson's "Fate." Where it had been a problematic duality, it now appears as a solution to life's problems. There is, he says, "One key, one solution to the mysteries of human condition" there is "one solution to the old knots of fate, freedom, and foreknowledge," and this is the propounding, namely, of the double consciousness."[21]

> A man must ride alternately on the horses of his private and his public nature, as the equestrians in the circus throw themselves nimbly from horse to horse, or plant one foot on the back of one, and the other foot on the back of the other. So when a man is the victim of his fate, has sciatica in his loins, and cramp in his mind; a club-foot and a club in his wit; a sour face, and a selfish temper; a strut in his gait, and a conceit in his affection; or is ground to powder by the vice of his race;—he is to rally on his relation to the Universe, which his ruin benefits. Leaving the demon who suffers, he is to take sides with the Deity who secures universal benefit by his pain.[22]

We have each, Emerson says, both a "private" and "a public nature." We are reminded here of Emerson's emphasis and alterations between "Society and Solitude." There is no solution on either side alone, but only in going back and forth. We must change perspective between that of common sense and every-day life, on the one hand, and private thought on the other—thus gaining insight from the disparity and conflict of perspectives. If your private view leaves you in defeat and ashes, then it is time to switch and take up the case of the opposition which benefits from your defeat and suffering. Admit your errors, when you see them, and join the opposition. In that way, you may also benefit from the defeat of your error. Emerson continues:

> To offset the drag of temperament and race, which pulls down, learn this lesson, namely, that by the cunning co-presence of two elements, which is throughout nature, whatever lames or paralyzes you, draws in with it the divinity, in some form, to repay. A good intention clothes itself with sudden power. When a god wishes to ride, any chip or pebble will bud and shoot out winged feet, and serve him for a horse.
>
> Let us build altars to the Blessed Unity which holds nature and souls in perfect solution, and compels every atom to serve a universal end.[23]

This is Emerson's doctrine of compensation and cosmic justice in another guise. Whatever pulls you down, whatever "lames or paralyzes you," benefits another, and if you join with that other, then you can benefit from the "compensation" yourself. In this way, you can continue to "serve a universal end." But, if we see, in some tension with Emerson's teaching, that there is little automatic in justice, that even the benefits which may ultimately arise from loss depend on our ability to greave (instead of running on into obsession), then so is it, also in every generalization of the point which Emerson explores. If there is no automatic compensation, and justice depends on our continuing to work to distinguish the "better and worse" among possibilities and human potentialities, the point still remains that internal honesty and rigorous intellectual and moral integrity may hold the solution even for those illusions which arise from our occasional stubbornness and blindness. From intellectual self-reliance, we may become our own best critics. We can understand in these terms how Emerson, the private scholar, could become the conscience of a nation willing and able to argue with great force and act with great masses in favor of the abolition of slavery.

"A good intention clothes itself with sudden power," says Emerson; and "when a god wishes to ride, any chip or pebble will bud and shoot out winged feet, and serve him for a horse." We do not know in any dependable way which side of the double consciousness may hold greater benefit on any given occasion, yet we know that creativity arises out of just this tension.

6. Historical Context: America, Power, and Culture

Writing to Thomas Carlyle in April 1854, Emerson thought that the British writer should come and see America, which was "growing furiously" and among its other attractions featured "wealth ... on a new scale." "New Kansas new Nebraska [are] looming up in these days." Congress was about to decide on the question of slavery in Kansas and Nebraska. Though Emerson focuses on the attraction of American growth and vitality, he is not optimistic that the politicians in Washington will be able to solve the problems outstanding. If "the politicians shall be sodden, the states escape, please God!" Carlyle should come to see the events unfolding on such a grand continental scale. The deeper moral issue is to be considered: "The fight of slave and freeman drawing nearer, the question is properly, whether slavery or whether freedom shall be abolished. Come and see."[24] Emerson was keenly aware of the state of American politics and the long development of its festering sectional divisions, which had only been exacerbated by the competition in adding new slave states and new free states—at least since the time of the Missouri compromise of 1820. He knew, as Abraham Lincoln was later to put the matter, that the nation "could not long exist half slave and half free," and that "a house divided against itself cannot stand." Emerson did not emphasize his political opinions in his books. He did, however, provide the following hint of his positions in the essay on "Culture" in the present book:

> Let us make our education brave and preventive. Politics is an after-work, a poor patching. We are always a little late. The evil is done, the law is passed, and we begin the up-hill agitation for repeal of that of which we ought to have prevented the enacting. We shall one day learn to supersede politics by education. What we call our root-and-branch reforms of slavery, war, gambling, intemperance, is only medicating the symptoms. We must begin higher up, namely, in Education.[25]

The political issues and problems might turn out in various ways, but Emerson was sure that there was a higher court of appeal than what we find in politics. "Politics is an after-work," he says, "a poor patching," and this is because politics is predominantly a working out of habits and values already established and therefore already represented firmly in political councils. No matter how perfect and desirable our systems of representation of established values, politics cannot fix the conflicts and defects of those established values and habits of action. Our "root and branch" political reforms therefore remain, too often, superficial, when measured against the genuine depth of our problems. War may indeed become inevitable in such circumstances, and that was how Emerson viewed the nation in the 1850s as he developed and wrote out his book on *The Conduct of Life*.

Far be it from Emerson, then, to want to subject American growth and economic vitality to a superior political control sufficient to dam it up. Instead we find him addressing education and culture as the final arbiters of success. "Whilst all the world is in pursuit of power, and of wealth as a means of power, culture corrects the theory of success."[26] That is why Emerson understands culture as largely a matter of our pursuit of higher values. "A man is the prisoner of his power," he says, and culture is needed to free the human being, or the nation, from the monomania of specific powers and their visible and obvious outcomes. So, for example, if America is gifted in making money and producing economic growth, then we should be most wary of excesses in just these matters. We must ask what is being sacrificed or ignored.

Emerson's image of America and of its problems in familiar, even after more than 150 years. "A topical memory makes" of us, "an almanac;" while "a talent for debate," tends to make merely "a disputant." "Skill to get money makes" of us "a miser, that is, a beggar," according to Emerson, though "Culture reduces these inflammations by invoking the aid of other powers against the dominant talent, and by appealing to the rank of powers. It watches success."[27] If we ignore or disregard this control by culture over power and "success," then we evade deeper realities and store up problems for ourselves and others.

Such was the unhappy course which brought America to its great mid-nineteenth-century tragedies: something was lacking and defective in our conduct of life. Instead of directly addressing the consequences in political debates, Emerson aimed to make up the deeper defects and omissions. However, a section of the "Lecture on Slavery" from 1855 discusses the political compromise concerning slavery in the Constitution. You might argue that the American Revolution would have been impossible without the South, and that action against slavery, in 1776, would have been an impediment to independence. In his original draft of the Declaration of Independence, Thomas Jefferson had included a complaint against King George III's forcing the slave trade upon the colonies. But this was removed from the final document.

The arguments from the necessities of war do not clearly extend to decisions made in the constitutional convention. Emerson argues, persuasively, that other options existed. (It is worth recalling that Jefferson and John Adams were not at the convention; they were away on foreign assignments.) Speaking of the Constitutional Convention, Emerson says:

> The fathers, in July 1787, consented to adopt population as the basis of representation, and to count only three-fifths of the slaves, and to concede the reclamation of fugitive slaves;—for the consideration, that there should be no slavery in the Northwestern Territory. They agreed to this false basis of representation and to this criminal complicity of restoring fugitives: and the splendor of the bribe, namely, the magnificent prosperity of America from 1787, is their excuse for the crime. They should have refused it at the risk of making no Union.[28]

The view is that the decisions on slavery at the Constitutional Convention were short-sighted. Emerson sees them as primarily motivated by economic considerations. The Northwest Ordinance, forbidding slavery north of the Ohio and east of the Mississippi was adopted on 13 July of the same year, one of the last acts of Congress under the Articles of Confederation, and Emerson suggests there was a *quid pro quo.*

The slaves themselves had no say in the matter, but acceptance of slavery benefited all others concerned, though only as far as they cared to look. Had the North and the South looked further, they might have come to different decisions. But high political compromise that neglected moral deliberation was the order of the day. One of the defects and a continuing blindness in the over-valuation of politics is that it does not see that politics mainly ministers to the problems of those who already have some considerable power and influence. Emerson thought the expressed ideals of the American Revolution, understood to include the slaves, should have overruled even the imperative of Union. Continuing the above passage, he suggests alternatives:

> Many ways could have been taken. If the southern section had made a separate alliance with England, or gone back into colonies, the slaves would have been emancipated with the West Indians, and then the colonies could have been annexed to us. The bribe, if they foresaw the prosperity we have seen, was one to dazzle common men, and I do not wonder that common men excuse and applaud it. But always so much crime brings so much ruin. A little crime a minor penalty; a great crime a great disaster.[29]

A central point, evoking themes from "Compensation," is the need for moral deliberation in political decisions. Ignoring great moral crimes, by and by, we will produce "great disaster."

The following quotation from Emerson's "Address on the Emancipation of the Negroes in the British West Indies" (1844) provides insight into the moral grounds for his opposition to slavery. The passage starts with a general description of the evils:

> Language must be raked, the secrets of slaughterhouses and infamous holes that cannot front the day, must be ransacked, to tell what Negro-slavery has been. These men, our benefactors, as they are producers of corn and wine, of coffee, of tobacco, of cotton, of sugar, of rum, and brandy, gentle and joyous themselves, and producers of comfort and luxury for the civilized world,—there seated in the finest climates of the globe, children of the sun,—I am heart-sick when I read how they came there, and how they are kept there. Their case was left out of the mind and out of the heart of their brothers.

Certainly, their case was left out at the Constitutional Convention, as Emerson was later to argue. But they were entitled to more. Emerson continues:

> The prizes of society, the trumpet of fame, the privileges of learning, of culture, of religion, the decencies and joys of marriage, honor, obedience, personal authority, and a perpetual melioration into a finer civility, these were for all, but not for them.[30]

By seeing Emerson as essentially a religious thinker, deeply concerned with the human soul, and the development of human potentialities, we will see that he thought slavery wrong, fundamentally wrong, because it denied to some human beings what belong by right to all. There are distinctively human potentialities, and Emerson leaves no doubt that they are independent of race. He was not the first, but his expression of the point was of great value in overturning the negligent and myopic common-sense of his day. Creative growth of the person is not something we can reserve for some people at the expense of others. According to Emerson, there is a moral law of the mind, and of the world, which forbids denial of free development to anyone, and the moral law determines the fate of the transgressor.

Similarly, regarding our America today, we might say that all its power and might, military, economic, and cultural, will not and cannot prevent the untoward and unhappy workings of our own growing social and economic inequalities. The threat implicit in this places limits on what we may do. We may of course evade the point for a time, but the workings of growing inequalities are ultimately quite sure. The consequences or effects of what we now do are already included in our present acts, which are indeed causes. There can be little doubt of what we typically neglect, if, too intensively, we pursue our own special talent and power of economic expansion. In consequence, then, there is, plausibly, even less room for doubt on the proper direction of our deeper and fuller success.

I

FATE

——•——

Delicate omens traced in air
To the lone bard true witness bare;
Birds with auguries on their wings
Chanted undeceiving things
Him to beckon, him to warn;
Well might then the poet scorn
To learn of scribe or courier
Hints writ in vaster character;
And on his mind, at dawn of day,
Soft shadows of the evening lay.
For the prevision is allied
Unto the thing so signified;
Or say, the foresight that awaits
Is the same Genius that creates.

FATE

It chanced during one winter, a few years ago, that our cities were bent on discussing the theory of the Age. By an odd coincidence, four or five noted men were each reading a discourse to the citizens of Boston or New York, on the Spirit of the Times. It so happened that the subject had the same prominence in some remarkable pamphlets and journals issued in London in the same season. To me, however, the question of the times resolved itself into a practical question of the conduct of life. How shall I live? We are incompetent to solve the times. Our geometry cannot span the huge orbits of the prevailing ideas, behold their return, and reconcile their opposition. We can only obey our own polarity. 'Tis fine for us to speculate and elect our course, if we must accept an irresistible dictation.[1]

In our first steps to gain our wishes, we come upon immovable limitations. We are fired with the hope to reform men. After many experiments, we find that we must begin earlier,—at school. But the boys and girls are not docile; we can make nothing of them. We decide that they are not of good stock. We must begin our reform earlier still,—at generation: that is to say, there is Fate, or laws of the world.[2]

But if there be irresistible dictation, this dictation understands itself. If we must accept Fate, we are not less compelled to affirm liberty, the significance of the individual, the grandeur of duty, the power of character. This is true, and that other is true. But our geometry cannot span these extreme points, and reconcile them. What to do? By obeying each thought frankly, by harping, or, if you will, pounding on each string, we learn at last its power. By the same obedience to other thoughts, we learn theirs, and then comes some reasonable hope of harmonizing them. We are sure that, though we know not how, necessity does comport with liberty, the individual with the world, my polarity with the spirit of the times. The riddle of the age has for each a private solution. If one would study his own time, it must be by this method of taking up in turn each of the leading topics which belong to our scheme of human life, and, by firmly stating all that is agreeable to experience on one, and doing the same justice to the opposing facts in the others, the true limitations will appear. Any excess of emphasis, on one part, would be corrected, and a just balance would be made.

But let us honestly state the facts. Our America has a bad name for superficialness. Great men, great nations, have not been boasters and buffoons, but perceivers of the terror of life, and have manned themselves to face it. The Spartan, embodying his religion in his country, dies before its majesty without a question. The Turk, who believes his doom is written on the iron leaf in the moment when he entered the world, rushes on the enemy's saber with undivided will. The Turk, the Arab, the Persian, accepts the foreordained fate.

> "On two days, it steads not to run from thy grave,
>   The appointed, and the unappointed day;
> On the first, neither balm nor physician can save,
>   Nor thee, on the second, the Universe slay."

The Hindu, under the wheel, is as firm. Our Calvinists,[3] in the last generation, had something of the same dignity. They felt that the weight of the Universe held them down to their place. What could *they* do? Wise men feel that there is something which cannot be talked or voted away,—a strap or belt which girds the world.

> "The Destiny, minister general,
> That executeth in the world o'er all,
> The purveyance which God hath seen beforne,
> So strong it is, that though the world had sworn
> The contrary of a thing by yea or nay,
> Yet sometime it shall fallen on a day
> That falleth not oft in a thousand year;
> For, certainly, our appetités here,
> Be it of war, or peace, or hate, or love,
> All this is ruléd by the sight above."
>   Chaucer: *The Knighte's Tale.*[4]

The Greek Tragedy expressed the same sense: "Whatever is fated, that will take place. The great immense mind of Jove is not to be transgressed."

Savages cling to a local god of one tribe or town. The broad ethics of Jesus were quickly narrowed to village theologies, which preach an election or favoritism.[5] And, now and then, an amiable parson, like Jung Stilling,[6] or Robert Huntington, believes in a pistareen-Providence,[7] which, whenever the good man wants a dinner, makes that somebody shall knock at his door, and leave a half-dollar. But Nature is no sentimentalist,—does not cosset or pamper us. We must see that the world is rough and surly, and will not mind drowning a man or a woman; but swallows your ship like a grain of dust.[8] The cold, inconsiderate of persons, tingles your blood, benumbs your feet, freezes a man like an apple. The diseases, the elements, fortune, gravity, lightning, respect no persons. The way of Providence is a little rude. The habit of snake and spider, the snap of the tiger and other leapers and bloody jumpers, the crackle of the bones of his prey in the coil of the anaconda,—these are in the system, and our habits are like theirs. You have just dined, and, however scrupulously the slaughter-house is concealed in the graceful distance of miles, there is complicity,—expensive races,—race living at the expense of race. The planet is liable to shocks from comets, perturbations from planets, rendings from earthquake and volcano, alterations of climate, precessions of equinoxes. Rivers dry up by opening of the forest. The sea changes its bed. Towns and counties fall into it. At Lisbon, an earthquake killed men like flies.[9] At Naples, three years ago, ten thousand persons were crushed in a few minutes. The scurvy at sea; the sword of the climate in the west of Africa, at Cayenne,[10] at Panama, at New Orleans, cut off men like a massacre. Our western prairie shakes with fever and ague.[11] The cholera, the small-pox, have proved as mortal to some tribes, as a frost to the crickets, which, having filled the summer with noise, are silenced by a fall of the temperature of one night. Without uncovering what does not concern us, or counting how many species of parasites hang on a bombyx;[12] or groping after intestinal parasites, or infusory biters, or the obscurities of alternate generation;—the forms of the shark, the *labrus*,[13] the jaw of the sea-wolf paved with crushing teeth, the weapons of the grampus,[14] and other warriors hidden in the sea,—are hints of ferocity in the interiors of nature. Let us not deny it up and down. Providence has a wild, rough, incalculable road to its end, and it is of no use to try to whitewash its huge, mixed instrumentalities, or to dress up that terrific benefactor in a clean shirt and white neckcloth of a student in divinity.

Will you say, the disasters which threaten mankind are exceptional, and one need not lay his account for cataclysms every day? Aye, but what happens once, may happen again, and so long as these strokes are not to be parried by us, they must be feared.

But these shocks and ruins are less destructive to us, than the stealthy power of other laws which act on us daily. An expense of ends to means is fate;—organization tyrannizing over character. The menagerie, or forms and powers of the spine, is a book of fate: the bill of the bird, the skull of the snake, determines tyrannically its limits. So is the scale of races, of temperaments; so is sex; so is climate; so is the reaction of talents imprisoning the vital power in certain directions. Every spirit makes its house; but afterwards the house confines the spirit.

The gross lines are legible to the dull: the cabman is phrenologist so far: he looks in your face to see if his shilling is sure. A dome of brow denotes one thing; a pot-belly another; a squint, a pug-nose, mats of hair, the pigment of the epidermis, betray character. People seem sheathed in their tough organization. Ask Spurzheim, ask the doctors, ask Quételet,[15] if temperaments decide nothing?—or if there be anything they do not decide? Read the description in medical books of the four temperaments, and you will think you are reading your own thoughts which you had not yet told. Find the part which black eyes, and which blue eyes, play severally in the company. How shall a man escape from his ancestors, or draw off from his veins the black drop which he drew from his father's or his mother's life? It often appears in a family, as if all the qualities of the progenitors were potted in several jars,—some ruling quality in each son or daughter of the house,—and sometimes the unmixed temperament, the rank unmitigated elixir, the family vice, is drawn off in a separate individual, and the others are proportionally relieved. We sometimes see a change of expression in our companion, and say, his father, or his mother, comes to the windows of his eyes, and sometimes a remote relative. In different hours, a man represents each of several of his ancestors, as if there were seven or eight of us rolled up in each man's skin,—seven or eight ancestors at least,—and they constitute the variety of notes for that new piece of music which his life is. At the corner of the street, you read the possibility of each passenger, in the facial angle, in the complexion, in the depth of his eye. His parentage determines it. Men are what their mothers made them. You may as well ask a loom which weaves huckaback,[16] why it does not make cashmere, as expect poetry from this engineer, or a chemical discovery from that jobber.[17] Ask the digger in the ditch to explain Newton's laws:[18] the fine organs of his brain have been pinched by overwork and squalid poverty from father to son, for a hundred years. When each comes forth from his mother's womb, the gate of gifts closes behind him. Let him value his hands and feet, he has but one pair. So he has but one future, and that is already predetermined in his lobes, and described in that little fatty face, pigeye, and squat form. All the privilege and all the legislation of the world cannot meddle or help to make a poet or a prince of him.

Jesus said, "When he looketh on her, he hath committed adultery."[19] But he is an adulterer before he has yet looked on the woman, by the superfluity of animal, and the defect of thought, in his constitution. Who meets him, or who meets her, in the street, sees that they are ripe to be each other's victim.

In certain men, digestion and sex absorb the vital force, and the stronger these are, the individual is so much weaker. The more of these drones perish, the better for the hive. If, later, they give birth to some superior individual, with force enough to add to this animal a new aim, and a complete apparatus to work it out, all the ancestors are gladly forgotten. Most men and most women are merely one couple more. Now and then, one has a new cell or *camarilla*[20] opened in his brain,—an architectural, a musical, or a philological knack, some stray taste or talent for flowers, or chemistry, or pigments, or story-telling, a good hand for drawing, a good foot for dancing, an athletic frame for wide journeying, and etc.—which skill nowise alters rank in the scale of nature, but serves to pass the time, the life of sensation going on as before. At last, these hints and tendencies are fixed in one, or in a succession. Each absorbs so much food and force, as to become itself a new center. The new talent draws off so rapidly the vital force, that not enough remains for the animal functions, hardly enough for health; so that, in the second generation, if the like genius appear, the health is visibly deteriorated, and the generative force impaired.

People are born with the moral or with the material bias;—uterine brothers with this diverging destination: and I suppose, with high magnifiers, Mr. Fraunhofer[21] or Dr. Carpenter might come to distinguish in the embryo at the fourth day,—this is a Whig, and that a Free-soiler.[22]

It was a poetic attempt to lift this mountain of Fate, to reconcile this despotism of race with liberty, which led the Hindus to say, "Fate is nothing but the deeds committed in a prior state of existence."[23] I find the coincidence of the extremes of eastern and western speculation in the daring statement of Schelling, "there is in every man a certain feeling, that he has been what he is from all eternity, and by no means became such in time."[24] To say it less sublimely,—in the history of the individual is always an account of his condition, and he knows himself to be a party to his present estate.

A good deal of our politics is physiological. Now and then a man of wealth in the heyday of youth adopts the tenet of broadest freedom. In England there is always some man of wealth and large connection, planting himself, during all his years of health, on the side of progress, who, as soon as he begins to die, checks his forward play, calls in his troops, and becomes conservative. All conservatives are such from personal defects. They have been effeminated by position or nature, born halt and blind, through luxury of their parents, and can only, like invalids, act on the defensive. But strong natures, backwoodsmen, New Hampshire giants, Napoleons, Burkes, Broughams, Websters, Kossuths,[25] are inevitable patriots, until their life ebbs, and their defects and gout, palsy and money, warp them.

The strongest idea incarnates itself in majorities and nations, in the healthiest and strongest. Probably, the election goes by avoirdupois weight, and, if you could weigh bodily the tonnage of any hundred of the Whig and the Democratic party in a town on the Dearborn balance, as they passed the hayscales, you could predict with certainty which party would carry it. On the whole it would be rather the speediest way of deciding the vote, to put the selectmen or the mayor and aldermen at the hayscales.

In science, we have to consider two things: power and circumstance. All we know of the egg, from each successive discovery, is, *another vesicle*;[26] and if, after five hundred years you get a better observer or a better glass, he finds, within the last observed, another. In vegetable and animal tissue it is just alike, and all that the primary power or spasm operates is still, vesicles, vesicles. Yes,—but the tyrannical Circumstance! A vesicle in new circumstances, a vesicle lodged in darkness, Oken[27] thought, became animal; in light, a plant. Lodged in the parent animal, it suffers changes which end in unsheathing miraculous capability in the unaltered vesicle, and it unlocks itself to fish, bird, or quadruped, head and foot, eye and claw. The Circumstance is Nature. Nature is what you may do. There is much you may not. We have two things, —the circumstance, and the life. Once we thought, positive power was all. Now we learn that negative power, or circumstance, is half. Nature is the tyrannous circumstance, the thick skull, the sheathed snake, the ponderous, rock-like jaw; necessitated activity; violent direction; the conditions of a tool, like the locomotive, strong enough on its track, but which can do nothing but mischief off of it; or skates, which are wings on the ice, but fetters on the ground.

The book of Nature is the book of Fate. She turns the gigantic pages,—leaf after leaf,—never re-turning one. One leaf she lays down, a floor of granite; then a thousand ages, and a bed of slate; a thousand ages, and a measure of coal; a thousand ages, and a layer of marl and mud: vegetable forms appear; her first misshapen animals, zoophyte, trilobium,[28] fish; then, saurians,—rude forms, in which she has only blocked her future statue, concealing under these unwieldly monsters the fine type of her coming king. The face of the planet cools and dries, the races meliorate, and man is born. But when a race[29] has lived its term, it comes no more again.

The population of the world is a conditional population; not the best, but the best that could live now; and the scale of tribes, and the steadiness with which victory adheres to one tribe, and defeat to another, is as uniform as the superposition of strata. We know in history what weight belongs to race. We see the English, French, and Germans planting themselves on every shore and market of America and Australia, and monopolizing the commerce of these countries. We like the nervous and victorious habit of our own branch of the family. We follow the step of the Jew, of the Indian, of the Negro. We see how much will has been expended to extinguish the Jew, in vain. Look at the unpalatable conclusions of Knox,[30] in his "Fragment of Races,"—a rash and unsatisfactory writer, but charged with pungent and unforgettable truths. "Nature respects race, and not hybrids." "Every race has its own *habitat*." "Detach a colony from the race, and it deteriorates to the crab."[31] See the shades of the picture. The German and Irish millions, like the Negro, have a great deal of guano[32] in their destiny. They are ferried over the Atlantic, and carted over America, to ditch and to drudge, to make corn cheap, and then to lie down prematurely to make a spot of green grass on the prairie.

One more fagot[33] of these adamantine[34] bandages, is, the new science of Statistics. It is a rule, that the most casual and extraordinary events—if the basis of population is broad enough—become matter of fixed calculation. It would not be safe to say when a captain like Bonaparte,[35] a singer like Jenny Lind,[36] or a navigator like Bowditch,[37] would be born in Boston: but, on a population of twenty or two hundred millions, something like accuracy may be had.[38]

'Tis frivolous to fix pedantically the date of particular inventions. They have all been invented over and over fifty times. Man is the arch machine, of which all these shifts drawn from himself are toy models. He helps himself on each emergency by copying or duplicating his own structure, just so far as the need is. 'Tis hard to find the right Homer, Zoroaster, or Menu;[39] harder still to find the Tubal Cain, or Vulcan, or Cadmus, or Copernicus, or Fust, or Fulton,[40] the indisputable inventor. There are scores and centuries of them. "The air is full of men."[41] This kind of talent so abounds, this constructive tool-making efficiency, as if it adhered to the chemic atoms, as if the air he breathes were made of Vaucansons, Franklins, and Watts.[42]

Doubtless, in every million there will be an astronomer, a mathematician, a comic poet, a mystic. No one can read the history of astronomy, without perceiving that Copernicus, Newton, Laplace,[43] are not new men, or a new kind of men, but that Thales, Anaximenes, Hipparchus, Empedocles, Aristarchus,

Pythagoras, Oenopides,[44] had anticipated them; each had the same tense geometrical brain, apt for the same vigorous computation and logic, a mind parallel to the movement of the world. The Roman mile probably rested on a measure of a degree of the meridian. Mohammedan and Chinese know what we know of leap-year, of the Gregorian calendar, and of the precession of the equinoxes. As, in every barrel of cowries,[45] brought to New Bedford, there shall be one *orangia*,[46] so there will, in a dozen millions of Malays and Mohammedans, be one or two astronomical skulls. In a large city, the most casual things, and things whose beauty lies in their casuality, are produced as punctually and to order as the baker's muffin for breakfast. Punch[47] makes exactly one capital joke a week; and the journals contrive to furnish one good piece of news every day.

And not less work the laws of repression, the penalties of violated functions. Famine, typhus, frost, war, suicide, and effete races, must be reckoned calculable parts of the system of the world.

These are pebbles from the mountain, hints of the terms by which our life is walled up, and which show a kind of mechanical exactness, as of a loom or mill, in what we call casual or fortuitous events.

The force with which we resist these torrents of tendency looks so ridiculously inadequate, that it amounts to little more than a criticism or a protest made by a minority of one, under compulsion of millions. I seemed, in the height of a tempest, to see men overboard struggling in the waves, and driven about here and there. They glanced intelligently at each other, but 'twas little they could do for one another; 'twas much if each could keep afloat alone. Well, they had a right to their eyebeams, and all the rest was Fate.

We cannot trifle with this reality, this cropping-out in our planted gardens of the core of the world. No picture of life can have any veracity that does not admit the odious facts. A man's power is hooped in by a necessity, which, by many experiments, he touches on every side, until he learns its arc.

The element running through entire nature, which we popularly call Fate, is known to us as limitation. Whatever limits us, we call Fate. If we are brute and barbarous, the fate takes a brute and dreadful shape. As we refine, our checks become finer. If we rise to spiritual culture, the antagonism takes a spiritual form. In the Hindu fables, Vishnu follows Maya[48] through all her ascending changes, from insect and crawfish up to elephant; whatever form she took, he took the male form of that kind, until she became at last woman and goddess, and he a man and a god. The limitations refine as the soul purifies, but the ring of necessity is always perched at the top.

When the gods in the Norse heaven were unable to bind the Fenris Wolf with steel or with weight of mountains,—the one he snapped and the other he spurned with his heel,—they put round his foot a limp band softer than silk or cobweb, and this held him: the more he spurned it, the stiffer it drew. So soft and so stanch is the ring of Fate. Neither brandy, nor nectar, nor sulfuric ether, nor hell-fire, nor ichor,[49] nor poetry, nor genius, can get rid of this limp band. For if we give it the high sense in which the poets use it, even thought itself is not above Fate: that too must act according to eternal laws, and all that is willful and fantastic in it is in opposition to its fundamental essence.[50]

And, last of all, high over thought, in the world of morals, Fate appears as vindicator, leveling the high, lifting the low, requiring justice in man, and always striking soon or late, when justice is not done. What is useful will last; what is hurtful will sink. "The doer must suffer," said the Greeks: "you would soothe a Deity not to be soothed." "God himself cannot procure good for the wicked," said the Welsh triad.[51] "God may consent, but only for a time," said the bard of Spain.[52] The limitation is impassable by any insight of man. In its last and loftiest ascensions, insight itself, and the freedom of the will, is one of its obedient members.[53] But we must not run into generalizations too large, but show the natural bounds or essential distinctions, and seek to do justice to the other elements as well.

Thus we trace Fate, in matter, mind, and morals,—in race, in retardations of strata, and in thought and character as well. It is everywhere bound or limitation. But Fate has its lord; limitation its limits; is different seen from above and from below; from within and from without. For, though Fate is immense, so is Power, which is the other fact in the dual world, immense. If Fate follows and limits Power, Power attends and antagonizes Fate.[54] We must respect Fate as natural history, but there is more than natural history. For who and what is this criticism that pries into the matter? Man is not order of nature, sack and sack, belly and members, link in a chain, nor any ignominious baggage, but a stupendous antagonism, a dragging together of the poles of the Universe. He betrays his relation to what is below him,—thick-skulled, small-brained, fishy, quadrumanous,[55]—quadruped ill-disguised, hardly escaped into biped, and has paid for the new powers by loss of some of the old ones. But the lightning which explodes and fashions planets, maker of planets and suns, is in him. On one side, elemental order, sandstone and granite, rock-edges, peat-bog, forest, sea and shore; and, on the other part, thought, the spirit which composes and decomposes nature,—here they are, side by side, god and devil, mind and matter, king and conspirator, belt and spasm, riding peacefully together in the eye and brain of every man.

Nor can he blink the freewill. To hazard the contradiction,—freedom is necessary. If you please to plant yourself on the side of Fate, and say, Fate is all; then we say, a part of Fate is the freedom of man. Forever wells up the impulse of choosing and acting in the soul. Intellect annuls Fate. So far as a man thinks, he is free. And though nothing is more disgusting than the crowing about liberty by slaves, as most men are, and the flippant mistaking for freedom of some paper preamble like a "Declaration of Independence," or the statute right to vote, by those who have never dared to think or to act, yet it is wholesome to man to look not at Fate, but the other way: the practical view is the other. His sound relation to these facts is to use and command, not to cringe to them. "Look not on nature, for her name is fatal,"[56] said the oracle. The too much contemplation of these limits induces meanness. They who talk much of destiny, their birth-star, and etc., are in a lower dangerous plane, and invite the evils they fear.

I cited the instinctive and heroic races as proud believers in Destiny. They conspire with it; a loving resignation is with the event. But the dogma makes a different impression, when it is held by the weak and lazy. 'Tis weak and vicious people who cast the blame on Fate. The right use of Fate is to bring up our conduct to the loftiness of nature. Rude and invincible except by themselves are the elements. So let man be. Let him empty his breast of his windy conceits, and show his lordship by manners and deeds on the scale of nature. Let him hold his purpose as with the tug of gravitation. No power, no persuasion, no bribe shall make him give up his point. A man ought to compare advantageously with a river, an oak, or a mountain. He shall have not less the flow, the expansion, and the resistance of these.

'Tis the best use of Fate to teach a fatal courage. Go face the fire at sea, or the cholera in your friend's house, or the burglar in your own, or what danger lies in the way of duty, knowing you are guarded by the cherubim of Destiny. If you believe in Fate to your harm, believe it, at least, for your good.

For, if Fate is so prevailing, man also is part of it, and can confront fate with fate. If the Universe have these savage accidents, our atoms are as savage in resistance. We should be crushed by the atmosphere, but for the reaction of the air within the body. A tube made of a film of glass can resist the shock of the ocean, if filled with the same water. If there be omnipotence in the stroke, there is omnipotence of recoil.

1. But Fate against Fate is only parrying and defense: there are, also, the noble creative forces. The revelation of Thought takes man out of servitude into freedom. We rightly say of ourselves, we were born, and afterward we were born again, and many times. We have successive experiences so important, that the new forgets the old, and hence the mythology of the seven or the nine heavens. The day of days, the great day of the feast of life, is that in which the inward eye opens to the Unity in things, to the omnipresence of law;—sees that what is must be, and ought to be, or is the best. This beatitude dips from on high down on us, and we see. It is not in us so much as we are in it. If the air come to our lungs, we breathe and live; if not, we die. If the light come to our eyes, we see; else not. And if truth come to our mind, we suddenly expand to its dimensions, as if we grew to worlds. We are as lawgivers; we speak for Nature; we prophesy and divine.

This insight throws us on the party and interest of the Universe, against all and sundry; against ourselves, as much as others. A man speaking from insight affirms of himself what is true of the mind: seeing its immortality, he says, I am immortal; seeing its invincibility, he says, I am strong. It is not in us, but we are in it.[57] It is of the maker, not of what is made. All things are touched and changed by it. This uses, and is not used. It distances those who share it, from those who share it not. Those who share it not are flocks and herds. It dates from itself;—not from former men or better men,—gospel, or constitution, or college, or custom. Where it shines, Nature is no longer intrusive, but all things make a musical or pictorial impression. The world of men show like a comedy without laughter:—populations, interests, government, history;—'tis all toy figures in a toy house. It does not overvalue particular truths. We hear eagerly every thought and word quoted from an intellectual man. But, in his presence, our own mind is roused to activity, and we forget very fast what he says, much more interested in the new play of our own thought, than in any thought of his. 'Tis the majesty into which we have suddenly mounted, the impersonality, the scorn of egotisms, the sphere of laws, that engage us. Once we were stepping a little this way, and a little that way; now, we are as men in a balloon, and do not think so much of the point we have left, or the point we would make, as of the liberty and glory of the way.

Just as much intellect as you add, so much organic power. He who sees through the design, presides over it, and must will that which must be. We sit and rule, and, though we sleep, our dream will come to pass. Our thought, though it were only an hour old, affirms an oldest necessity, not to be separated from thought, and not to be separated from will. They must always have coexisted. It apprises us of its sovereignty and godhead, which refuse to be severed from it. It is not mine or thine, but the will of all mind. It is poured into the souls of all men, as the soul itself which constitutes them men. I know not whether there be, as is alleged, in the upper region of our atmosphere, a permanent westerly current, which carries with it all atoms which rise to that height, but I see, that when souls reach a certain clearness of perception, they accept a knowledge and motive above selfishness. A breath of will blows eternally through the universe of souls in the direction of the Right and Necessary. It is the air which all intellects inhale and exhale, and it is the wind which blows the worlds into order and orbit.

Thought dissolves the material universe, by carrying the mind up into a sphere where all is plastic. Of two men, each obeying his own thought, he whose thought is deepest will be the strongest character. Always one man more than another represents the will of Divine Providence to the period.

2. If thought makes free, so does the moral sentiment. The mixtures of spiritual chemistry refuse to be analyzed. Yet we can see that with the perception of truth is joined the desire that it shall prevail. That affection is essential to will. Moreover, when a strong will appears, it usually results from a certain unity of organization, as if the whole energy of body and mind flowed in one direction. All great force is real and elemental. There is no manufacturing a strong will. There must be a pound to balance a pound. Where power is shown in will, it must rest on the universal force. Alaric[58] and Bonaparte must believe they rest on a truth, or their will can be bought or bent. There is a bribe possible for any finite will. But the pure sympathy with universal ends is an infinite force, and cannot be bribed or bent. Whoever has had experience of the moral sentiment cannot choose but believe in unlimited power. Each pulse from that heart is an oath from the Most High. I know not what the word *sublime* means, if it be not the intimations in this infant of a terrific force. A text of heroism, a name and anecdote of courage, are not arguments, but sallies of freedom. One of these is the verse of the Persian Hafiz,[59] "'Tis written on the gate of Heaven, 'Wo unto him who suffers himself to be betrayed by Fate!'" Does the reading of history

make us fatalists? What courage does not the opposite opinion show! A little whim of will to be free gallantly contending against the universe of chemistry.

But insight is not will, nor is affection will. Perception is cold, and goodness dies in wishes; as Voltaire[60] said, 'tis the misfortune of worthy people that they are cowards; "*un des plus grands malheurs des honnêtes gens c'est qu'ils sont des lâches.*" There must be a fusion of these two to generate the energy of will. There can be no driving force, except through the conversion of the man into his will, making him the will, and the will him. And one may say boldly, that no man has a right perception of any truth, who has not been reacted on by it, so as to be ready to be its martyr.

The one serious and formidable thing in nature is a will. Society is servile from want of will, and therefore the world wants saviors and religions. One way is right to go: the hero sees it, and moves on that aim, and has the world under him for root and support. He is to others as the world. His approbation is honor; his dissent, infamy. The glance of his eye has the force of sunbeams. A personal influence towers up in memory only worthy, and we gladly forget numbers, money, climate, gravitation, and the rest of Fate.

We can afford to allow the limitation, if we know it is the meter of the growing man. We stand against Fate, as children stand up against the wall in their father's house, and notch their height from year to year. But when the boy grows to man, and is master of the house, he pulls down that wall, and builds a new and bigger. 'Tis only a question of time. Every brave youth is in training to ride and rule this dragon. His science is to make weapons and wings of these passions and retarding forces. Now whether, seeing these two things, fate and power, we are permitted to believe in unity?[61] The bulk of mankind believe in two gods. They are under one dominion here in the house, as friend and parent, in social circles, in letters, in art, in love, in religion: but in mechanics, in dealing with steam and climate, in trade, in politics, they think they come under another; and that it would be a practical blunder to transfer the method and way of working of one sphere, into the other. What good, honest, generous men at home, will be wolves and foxes on change![62] What pious men in the parlor will vote for what reprobates[63] at the polls! To a certain point, they believe themselves the care of a Providence. But, in a steamboat, in an epidemic, in war, they believe a malignant energy rules.

But relation and connection are not somewhere and sometimes, but everywhere and always. The divine order does not stop where their sight stops. The friendly power works on the same rules, in the next farm, and the next planet. But, where they have not experience, they run against it, and hurt themselves. Fate, then, is a name for facts not yet passed under the fire of thought;—for causes which are unpenetrated.

But every jet of chaos which threatens to exterminate us, is convertible by intellect into wholesome force. Fate is unpenetrated causes. The water drowns ship and sailor, like a grain of dust. But learn to swim, trim your bark, and the wave which drowned it, will be cloven by it, and carry it, like its own foam, a plume and a power. The cold is inconsiderate of persons, tingles your blood, freezes a man like a dew-drop. But learn to skate, and the ice will give you a graceful, sweet, and poetic motion. The cold will brace your limbs and brain to genius, and make you foremost men of time. Cold and sea will train an imperial Saxon race, which nature cannot bear to lose, and, after cooping it up for a thousand years in yonder England, gives a hundred Englands, a hundred Mexicos. All the bloods it shall absorb and domineer: and more than Mexicos,—the secrets of water and steam, the spasms of electricity, the ductility of metals, the chariot of the air, the ruddered balloon are awaiting you.

The annual slaughter from typhus far exceeds that of war; but right drainage destroys typhus. The plague in the sea-service from scurvy is healed by lemon juice and other diets portable or procurable: the depopulation by cholera and small-pox is ended by drainage and vaccination; and every other pest is not less in the chain of cause and effect, and may be fought off. And, whilst art draws out the venom, it commonly extorts some benefit from the vanquished enemy. The mischievous torrent is taught to drudge for man: the wild beasts he makes useful for food, or dress, or labor; the chemic explosions are controlled like his watch. These are now the steeds on which he rides. Man moves in all modes, by legs of horses, by wings of wind, by steam, by gas of balloon, by electricity, and stands on tiptoe threatening to hunt the eagle in his own element. There's nothing he will not make his carrier.

Steam was, till the other day, the devil which we dreaded. Every pot made by any human potter or brazier had a hole in its cover, to let off the enemy, lest he should lift pot and roof, and carry the house away. But the Marquis of Worcester,[64] Watt, and Fulton bethought themselves, that, where was power, was not devil, but was God; that it must be availed of, and not by any means let off and wasted. Could he lift pots and roofs and houses so handily? he was the workman they were in search of. He could be used to lift away, chain, and compel other devils, far more reluctant and dangerous, namely, cubic miles of earth, mountains, weight or resistance of water, machinery, and the labors of all men in the world; and time he shall lengthen, and shorten space.

It has not fared much otherwise with higher kinds of steam. The opinion of the million was the terror of the world, and it was attempted, either to dissipate it, by amusing nations, or to pile it over with strata of society,—a layer of soldiers; over that, a layer of lords; and a king on the top; with clamps and hoops of castles, garrisons, and police. But, sometimes, the religious principle would get in, and burst the hoops, and rive every mountain laid on top of it. The Fultons and Watts of politics, believing in unity, saw that it was a power, and, by satisfying it (as justice satisfies everybody,) through a different disposition of society,—grouping it on a level, instead of piling it into a mountain,—they have contrived to make of his terror the most harmless and energetic form of a State.[65]

Very odious, I confess, are the lessons of Fate. Who likes to have a dapper phrenologist pronouncing on his fortunes? Who likes to believe that he has hidden in his skull, spine, and pelvis, all the vices of a Saxon or Celtic race,[66] which will be sure to pull him down,—with what grandeur of hope and resolve he is fired,—into a selfish, huckstering, servile, dodging animal? A learned physician tells us, the fact is invariable with the Neapolitan, that, when mature, he assumes the forms of the unmistakable scoundrel. That is a little overstated,—but may pass.

But these are magazines and arsenals. A man must thank his defects, and stand in some terror of his talents. A transcendent talent draws so largely on his forces, as to lame him; a defect pays him revenues on the other side. The sufferance, which is the badge of the Jew, has made him, in these days, the ruler of the rulers of the earth. If Fate is ore and quarry, if evil is good in the making, if limitation is power that shall be, if calamities, oppositions, and weights are wings and means,—we are reconciled.

Fate involves the melioration. No statement of the Universe can have any soundness, which does not admit its ascending effort. The direction of the whole, and of the parts, is toward benefit, and in proportion to the health. Behind every individual, closes organization: before him, opens liberty,—the Better, the Best. The first and worst races are dead. The second and imperfect races are dying out, or remain for the maturing of higher. In the latest race, in man,[67] every generosity, every new perception, the love and praise he extorts from his fellows, are certificates of advance out of fate into freedom. Liberation of the will from the sheaths and clogs of organization which he has outgrown, is the end and aim of this world. Every calamity is a spur and valuable hint; and where his endeavors do not yet fully avail, they tell as tendency. The whole circle of animal life,—tooth against tooth,—devouring war, war for food, a yelp of pain and a grunt of triumph, until, at last, the whole menagerie, the whole chemical mass is mellowed and refined for higher use,—pleases at a sufficient perspective.

But to see how fate slides into freedom, and freedom into fate, observe how far the roots of every creature run, or find, if you can, a point where there is no thread of connection. Our life is consentaneous[68] and far-related. This knot of nature is so well tied, that nobody was ever cunning enough to find the two ends. Nature is intricate, overlapped, interweaved, and endless. Christopher Wren[69] said of the beautiful King's College chapel, "that, if anybody would tell him where to lay the first stone, he would build such another." But where shall we find the first atom in this house of man, which is all consent, inosculation,[70] and balance of parts?

The web of relation is shown in *habitat*, shown in hibernation. When hibernation was observed, it was found, that, whilst some animals became torpid in winter, others were torpid in summer: hibernation then was a false name. The *long sleep* is not an effect of cold, but is regulated by the supply of food proper to the animal. It becomes torpid when the fruit or prey it lives on is not in season, and regains its activity when its food is ready.

Eyes are found in light; ears in auricular air; feet on land; fins in water; wings in air; and each creature where it was meant to be, with a mutual fitness. Every zone has its own *Fauna*. There is adjustment between the animal and its food, its parasite, its enemy. Balances are kept. It is not allowed to diminish in numbers, nor to exceed. The like adjustments exist for man. His food is cooked, when he arrives; his coal in the pit; the house ventilated; the mud of the deluge dried; his companions arrived at the same hour, and awaiting him with love, concert, laughter, and tears. These are coarse adjustments, but the invisible are not less. There are more belongings to every creature than his air and his food. His instincts must be met, and he has predisposing power that bends and fits what is near him to his use. He is not possible until the invisible things are right for him, as well as the visible. Of what changes, then, in sky and earth, and in finer skies and earths, does the appearance of some Dante or Columbus[71] apprise us!

How is this effected? Nature is no spendthrift, but takes the shortest way to her ends. As the general says to his soldiers, "if you want a fort, build a fort," so nature makes every creature do its own work and get its living,—is it planet, animal, or tree. The planet makes itself. The animal cell makes itself;—then, what it wants. Every creature,—wren or dragon,—shall make its own lair. As soon as there is life, there is self-direction, and absorbing and using of material. Life is freedom,—life in the direct ratio of its amount. You may be sure, the new-born man is not inert. Life works both voluntarily and supernaturally in its neighborhood. Do you suppose, he can be estimated by his weight in pounds, or, that he is contained in his skin,—this reaching, radiating, jaculating fellow? The smallest candle fills a mile with its rays, and the papillae of a man run out to every star.

When there is something to be done, the world knows how to get it done. The vegetable eye makes leaf, pericarp,[72] root, bark, or thorn, as the need is; the first cell converts itself into stomach, mouth, nose, or nail, according to the want: the world throws its life into a hero or a shepherd; and puts him where he is wanted. Dante and Columbus were Italians, in their time: they would be Russians or Americans today. Things ripen, new men come. The adaptation is not capricious. The ulterior aim, the purpose beyond itself, the correlation by which planets subside and crystallize, then animate beasts and men, will not stop, but will work into finer particulars, and from finer to finest.

The secret of the world is, the tie between person and event. Person makes event, and event person. The "times," "the age," what is that, but a few profound persons and a few active persons who epitomize the times?—Goethe, Hegel, Metternich, Adams, Calhoun, Guizot, Peel, Cobden, Kossuth, Rothschild, Astor, Brunel,[73] and the rest. The same fitness must be presumed between a man and the time and event, as between the sexes, or between a race of animals and the food it eats, or the inferior races it uses. He thinks his fate alien, because the copula is hidden. But the soul contains the event that shall befall it, for the event is only the actualization of its thoughts; and what we pray to ourselves for is always granted. The event is the print of your form. It fits you like your skin. What each does is proper to him. Events are the children of his body and mind. We learn that the soul of Fate is the soul of us, as Hafiz sings,

> Alas! till now I had not known,
> My guide and fortune's guide are one.

All the toys that infatuate men, and which they play for,—houses, land, money, luxury, power, fame, are the selfsame thing, with a new gauze or two of illusion overlaid. And of all the drums and rattles by which men are made willing to have their heads broke, and are led out solemnly every morning to parade,—the most admirable is this by which we are brought to believe that events are arbitrary, and independent of actions. At the conjuror's, we detect the hair by which he moves his puppet, but we have not eyes sharp enough to descry the thread that ties cause and effect.

Nature magically suits the man to his fortunes, by making these the fruit of his character. Ducks take to the water, eagles to the sky, waders to the sea margin, hunters to the forest, clerks to counting-rooms, soldiers to the frontier. Thus events grow on the same stem with persons; are sub-persons. The pleasure of life is according to the man that lives it, and not according to the work or the place. Life is an ecstasy. We know what madness belongs to love,—what power to paint a vile object in hues of heaven. As insane persons are indifferent to their dress, diet, and other accommodations, and, as we do in dreams, with equanimity, the most absurd acts, so, a drop more of wine in our cup of life will reconcile us to strange company and work. Each creature puts forth from itself its own condition and sphere, as the slug sweats out its slimy house on the pear-leaf, and the woolly aphides on the apple perspire their own bed, and the fish its shell. In youth, we clothe ourselves with rainbows, and go as brave as the zodiac. In age, we put out another sort of perspiration,—gout, fever, rheumatism, caprice, doubt, fretting, and avarice.

A man's fortunes are the fruit of his character. A man's friends are his magnetisms. We go to Herodotus and Plutarch[74] for examples of Fate; but we are examples. "*Quisque suos patimur manes.*"[75] The tendency of every man to enact all that is in his constitution is expressed in the old belief that the efforts which we make to escape from our destiny only serve to lead us into it: and I have noticed, a man likes better to be complimented on his position, as the proof of the last or total excellence, than on his merits.

A man will see his character emitted in the events that seem to meet, but which exude from and accompany him. Events expand with the character. As once he found himself among toys, so now he plays a part in colossal systems, and his growth is declared in his ambition, his companions, and his performance. He looks like a piece of luck, but is a piece of causation;—the mosaic, angulated and ground to fit into the gap he fills. Hence in each town there is some man who is, in his brain and performance, an explanation of the tillage, production, factories, banks, churches, ways of living, and society, of that town. If you do not chance to meet him, all that you see will leave you a little puzzled: if you see him, it will become plain. We know in Massachusetts who built New Bedford, who built Lynn, Lowell, Lawrence, Clinton, Fitchburg, Holyoke, Portland, and many another noisy mart. Each of these men, if they were transparent, would seem to you not so much men, as walking cities, and, wherever you put them, they would build one.

History is the action and reaction of these two,—Nature and Thought;—two boys pushing each other on the curb-stone of the pavement. Everything is pusher or pushed: and matter and mind are in perpetual tilt and balance, so. Whilst the man is weak, the earth takes up him. He plants his brain and affections. By and by he will take up the earth, and have his gardens and vineyards in the beautiful order and productiveness of his thought. Every solid in the universe is ready to become fluid on the approach of the mind, and the power to flux it is the measure of the mind. If the wall remain adamant, it accuses the want of thought. To a subtler force, it will stream into new forms, expressive of the character of the mind. What is the city in which we sit here, but an aggregate of incongruous materials, which have obeyed the will of some man? The granite was reluctant, but his hands were stronger, and it came. Iron was deep in the ground, and well combined with stone; but could not hide from his fires. Wood, lime, stuffs, fruits, gums, were dispersed over the earth and sea, in vain. Here they are, within reach of every man's day-labor,—what he wants of them. The whole world is the flux of matter over the wires of thought to the poles or points where it would build. The races of men[76] rise out of the ground preoccupied with a thought which rules them, and divided into parties ready armed and angry to fight for this metaphysical abstraction. The quality of the thought differences the Egyptian and the Roman, the Austrian and the American. The men who come on the stage at one period are all found to be related to each other. Certain ideas are in the air. We are all impressionable, for we are made of them; all impressionable, but some more than others, and these first express them. This explains the curious contemporaneousness of inventions and discoveries. The truth is in the air, and the most impressionable brain will announce it first, but all will announce it a few minutes later. So women, as most susceptible, are the best index of the coming hour. So the great man, that is, the man most imbued with the spirit of the time, is the impressionable man,—of a fiber irritable and delicate, like iodine to light.[77] He feels the infinitesimal attractions. His mind is righter than others, because he yields to a current so feeble as can be felt only by a needle delicately poised.

The correlation is shown in defects. Möller, in his Essay on Architecture, taught that the building which was fitted accurately to answer its end, would

turn out to be beautiful, though beauty had not been intended.[78] I find the like
unity in human structures rather virulent and pervasive; that a crudity in the
blood will appear in the argument; a hump in the shoulder will appear in the
speech and handiwork. If his mind could be seen, the hump would be seen. If a
man has a seesaw in his voice, it will run into his sentences, into his poem, into
the structure of his fable, into his speculation, into his charity. And, as every
man is hunted by his own demon, vexed by his own disease, this checks all his
activity.

So each man, like each plant, has his parasites. A strong, astringent,
bilious[79] nature has more truculent[80] enemies than the slugs and moths that fret
my leaves. Such an one has curculios,[81] borers, knife-worms: a swindler ate
him first, then a client, then a quack, then smooth, plausible gentlemen, bitter
and selfish as Moloch.[82]

This correlation really existing can be divined. If the threads are there,
thought can follow and show them. Especially when a soul is quick and docile;
as Chaucer sings,[83]

> "Or if the soul of proper kind
> Be so perfect as men find,
> That it wot what is to come,
> And that he warneth all and some
> Of every of their aventures,
> By previsions or figures;
> But that our flesh hath not might
> It to understand aright
> For it is warned too darkly." —

Some people are made up of rhyme, coincidence, omen, periodicity, and
presage: they meet the person they seek; what their companion prepares to
say to them, they first say to him; and a hundred signs apprise them of what
is about to befall.

Wonderful intricacy in the web, wonderful constancy in the design this
vagabond life admits. We wonder how the fly finds its mate, and yet year after
year we find two men, two women, without legal or carnal tie, spend a great
part of their best time within a few feet of each other. And the moral is, that
what we seek we shall find;[84] what we flee from flees from us; as Goethe said,
"what we wish for in youth, comes in heaps on us in old age,"[85] too often
cursed with the granting of our prayer: and hence the high caution, that, since
we are sure of having what we wish, we beware to ask only for high things.

One key, one solution to the mysteries of human condition, one solution to the old knots of fate, freedom, and foreknowledge, exists, the propounding, namely, of the double consciousness.[86] A man must ride alternately on the horses of his private and his public nature, as the equestrians in the circus throw themselves nimbly from horse to horse, or plant one foot on the back of one, and the other foot on the back of the other. So when a man is the victim of his fate, has sciatica[87] in his loins, and cramp in his mind; a club-foot and a club in his wit; a sour face, and a selfish temper; a strut in his gait, and a conceit in his affection; or is ground to powder by the vice of his race;—he is to rally on his relation to the Universe, which his ruin benefits. Leaving the demon who suffers, he is to take sides with the Deity who secures universal benefit by his pain.

To offset the drag of temperament and race, which pulls down, learn this lesson, namely, that by the cunning co-presence of two elements, which is throughout nature, whatever lames or paralyzes you, draws in with it the divinity, in some form, to repay. A good intention clothes itself with sudden power. When a god wishes to ride, any chip or pebble will bud and shoot out winged feet, and serve him for a horse.

Let us build altars to the Blessed Unity[88] which holds nature and souls in perfect solution, and compels every atom to serve a universal end. I do not wonder at a snow-flake, a shell, a summer landscape, or the glory of the stars; but at the necessity of beauty under which the universe lies; that all is and must be pictorial; that the rainbow, and the curve of the horizon, and the arch of the blue vault are only results from the organism of the eye. There is no need for foolish amateurs to fetch me to admire a garden of flowers, or a sun-gilt cloud, or a waterfall, when I cannot look without seeing splendor and grace. How idle to choose a random sparkle here or there, when the indwelling necessity plants the rose of beauty on the brow of chaos, and discloses the central intention of Nature to be harmony and joy.[89]

Let us build altars to the Beautiful Necessity.[90] If we thought men were free in the sense, that, in a single exception one fantastical will could prevail over the law of things, it were all one as if a child's hand could pull down the sun. If, in the least particular, one could derange the order of nature,—who would accept the gift of life?

Let us build altars to the Beautiful Necessity, which secures that all is made of one piece; that plaintiff and defendant, friend and enemy, animal and planet, food and eater, are of one kind. In astronomy, is vast space, but no foreign system; in geology, vast time, but the same laws as today. Why should we be afraid of Nature, which is no other than "philosophy and theology embodied"? Why should we fear to be crushed by savage elements, we who are made up of the same elements? Let us build to the Beautiful Necessity, which makes man brave in believing that he cannot shun a danger that is appointed, nor incur one that is not; to the Necessity which rudely or softly educates him to the perception that there are no contingencies;[91] that Law rules throughout existence, a Law which is not intelligent but intelligence;—not personal nor impersonal,—it disdains words and passes understanding; it dissolves persons; it vivifies nature; yet solicits the pure in heart to draw on all its omnipotence.

II

POWER

———•———

His tongue was framed to music,
And his hand was armed with skill,
His face was the mould of beauty,
And his heart the throne of will.

POWER

There is not yet any inventory of a man's faculties, any more than a bible of his opinions. Who shall set a limit to the influence of a human being? There are men, who, by their sympathetic attractions, carry nations with them, and lead the activity of the human race. And if there be such a tie, that, wherever the mind of man goes, nature will accompany him, perhaps there are men whose magnetisms are of that force to draw material and elemental powers, and, where they appear, immense instrumentalities organize around them. Life is a search after power; and this is an element with which the world is so saturated,—there is no chink or crevice in which it is not lodged,—that no honest seeking goes unrewarded. A man should prize events and possessions as the ore in which this fine mineral is found; and he can well afford to let events and possessions, and the breath of the body go, if their value has been added to him in the shape of power. If he have secured the elixir, he can spare the wide gardens from which it was distilled.[1] A cultivated man, wise to know and bold to perform, is the end to which nature works, and the education of the will is the flowering and result of all this geology and astronomy.

All successful men have agreed in one thing,—they were *causationists*. They believed that things went not by luck, but by law; that there was not a weak or a cracked link in the chain that joins the first and last of things. A belief in causality, or strict connection between every pulse-beat and the principle of being, and, in consequence, belief in compensation,[2] or, that nothing is got for nothing,—characterizes all valuable minds, and must control every effort that is made by an industrious one. The most valiant men are the best believers in the tension of the laws. "All the great captains," said Bonaparte, "have performed vast achievements by conforming with the rules of the art,—by adjusting efforts to obstacles."

The key to the age may be this, or that, or the other, as the young orators describe;—the key to all ages is—Imbecility; imbecility in the vast majority of men, at all times, and even in heroes in all but certain eminent moments; victims of gravity, custom, and fear. This gives force to the strong,—that the multitude have no habit of self-reliance or original action.

We must reckon success a constitutional trait. Courage,—the old physicians taught, (and their meaning holds, if their physiology is a little mythical,)— courage, or the degree of life, is as the degree of circulation of the blood in the arteries. "During passion, anger, fury, trials of strength, wrestling, fighting, a large amount of blood is collected in the arteries, the maintenance of bodily strength requiring it, and but little is sent into the veins. This condition is constant with intrepid[3] persons." Where the arteries hold their blood, is courage and adventure possible. Where they pour it unrestrained into the veins, the spirit is low and feeble. For performance of great mark, it needs extraordinary health. If Eric is in robust health, and has slept well, and is at the top of his condition, and thirty years old, at his departure from Greenland, he will steer west, and his ships will reach Newfoundland. But take out Eric and put in a stronger and bolder man,—Biorn, or Thorfin,[4]—and the ships will, with just as much ease, sail six hundred, one thousand, fifteen hundred miles further, and reach Labrador and New England. There is no chance in results. With adults, as with children, one class enter cordially into the game, and whirl with the whirling world; the others have cold hands, and remain bystanders; or are only dragged in by the humor and vivacity of those who can carry a dead weight. The first wealth is health. Sickness is poor-spirited, and cannot serve any one: it must husband its resources to live. But health or fullness answers its own ends and has to spare, runs over, and inundates the neighborhoods and creeks of other men's necessities.

All power is of one kind, a sharing of the nature of the world. The mind that is parallel with the laws of nature will be in the current of events, and strong with their strength. One man is made of the same stuff of which events are made; is in sympathy with the course of things; can predict it. Whatever befalls, befalls him first; so that he is equal to whatever shall happen. A man who knows men, can talk well on politics, trade, law, war, religion. For, everywhere, men are led in the same manners.

The advantage of a strong pulse is not to be supplied by any labor, art, or concert. It is like the climate, which easily rears a crop, which no glass, or irrigation, or tillage, or manures, can elsewhere rival. It is like the opportunity of a city like New York, or Constantinople, which needs no diplomacy to force capital or genius or labor to it. They come of themselves, as the waters flow to it. So a broad, healthy, massive understanding seems to lie on the shore of unseen rivers, of unseen oceans, which are covered with barks, that, night and day, are drifted to this point. That is poured into its lap, which other men lie plotting for. It is in everybody's secret; anticipates everybody's discovery; and if it do not command every fact of the genius and the scholar, it is because it is large and sluggish, and does not think them worth the exertion which you do.

This affirmative force is in one, and is not in another, as one horse has the spring in him, and another in the whip. "On the neck of the young man," said Hafiz, "sparkles no gem so gracious as enterprise." Import into any stationary district, as into an old Dutch population in New York or Pennsylvania, or among the planters of Virginia, a colony of hardy Yankees, with seething brains, heads full of steam-hammer, pulley, crank, and toothed wheel,—and everything begins to shine with values. What enhancement to all the water and land in England, is the arrival of James Watt or Brunel! In every company, there is not only the active and passive sex, but, in both men and women, a deeper and more important *sex of mind*, namely, the inventive or creative class of both men and women, and the uninventive or accepting class. Each *plus* man represents his set, and, if he have the accidental advantage of personal ascendancy,—which implies neither more nor less of talent, but merely the temperamental or taming eye of a soldier or a schoolmaster, (which one has, and one has not, as one has a black mustache and one a blond,) then quite easily and without envy or resistance, all his coadjutors and feeders will admit his right to absorb them. The merchant works by book-keeper and cashier; the lawyer's authorities are hunted up by clerks; the geologist reports the surveys of his subalterns; Commander Wilkes[5] appropriates the results of all the naturalists attached to the Expedition; Thorvaldsen's statue[6] is finished by stone-cutters; Dumas[7] has journeymen; and Shakespeare was theater-manager, and used the labor of many young men, as well as the playbooks.

There is always room for a man of force, and he makes room for many. Society is a troop of thinkers, and the best heads among them take the best places. A feeble man can see the farms that are fenced and tilled, the houses that are built. The strong man sees the possible houses and farms. His eye makes estates, as fast as the sun breeds clouds.

When a new boy comes into school, when a man travels, and encounters strangers every day, or, when into any old club a new comer is domesticated,— that happens which befalls, when a strange ox is driven into a pen or pasture where cattle are kept; there is at once a trial of strength between the best pair of horns and the new comer, and it is settled thenceforth which is the leader. So now, there is a measuring of strength, very courteous, but decisive, and an acquiescence thenceforward when these two meet. Each reads his fate in the other's eyes. The weaker party finds, that none of his information or wit quite fits the occasion. He thought he knew this or that: he finds that he omitted to learn the end of it. Nothing that he knows will quite hit the mark, whilst all the rival's arrows are good, and well thrown. But if he knew all the facts in the encyclopedia, it would not help him: for this is an affair of presence of mind, of attitude, of aplomb:[8] the opponent has the sun and wind, and, in every cast, the choice of weapon and mark; and, when he himself is matched with some other antagonist, his own shafts fly well and hit. 'Tis a question of stomach and constitution. The second man is as good as the first,—perhaps better; but has not stoutness or stomach, as the first has, and so his wit seems over-fine or under-fine.

Health is good,—power, life, that resists disease, poison, and all enemies, and is conservative, as well as creative. Here is question, every spring, whether to graft with wax, or whether with clay; whether to whitewash or to potash, or to prune; but the one point is the thrifty tree. A good tree, that agrees with the soil, will grow in spite of blight, or bug, or pruning, or neglect, by night and by day, in all weathers and all treatments. Vivacity, leadership, must be had, and we are not allowed to be nice in choosing. We must fetch the pump with dirty water, if clean cannot be had. If we will make bread, we must have contagion, yeast, emptyings, or what not, to induce fermentation into the dough: as the torpid artist seeks inspiration at any cost, by virtue or by vice, by friend or by fiend, by prayer or by wine. And we have a certain instinct that where is great amount of life, though gross and peccant,[9] it has its own checks and purifications, and will be found at last in harmony with moral laws.

We watch in children with pathetic interest, the degree in which they possess recuperative force. When they are hurt by us, or by each other, or go to the bottom of the class, or miss the annual prizes, or are beaten in the game,—if they lose heart, and remember the mischance in their chamber at home, they have a serious check. But if they have the buoyancy and resistance that pre-occupies them with new interest in the new moment,—the wounds cicatrize, and the fiber is the tougher for the hurt.

One comes to value this *plus* health, when he sees that all difficulties vanish before it. A timid man listening to the alarmists in Congress, and in the newspapers, and observing the profligacy of party,—sectional interests urged with a fury which shuts its eyes to consequences, with a mind made up to desperate extremities, ballot in one hand, and rifle in the other,—might easily believe that he and his country have seen their best days, and he hardens himself the best he can against the coming ruin. But, after this has been foretold with equal confidence fifty times, and government six per cents have not declined a quarter of a mill, he discovers that the enormous elements of strength which are here in play, make our politics unimportant. Personal power, freedom, and the resources of nature strain every faculty of every citizen. We prosper with such vigor, that, like thrifty trees, which grow in spite of ice, lice, mice, and borers, so we do not suffer from the profligate swarms that fatten on the national treasury. The huge animals nourish huge parasites, and the rancor of the disease attests the strength of the constitution. The same energy in the Greek *Demos*[10] drew the remark, that the evils of popular government appear greater than they are; there is compensation for them in the spirit and energy it awakens. The rough and ready style which belongs to a people of sailors, foresters, farmers, and mechanics, has its advantages. Power educates the potentate. As long as our people quote English standards they dwarf their own proportions. A Western lawyer of eminence said to me he wished it were a penal offense to bring an English law-book into a court in this country, so pernicious[11] had he found in his experience our deference to English precedent.[12] The very word 'commerce' has only an English meaning,[13] and is pinched to the cramp exigencies[14] of English experience. The commerce of rivers, the commerce of railroads, and who knows but the commerce of air-balloons, must add an American extension to the pond-hole of admiralty. As long as our people quote English standards, they will miss the sovereignty of power; but let these rough riders,—legislators in shirt-sleeves,—Hoosier,[15] Sucker, Wolverine, Badger,—or whatever hard head Arkansas, Oregon, or Utah sends, half orator, half assassin, to represent its wrath and cupidity[16] at Washington,— let these drive as they may; and the disposition of territories and public lands, the necessity of balancing and keeping at bay the snarling majorities of German, Irish, and of native millions, will bestow promptness, address, and reason, at last, on our buffalo-hunter, and authority and majesty of manners. The instinct of the people is right. Men expect from good Whigs, put into office by the respectability of the country, much less skill to deal with Mexico, Spain, Britain, or with our own malcontent members, than from some strong transgressor, like Jefferson, or Jackson,[17] who first conquers his own government, and then uses the same genius to conquer the foreigner. The senators who dissented from Mr. Polk's Mexican war, were not those who knew better, but those who, from political position, could afford it; not Webster, but Benton and Calhoun.[18]

This power, to be sure, is not clothed in satin. 'Tis the power of lynch law, of soldiers and pirates; and it bullies the peaceable and loyal. But it brings its own antidote; and here is my point,—that all kinds of power usually emerge at the same time; good energy, and bad; power of mind, with physical health; the ecstasies of devotion, with the exasperations of debauchery. The same elements are always present, only sometimes these conspicuous, and sometimes those; what was yesterday foreground, being today background,—what was surface, playing now a not less effective part as basis. The longer the drought lasts, the more is the atmosphere surcharged with water. The faster the ball falls to the sun, the force to fly off is by so much augmented. And, in morals, wild liberty breeds iron conscience; natures with great impulses have great resources, and return from far. In politics, the sons of democrats will be whigs; whilst red republicanism, in the father, is a spasm of nature to engender an intolerable tyrant in the next age.[19] On the other hand, conservatism, ever more timorous and narrow, disgusts the children, and drives them for a mouthful of fresh air into radicalism.

Those who have most of this coarse energy,—the 'bruisers,' who have run the gauntlet of caucus and tavern through the county or the state, have their own vices, but they have the good nature of strength and courage. Fierce and unscrupulous, they are usually frank and direct, and above falsehood. Our politics fall into bad hands, and churchmen and men of refinement, it seems agreed, are not fit persons to send to Congress. Politics is a deleterious profession, like some poisonous handicrafts. Men in power have no opinions, but may be had cheap for any opinion, for any purpose,—and if it be only a question between the most civil and the most forcible, I lean to the last. These Hoosiers and Suckers are really better than the sniveling opposition. Their wrath is at least of a bold and manly cast. They see, against the unanimous declarations of the people, how much crime the people will bear; they proceed from step to step, and they have calculated but too justly upon their Excellencies, the New England governors, and upon their Honors, the New England legislators. The messages of the governors and the resolutions of the legislatures, are a proverb for expressing a sham virtuous indignation, which, in the course of events, is sure to be belied.

In trade, also, this energy usually carries a trace of ferocity.[20] Philanthropic and religious bodies do not commonly make their executive officers out of saints. The communities hitherto founded by Socialists,—the Jesuits, the Port-Royalists, the American communities[21] at New Harmony, at Brook Farm, at

Zoar, are only possible, by installing Judas as steward. The rest of the offices may be filled by good burgesses.[22] The pious and charitable proprietor has a foreman not quite so pious and charitable. The most amiable of country gentlemen has a certain pleasure in the teeth of the bull-dog which guards his orchard. Of the Shaker society,[23] it was formerly a sort of proverb in the country, that they always sent the devil to market. And in representations of the Deity, painting, poetry, and popular religion have ever drawn the wrath from Hell. It is an esoteric doctrine of society, that a little wickedness is good to make muscle; as if conscience were not good for hands and legs, as if poor decayed formalists of law and order cannot run like wild goats, wolves, and conies;[24] that, as there is a use in medicine for poisons, so the world cannot move without rogues; that public spirit and the ready hand are as well found among the malignants.[25] 'Tis not very rare, the coincidence of sharp private and political practice, with public spirit, and good neighborhood.

I knew a burly Boniface[26] who for many years kept a public-house in one of our rural capitals. He was a knave whom the town could ill spare. He was a social, vascular creature, grasping and selfish. There was no crime which he did not or could not commit. But he made good friends of the selectmen, served them with his best chop, when they supped at his house, and also with his honor the Judge, he was very cordial, grasping his hand. He introduced all the fiends, male and female, into the town, and united in his person the functions of bully, incendiary, swindler, barkeeper and burglar. He girdled the trees, and cut off the horses' tails of the temperance people, in the night. He led the 'rummies' and radicals in town-meeting with a speech. Meantime, he was civil, fat, and easy, in his house, and precisely the most public-spirited citizen. He was active in getting the roads repaired and planted with shade-trees; he subscribed for the fountains, the gas, and the telegraph; he introduced the new horse-rake,[27] the new scraper, the baby-jumper,[28] and what not, that Connecticut sends to the admiring citizens. He did this the easier, that the peddler stopped at his house, and paid his keeping, by setting up his new trap on the landlord's premises.

Whilst thus the energy for originating and executing work, deforms itself by excess, and so our ax chops off our own fingers,—this evil is not without remedy. All the elements whose aid man calls in, will sometimes become his masters, especially those of most subtle force. Shall he, then, renounce steam, fire, and electricity, or, shall he learn to deal with them? The rule for this whole class of agencies is,—all *plus* is good; only put it in the right place.

Men of this surcharge of arterial blood cannot live on nuts, herb-tea, and elegies;[29] cannot read novels, and play whist; cannot satisfy all their wants at the Thursday Lecture, or the Boston Athenaeum. They pine for adventure, and must go to Pike's Peak;[30] had rather die by the hatchet of a Pawnee, than sit all day and every day at a counting-room desk. They are made for war, for the sea, for mining, hunting, and clearing; for hair-breadth adventures, huge risks, and the joy of eventful living. Some men cannot endure an hour of calm at sea. I remember a poor Malay cook, on board a Liverpool packet, who, when the wind blew a gale, could not contain his joy; "Blow!" he cried, "me do tell you, blow!" Their friends and governors must see that some vent for their explosive complexion is provided. The roisters[31] who are destined for infamy at home, if sent to Mexico, will "cover you with glory," and come back heroes and generals. There are Oregons, Californias, and Exploring Expeditions enough appertaining to America, to find them in files to gnaw, and in crocodiles to eat. The young English are fine animals, full of blood, and when they have no wars to breathe their riotous valors in, they seek for travels as dangerous as war, diving into Maelstroms;[32] swimming Hellesponts;[33] wading up the snowy Himalayas; hunting lion, rhinoceros, elephant, in South Africa; gypsying with Borrow in Spain and Algiers; riding alligators in South America with Waterton;[34] utilizing Bedouin, Sheik, and Pacha,[35] with Layard;[36] yachting among the icebergs of Lancaster Sound; peeping into craters on the equator; or running on the creases of Malays in Borneo.

The excess of virility has the same importance in general history, as in private and industrial life. Strong race or strong individual rests at last on natural forces, which are best in the savage, who, like the beasts around him, is still in reception of the milk from the teats of Nature. Cut off the connection between any of our works, and this aboriginal source, and the work is shallow. The people lean on this, and the mob is not quite so bad an argument as we sometimes say, for it has this good side. "March without the people," said a French deputy from the tribune, "and you march into night: their instincts are a finger-pointing of Providence, always turned toward real benefit. But when you espouse an Orleans party, or a Bourbon, or a Montalembert party,[37] or any other but an organic party, though you mean well, you have a personality instead of a principle, which will inevitably drag you into a corner."

The best anecdotes of this force are to be had from savage life, in explorers, soldiers, and buccaneers. But who cares for fallings-out of assassins, and fights of bears, or grindings of icebergs? Physical force has no value, where there is nothing else. Snow in snow-banks, fire in volcanoes and solfataras[38] is cheap. The luxury of ice is in tropical countries, and midsummer days. The luxury of fire is, to have a little on our hearth: and of electricity, not volleys of the charged cloud, but the manageable stream on the battery-wires. So of spirit, or energy; the rests or remains of it in the civil and moral man, are worth all the cannibals in the Pacific.

In history, the great moment is, when the savage is just ceasing to be a savage, with all his hairy Pelasgic[39] strength directed on his opening sense of beauty:—and you have Pericles and Phidias,[40]—not yet passed over into the Corinthian civility.[41] Everything good in nature and the world is in that moment of transition, when the swarthy juices still flow plentifully from nature, but their astringency[42] or acridity is got out by ethics and humanity.

The triumphs of peace have been in some proximity to war. Whilst the hand was still familiar with the sword-hilt, whilst the habits of the camp were still visible in the port and complexion of the gentleman, his intellectual power culminated: the compression and tension of these stern conditions is a training for the finest and softest arts, and can rarely be compensated in tranquil times, except by some analogous vigor drawn from occupations as hardy as war.

We say that success is constitutional; depends on a *plus* condition of mind and body, on power of work, on courage; that it is of main efficacy in carrying on the world, and, though rarely found in the right state for an article of commerce, but oftener in the supersaturate or excess, which makes it dangerous and destructive, yet it cannot be spared, and must be had in that form, and absorbents provided to take off its edge.

The affirmative class monopolize the homage of mankind. They originate and execute all the great feats. What a force was coiled up in the skull of Napoleon! Of the sixty thousand men making his army at Eylau,[43] it seems some thirty thousand were thieves and burglars. The men whom, in peaceful communities, we hold if we can, with iron at their legs, in prisons, under the muskets of sentinels, this man dealt with, hand to hand, dragged them to their duty, and won his victories by their bayonets.

This aboriginal might gives a surprising pleasure when it appears under conditions of supreme refinement, as in the proficients in high art. When Michelangelo[44] was forced to paint the Sistine Chapel in fresco, of which art he knew nothing, he went down into the Pope's gardens behind the Vatican, and with a shovel dug out ochres, red and yellow, mixed them with glue and water with his own hands, and having, after many trials, at last suited himself, climbed his ladders, and painted away, week after week, month after month, the sibyls[45] and prophets. He surpassed his successors in rough vigor, as much as in purity of intellect and refinement. He was not crushed by his one picture left unfinished at last. Michel was wont to draw his figures first in skeleton, then to clothe them with flesh, and lastly to drape them. "Ah!" said a brave painter to me, thinking on these things, "if a man has failed, you will find he has dreamed instead of working. There is no way to success in our art, but to take off your coat, grind paint, and work like a digger on the railroad, all day and every day."

Success goes thus invariably with a certain *plus* or positive power: an ounce of power must balance an ounce of weight. And, though a man cannot return into his mother's womb, and be born with new amounts of vivacity, yet there are two economies, which are the best *succedanea*[46] which the case admits. The first is, the stopping off decisively our miscellaneous activity, and concentrating our force on one or a few points; as the gardener, by severe pruning, forces the sap of the tree into one or two vigorous limbs, instead of suffering it to spindle into a sheaf of twigs.

"Enlarge not thy destiny," said the oracle: "endeavor not to do more than is given thee in charge." The one prudence in life is concentration; the one evil is dissipation: and it makes no difference whether our dissipations are coarse or fine; property and its cares, friends, and a social habit, or politics, or music, or feasting. Everything is good which takes away one plaything and delusion more, and drives us home to add one stroke of faithful work. Friends, books, pictures, lower duties, talents, flatteries, hopes,—all are distractions which cause oscillations in our giddy balloon, and make a good poise and a straight course impossible. You must elect your work; you shall take what your brain can, and drop all the rest. Only so, can that amount of vital force accumulate, which can make the step from knowing to doing. No matter how much faculty of idle seeing a man has, the step from knowing to doing is rarely taken. 'Tis a step out of a chalk circle of imbecility into fruitfulness. Many an artist lacking this, lacks all: he sees the masculine Angelo or Cellini[47] with despair. He, too, is up to Nature and the First Cause[48] in his thought. But the spasm to collect and swing his whole being into one act, he has not. The poet Campbell[49] said, that "a man accustomed to work was equal to any achievement he resolved on, and, that, for himself, necessity not inspiration was the prompter of his muse."

Concentration is the secret of strength in politics, in war, in trade, in short, in all management of human affairs. One of the high anecdotes of the world is the reply of Newton to the inquiry, "how he had been able to achieve his discoveries?"—"By always intending my mind." Or if you will have a text from politics, take this from Plutarch: "There was, in the whole city, but one street in which Pericles[50] was ever seen, the street which led to the market-place and the council house. He declined all invitations to banquets, and all gay assemblies and company. During the whole period of his administration, he never dined at the table of a friend." Or if we seek an example from trade,—"I hope," said a good man to Rothschild, "your children are not too fond of money and business: I am sure you would not wish that."—"I am sure I should wish that: I wish them to give mind, soul, heart, and body to business,—that is the way to be happy. It requires a great deal of boldness and a great deal of caution, to make a great fortune, and when you have got it, it requires ten times as much wit to keep it. If I were to listen to all the projects proposed to me, I should ruin myself very soon. Stick to one business, young man. Stick to your brewery, (he said this to young Buxton,[51]) and you will be the great brewer of London. Be brewer, and banker, and merchant, and manufacturer, and you will soon be in the Gazette."

Many men are knowing, many are apprehensive and tenacious, but they do not rush to a decision. But in our flowing affairs a decision must be made,—the best, if you can; but any is better than none. There are twenty ways of going to a point, and one is the shortest; but set out at once on one. A man who has that presence of mind which can bring to him on the instant all he knows, is worth for action a dozen men who know as much, but can only bring it to light slowly. The good Speaker in the House is not the man who knows the theory of parliamentary tactics, but the man who decides off-hand. The good judge is not he who does hair-splitting justice to every allegation, but who, aiming at sub-stantial justice, rules something intelligible for the guidance of suitors. The good lawyer is not the man who has an eye to every side and angle of contin-gency, and qualifies all his qualifications, but who throws himself on your part so heartily, that he can get you out of a scrape. Dr. Johnson[52] said, in one of his flowing sentences, "Miserable beyond all names of wretchedness is that un-happy pair, who are doomed to reduce beforehand to the principles of abstract reason all the details of each domestic day. There are cases where little can be said, and much must be done."

The second substitute for temperament is drill, the power of use and routine. The hack is a better roadster than the Arab barb.[53] In chemistry, the galvanic stream, slow, but continuous, is equal in power to the electric spark, and is, in our arts, a better agent. So in human action, against the spasm of energy, we offset the continuity of drill. We spread the same amount of force over much time, instead of condensing it into a moment. 'Tis the same ounce of gold here in a ball, and there in a leaf. At West Point, Col. Buford, the chief engineer, pounded with a hammer on the trunnions[54] of a cannon, until he broke them off. He fired a piece of ordnance some hundred times in swift succession, until it burst. Now which stroke broke the trunnion? Every stroke. Which blast burst the piece? Every blast. *"Diligence passe sens,"* Henry VIII. was wont to say, or, great is drill. John Kemble[55] said, that the worst provincial company of actors would go through a play better than the best amateur company. Basil Hall[56] likes to show that the worst regular troops will beat the best volunteers. Practice is nine tenths. A course of mobs is good practice for orators. All the great speakers were bad speakers at first. Stumping it[57] through England for seven years, made Cobden a consummate debater. Stumping it through New England for twice seven, trained Wendell Phillips.[58] The way to learn German, is, to read the same dozen pages over and over a hundred times, till you know every word and particle in them, and can pronounce and repeat them by heart. No genius can recite a ballad at first reading, so well as mediocrity can at the fifteenth or twentieth reading. The rule for hospitality and Irish 'help,' is, to have the same dinner every day throughout the year. At last, Mrs. O'Shaughnessy learns to cook it to a nicety, the host learns to carve it, and the guests are well served. A humorous friend of mine thinks, that the reason why Nature is so perfect in her art, and gets up such inconceivably fine sunsets, is, that she has learned how, at last, by dint of doing the same thing so very often. Cannot one converse better on a topic on which he has experience, than on one which is new? Men whose opinion is valued on 'Change, are only such as have a special experience, and off that ground their opinion is not valuable. "More are made good by exercitation,[59] than by nature," said Democritus.[60] The friction in nature is so enormous that we cannot spare any power. It is not question to express our thought, to elect our way, but to overcome resistances of the medium and material in everything we do. Hence the use of drill, and the worthlessness of amateurs to cope with practitioners. Six hours every day at the piano, only to give facility of touch; six hours a day at painting, only to give command of the odious materials, oil, ochres, and brushes. The masters say, that they know a master in music, only by seeing the pose of the hands on the keys;—so difficult and vital an act is the command of the instrument. To have learned the use of the tools, by thousands of manipulations; to have learned the arts of reckoning, by endless adding and dividing, is the power of the mechanic and the clerk.

I remarked in England, in confirmation of a frequent experience at home, that, in literary circles, the men of trust and consideration, bookmakers,[61] editors, university deans and professors, bishops, too, were by no means men of the largest literary talent, but usually of a low and ordinary intellectuality, with a sort of mercantile activity and working talent. Indifferent hacks and mediocrities tower, by pushing their forces to a lucrative point, or by working power, over multitudes of superior men, in Old as in New England.

I have not forgotten that there are sublime considerations which limit the value of talent and superficial success. We can easily overpraise the vulgar hero. There are sources on which we have not drawn. I know what I abstain from. I adjourn what I have to say on this topic to the chapters on Culture and Worship. But this force or spirit, being the means relied on by Nature for bringing the work of the day about,—as far as we attach importance to household life, and the prizes of the world, we must respect that. And I hold, that an economy may be applied to it; it is as much a subject of exact law and arithmetic as fluids and gases are; it may be husbanded, or wasted; every man is efficient only as he is a container or vessel of this force, and never was any signal act or achievement in history, but by this expenditure. This is not gold, but the gold-maker; not the fame, but the exploit.

If these forces and this husbandry are within reach of our will, and the laws of them can be read, we infer that all success, and all conceivable benefit for man, is also, first or last, within his reach, and has its own sublime economies by which it may be attained. The world is mathematical, and has no casualty, in all its vast and flowing curve. Success has no more eccentricity, than the gingham and muslin we weave in our mills. I know no more affecting lesson to our busy, plotting New England brains, than to go into one of the factories with which we have lined all the watercourses in the States. A man hardly knows how much he is a machine, until he begins to make telegraph, loom, press, and locomotive, in his own image. But in these, he is forced to leave out his follies and hindrances, so that when we go to the mill, the machine is more moral than we. Let a man dare go to a loom, and see if he be equal to it. Let machine confront machine, and see how they come out. The world-mill is more complex than the calico-mill, and the architect stooped less. In the gingham-mill, a broken thread or a shred spoils the web through a piece of a hundred yards, and is traced back to the girl that wove it, and lessens her wages. The stockholder, on being shown this, rubs his hands with delight. Are you so cunning, Mr. Profitloss, and do you expect to swindle *your* master and employer, in the web you weave?[62] A day is a more magnificent cloth than any muslin, the mechanism that makes it is infinitely cunninger, and you shall not conceal the sleazy, fraudulent, rotten hours you have slipped into the piece, nor fear that any honest thread, or straighter steel, or more inflexible shaft, will not testify in the web.

III

WEALTH

———•———

Who shall tell what did befall,
Far away in time, when once,
Over the lifeless ball,
Hung idle stars and suns?
What god the element obeyed?
Wings of what wind the lichen bore,
Wafting the puny seeds of power,
Which, lodged in rock, the rock abrade?
And well the primal pioneer
Knew the strong task to it assigned,
Patient through Heaven's enormous year
To build in matter home for mind.
From air the creeping centuries drew
The matted thicket low and wide,
This must the leaves of ages strew
The granite slab to clothe and hide,
Ere wheat can wave its golden pride.
What smiths, and in what furnace, rolled
(In dizzy æons dim and mute
The reeling brain can ill compute)
Copper and iron, lead, and gold?
What oldest star the fame can save
Of races perishing to pave

The planet with a floor of lime?
Dust is their pyramid and mole:
Who saw what ferns and palms were pressed
Under the tumbling mountain's breast,
In the safe herbal of the coal?
But when the quarried means were piled,
All is waste and worthless, till
Arrives the wise selecting will,
And, out of slime and chaos, Wit
Draws the threads of fair and fit.
Then temples rose, and towns, and marts,
The shop of toil, the hall of arts;
Then flew the sail across the seas
To feed the North from tropic trees;
The storm-wind wove, the torrent span,
Where they were bid the rivers ran;
New slaves fulfilled the poet's dream,
Galvanic wire, strong-shouldered steam.
Then docks were built, and crops were stored,
And ingots added to the hoard.
But, though light-headed man forget,
Remembering Matter pays her debt:
Still, through her motes and masses, draw
Electric thrills and ties of Law,
Which bind the strengths of Nature wild
To the conscience of a child.

WEALTH

As soon as a stranger is introduced into any company one of the first questions which all wish to have answered, is, How does that man get his living? And with reason. He is no whole man until he knows how to earn a blameless livelihood. Society is barbarous, until every industrious man can get his living without dishonest customs.

Every man is a consumer, and ought to be a producer. He fails to make his place good in the world unless he not only pays his debt, but also adds something to the common wealth. Nor can he do justice to his genius without making some larger demand on the world than a bare subsistence. He is by constitution expensive, and needs to be rich.

Wealth has its source in applications of the mind to nature, from the rudest strokes of spade and axe, up to the last secrets of art. Intimate ties subsist between thought and all production; because a better order is equivalent to vast amounts of brute labor. The forces and the resistances are Nature's, but the mind acts in bringing things from where they abound to where they are wanted; in wise combining; in directing the practice of the useful arts, and in the creation of finer values, by fine art, by eloquence, by song, or the reproductions of memory. Wealth is in applications of mind to nature; and the art of getting rich consists not in industry, much less in saving, but in a better order, in timeliness, in being at the right spot. One man has stronger arms, or longer legs; another sees by the course of streams, and growth of markets, where land will be wanted, makes a clearing to the river, goes to sleep, wakes up rich. Steam is no stronger now, than it was a hundred years ago; but is put to better use. A clever fellow was acquainted with the expansive force of steam; he also saw the wealth of wheat and grass rotting in Michigan. Then he cunningly screws on the steam-pipe to the wheat-crop. Puff now, O Steam! The steam puffs and expands as before, but this time it is dragging all Michigan at its back to hungry New York and hungry England. Coal lay in ledges under the ground since the Flood, until a laborer with pick and windlass brings it to the surface. We may well call it black diamonds. Every basket is power and civilization. For coal is a portable climate. It carries the heat of the tropics to Labrador and the polar circle: and it is the means of transporting itself whithersoever it is wanted. Watt and Stephenson[1] whispered in the ear of mankind their secret, that *a half-ounce of coal will draw two tons a mile*, and coal carries coal, by rail and by boat, to make Canada as warm as Calcutta, and with its comfort brings its industrial power.

When the farmer's peaches are taken from under the tree and carried into town, they have a new look and a hundredfold value over the fruit which grew on the same bough and lies fulsomely[2] on the ground. The craft of the merchant is this bringing a thing from where it abounds to where it is costly.

Wealth begins in a tight roof that keeps the rain and wind out; in a good pump that yields you plenty of sweet water; in two suits of clothes, so to change your dress when you are wet; in dry sticks to burn; in a good double-wick lamp; and three meals; in a horse, or a locomotive, to cross the land; in a boat to cross the sea; in tools to work with; in books to read; and so, in giving, on all sides, by tools and auxiliaries, the greatest possible extension to our powers, as if it added feet, and hands, and eyes, and blood, length to the day, and knowledge, and good-will.

Wealth begins with these articles of necessity. And here we must recite the iron law which Nature thunders in these northern climates. First, she requires that each man should feed himself. If, happily, his fathers have left him no inheritance, he must go to work, and by making his wants less, or his gains more, he must draw himself out of that state of pain and insult in which she forces the beggar to lie. She gives him no rest until this is done: she starves, taunts, and torments him, takes away warmth, laughter, sleep, friends, and day-light, until he has fought his way to his own loaf. Then, less peremptorily, but still with sting enough, she urges him to the acquisition of such things as belong to him. Every warehouse and shop-window, every fruit-tree, every thought of every hour, opens a new want to him, which it concerns his power and dignity to gratify. It is of no use to argue the wants down: the philosophers have laid the greatness of man in making his wants few; but will a man content himself with a hut and a handful of dried peas?[3] He is born to be rich. He is thoroughly related; and is tempted out by his appetites and fancies to the conquest of this and that piece of nature, until he finds his well-being in the use of his planet, and of more planets than his own. Wealth requires, besides the crust of bread and the roof,—the freedom of the city, the freedom of the earth, traveling, machinery, the benefits of science, music, and fine arts, the best culture, and the best company. He is the rich man who can avail himself of all men's faculties. He is the richest man who knows how to draw a benefit from the labors of the greatest number of men, of men in distant countries, and in past times. The same correspondence that is between thirst in the stomach, and water in the spring, exists between the whole of man and the whole of nature. The elements offer their service to him. The sea, washing the equator and the poles, offers its perilous aid, and the power and empire that follow it,—day by day to his craft and audacity. "Beware of me," it says, "but if you can hold me, I am the key to all the lands." Fire offers, on its side, an equal power. Fire, steam, lightning, gravity, ledges of rock, mines of iron, lead, quicksilver, tin, and gold; forests of all woods; fruits of all climates; animals of all habits; the powers of tillage; the fabrics of his chemic laboratory; the webs of his loom; the masculine draught of his locomotive, the talismans of the machine-shop; all grand and subtle things, minerals, gases, ethers, passions, war, trade, government, are his natural playmates, and, according to the excellence of the machinery in each human being, is his attraction for the instruments he is to employ. The world is his tool-chest, and he is successful, or his education is carried on just so far, as is the marriage of his faculties with nature, or, the degree in which he takes up things into himself.

The strong race is strong on these terms. The Saxons are the merchants of the world; now, for a thousand years, the leading race, and by nothing more than their quality of personal independence, and, in its special modification, pecuniary independence. No reliance for bread and games[4] on the government, no clanship, no patriarchal style of living by the revenues of a chief, no marrying-on,—no system of clientship suits them; but every man must pay his scot.[5] The English are prosperous and peaceable, with their habit of considering that every man must take care of himself, and has himself to thank, if he do not maintain and improve his position in society.

The subject of economy mixes itself with morals, inasmuch as it is a peremptory point of virtue that a man's independence be secured. Poverty demoralizes. A man in debt is so far a slave; and Wall Street thinks it easy for a *millionaire* to be a man of his word, a man of honor, but, that, in failing circumstances, no man can be relied on to keep his integrity. And when one observes in the hotels and palaces of our Atlantic capitals, the habit of expense, the riot of the senses, the absence of bonds, clanship, fellow-feeling of any kind, he feels, that, when a man or a woman is driven to the wall, the chances of integrity are frightfully diminished, as if virtue were coming to be a luxury which few could afford, or, as Burke said, "at a market almost too high for humanity."[6] He may fix his inventory of necessities and of enjoyments on what scale he pleases, but if he wishes the power and privilege of thought, the chalking out his own career, and having society on his own terms, he must bring his wants within his proper power to satisfy.

The manly part is to do with might and main what you can do. The world is full of fops[7] who never did anything, and who have persuaded beauties and men of genius to wear their fop livery, and these will deliver the fop opinion, that it is not respectable to be seen earning a living; that it is much more respectable to spend without earning; and this doctrine of the snake will come also from the elect sons of light; for wise men are not wise at all hours, and will speak five times from their taste or their humor, to once from their reason. The brave workman, who might betray his feeling of it in his manners, if he do not succumb in his practice, must replace the grace or elegance forfeited, by the merit of the work done. No matter whether he make shoes, or statues, or laws. It is the privilege of any human work which is well done to invest the doer with a certain haughtiness. He can well afford not to conciliate, whose faithful work will answer for him. The mechanic at his bench carries a quiet heart and assured manners, and deals on even terms with men of any condition. The artist has made his picture so true, that it disconcerts criticism. The statue is so beautiful, that it contracts no stain from the market, but makes the market a silent gallery for itself. The case of the young lawyer was pitiful to disgust,—a paltry matter of buttons or tweezer-cases; but the determined youth saw in it an aperture to insert his dangerous wedges, made the insignificance of the thing forgotten, and gave fame by his sense and energy to the name and affairs of the Tittleton snuffbox factory.

Society in large towns is babyish, and wealth is made a toy. The life of pleasure is so ostentatious,[8] that a shallow observer must believe that this is the agreed best use of wealth, and, whatever is pretended, it ends in cosseting. But, if this were the main use of surplus capital, it would bring us to barricades, burned towns, and tomahawks, presently. Men of sense esteem wealth to be the assimilation of nature to themselves, the converting of the sap and juices of the planet to the incarnation and nutriment of their design. Power is what they want,—not candy;—power to execute their design, power to give legs and feet, form and actuality to their thought, which, to a clear-sighted man, appears the end for which the Universe exists, and all its resources might be well applied. Columbus thinks that the sphere is a problem for practical navigation, as well as for closet geometry, and looks on all kings and peoples as cowardly landsmen, until they dare fit him out. Few men on the planet have more truly belonged to it. But he was forced to leave much of his map blank. His successors inherited his map, and inherited his fury to complete it.

So the men of the mine, telegraph, mill, map, and survey,—the monomaniacs, who talk up their project in marts, and offices, and entreat men to subscribe:—how did our factories get built? how did North America get netted with iron rails, except by the importunity[9] of these orators, who dragged all the prudent men in? Is party the madness of many for the gain of a few?[10] This *speculative* genius is the madness of few for the gain of the world. The projectors are sacrificed, but the public is the gainer. Each of these idealists, working after his thought, would make it tyrannical, if he could. He is met and antagonized by other speculators, as hot as he. The equilibrium is preserved by these counteractions, as one tree keeps down another in the forest, that it may not absorb all the sap in the ground. And the supply in nature of railroad presidents, copper-miners, grand-junctioners,[11] smokeburners, fire-annihilators, and etc., is limited by the same law which keeps the proportion in the supply of carbon, of alum, and of hydrogen.

To be rich is to have a ticket of admission to the master-works and chief men of each race. It is to have the sea, by voyaging; to visit the mountains, Niagara, the Nile, the desert, Rome, Paris, Constantinople; to see galleries, libraries, arsenals, manufactories. The reader of Humboldt's[12] "Cosmos" follows the marches of a man whose eyes, ears, and mind are armed by all the science, arts, and implements which mankind have anywhere accumulated, and who is using these to add to the stock. So is it with Denon, Beckford, Belzoni, Wilkinson, Layard, Kane, Lepsius, and Livingstone.[13] "The rich man," says Saadi,[14] "is everywhere expected and at home." The rich take up something more of the world into man's life. They include the country as well as the town, the ocean-side, the White Hills, the Far West, and the old European homesteads of man, in their notion of available material. The world is his, who has money to go over it. He arrives at the sea-shore, and a sumptuous ship has floored and carpeted for him the stormy Atlantic, and made it a luxurious hotel, amid the horrors of tempests. The Persians say, "'Tis the same to him who wears a shoe, as if the whole earth were covered with leather."

Kings are said to have long arms, but every man should have long arms, and should pluck his living, his instruments, his power, and his knowing, from the sun, moon, and stars. Is not then the demand to be rich legitimate? Yet, I have never seen a rich man. I have never seen a man as rich as all men ought to be, or, with an adequate command of nature. The pulpit and the press have many commonplaces denouncing the thirst for wealth; but if men should take these moralists at their word, and leave off aiming to be rich, the moralists would rush to rekindle at all hazards this love of power in the people, lest civilization should be undone. Men are urged by their ideas to acquire the command over nature. Ages derive a culture from the wealth of Roman Caesars, Leo Tenths, magnificent Kings of France, Grand Dukes of Tuscany, Dukes of Devonshire, Townleys, Vernons, and Peels,[15] in England; or whatever great proprietors. It is the interest of all men, that there should be Vaticans and Louvres full of noble works of art; British Museums, and French Gardens of Plants, Philadelphia Academies of Natural History, Bodleian, Ambrosian,[16] Royal, Congressional Libraries. It is the interest of all that there should be Exploring Expeditions; Captain Cooks to voyage round the world, Rosses, Franklins, Richardsons, and Kanes,[17] to find the magnetic and the geographic poles. We are all richer for the measurement of a degree of latitude on the earth's surface. Our navigation is safer for the chart. How intimately our knowledge of the system of the Universe rests on that!—and a true economy in a state or an individual will forget its frugality in behalf of claims like these.

Whilst it is each man's interest, that, not only ease and convenience of living, but also wealth or surplus product should exist somewhere, it need not be in his hands. Often it is very undesirable to him. Goethe said well, "nobody should be rich but those who understand it." Some men are born to own, and can animate all their possessions. Others cannot: their owning is not graceful; seems to be a compromise of their character: they seem to steal their own dividends. They should own who can administer; not they who hoard and conceal; not they who, the greater proprietors they are, are only the greater beggars, but they whose work carves out work for more, opens a path for all. For he is the rich man in whom the people are rich, and he is the poor man in whom the people are poor: and how to give all access to the masterpieces of art and nature, is the problem of civilization. The socialism of our day has done good service in setting men on thinking how certain civilizing benefits, now only enjoyed by the opulent, can be enjoyed by all. For example, the providing to each man the means and apparatus of science, and of the arts. There are many articles good for occasional use, which few men are able to own. Every man wishes to see the ring of Saturn, the satellites and belts of Jupiter and Mars; the mountains and craters in the moon: yet how few can buy a telescope! and of those, scarcely one would like the trouble of keeping it in order, and exhibiting it. So of electrical and chemical apparatus, and many the like things. Every man may have occasion to consult books which he does not care to possess, such as cyclopedias, dictionaries, tables, charts, maps, and public documents: pictures also of birds, beasts, fishes, shells, trees, flowers, whose names he desires to know.

There is a refining influence from the arts of Design on a prepared mind, which is as positive as that of music, and not to be supplied from any other source. But pictures, engravings, statues, and casts, beside their first cost, entail expenses, as of galleries and keepers for the exhibition; and the use which any man can make of them is rare, and their value, too, is much enhanced by the numbers of men who can share their enjoyment. In the Greek cities, it was reckoned profane, that any person should pretend a property in a work of art, which belonged to all who could behold it. I think sometimes,—could I only have music on my own terms;—could I live in a great city, and know where I could go whenever I wished the ablution[18] and inundation[19] of musical waves,—that were a bath and a medicine.

If properties of this kind were owned by states, towns, and lyceums, they would draw the bonds of neighborhood closer. A town would exist to an intellectual purpose. In Europe, where the feudal forms secure the permanence of wealth in certain families, those families buy and preserve these things, and lay them open to the public. But in America, where democratic institutions divide every estate into small portions, after a few years, the public should step into the place of these proprietors, and provide this culture and inspiration for the citizen.

Man was born to be rich, or, inevitably grows rich by the use of his faculties; by the union of thought with nature. Property is an intellectual production. The game requires coolness, right reasoning, promptness, and patience in the players. Cultivated labor drives out brute labor. An infinite number of shrewd men, in infinite years, have arrived at certain best and shortest ways of doing, and this accumulated skill in arts, cultures, harvestings, curings, manufactures, navigations, exchanges, constitutes the worth of our world today.

Commerce is a game of skill, which every man cannot play, which few men can play well. The right merchant is one who has the just average of faculties we call *common-sense*; a man of a strong affinity for facts, who makes up his decision on what he has seen. He is thoroughly persuaded of the truths of arithmetic. There is always a reason, *in the man*, for his good or bad fortune, and so, in making money. Men talk as if there were some magic about this, and believe in magic, in all parts of life. He knows, that all goes on the old road, pound for pound, cent for cent,—for every effect a perfect cause,—and that good luck is another name for tenacity of purpose. He insures himself in every transaction, and likes small and sure gains. Probity and closeness to the facts are the basis, but the masters of the art add a certain long arithmetic. The problem is, to combine many and remote operations, with the accuracy and adherence to the facts, which is easy in near and small transactions; so to arrive at gigantic results, without any compromise of safety. Napoleon was fond of telling the story of the Marseilles banker, who said to his visitor, surprised at the contrast between the splendor of the banker's chateau and hospitality, and the meanness of the counting-room in which he had seen him,—"Young man, you are too young to understand how masses are formed,—the true and only power,—whether composed of money, water, or men, it is all alike,—a mass is an immense center of motion, but it must be begun, it must be kept up:"—and he might have added, that the way in which it must be begun and kept up, is, by obedience to the law of particles.

Success consists in close appliance to the laws of the world, and, since those laws are intellectual and moral, an intellectual and moral obedience. Political Economy is as good a book wherein to read the life of man, and the ascendancy of laws over all private and hostile influences, as any Bible which has come down to us.

Money is representative, and follows the nature and fortunes of the owner. The coin is a delicate meter of civil, social, and moral changes. The farmer is covetous of his dollar, and with reason. It is no waif[20] to him. He knows how many strokes of labor it represents. His bones ache with the day's work that earned it. He knows how much land it represents;—how much rain, frost, and sunshine. He knows that, in the dollar, he gives you so much discretion and patience so much hoeing, and threshing. Try to lift his dollar; you must lift all that weight. In the city, where money follows the skit[21] of a pen, or a lucky rise in exchange, it comes to be looked on as light. I wish the farmer held it dearer, and would spend it only for real bread; force for force.

The farmer's dollar is heavy, and the clerk's is light and nimble; leaps out of his pocket; jumps on to cards and faro-tables:[22] but still more curious is its susceptibility to metaphysical changes. It is the finest barometer of social storms, and announces revolutions.

Every step of civil advancement makes every man's dollar worth more. In California, the country where it grew,—what would it buy? A few years since, it would buy a shanty, dysentery, hunger, bad company, and crime. There are wide countries, like Siberia, where it would buy little else today, than some petty mitigation of suffering. In Rome, it will buy beauty and magnificence. Forty years ago, a dollar would not buy much in Boston. Now it will buy a great deal more in our old town, thanks to railroads, telegraphs, steamers, and the contemporaneous growth of New York, and the whole country. Yet there are many goods appertaining to a capital city, which are not yet purchasable here, no, not with a mountain of dollars. A dollar in Florida is not worth a dollar in Massachusetts. A dollar is not value, but representative of value, and, at last, of moral values. A dollar is rated for the corn it will buy, or to speak strictly, not for the corn or house-room, but for Athenian corn, and Roman house-room,—for the wit, probity, and power, which we eat bread and dwell in houses to share and exert. Wealth is mental; wealth is moral. The value of a dollar is, to buy just things: a dollar goes on increasing in value with all the genius, and all the virtue of the world. A dollar in a university, is worth more than a dollar in a jail; in a temperate, schooled, law-abiding community, than in some sink of crime, where dice, knives, and arsenic, are in constant play.

The "Bank-Note Detector"[23] is a useful publication. But the current dollar, silver or paper, is itself the detector of the right and wrong where it circulates. Is it not instantly enhanced by the increase of equity? If a trader refuses to sell his vote, or adheres to some odious right, he makes so much more equity in Massachusetts; and every acre in the State is more worth, in the hour of his action. If you take out of State-street the ten honestest merchants, and put in ten roguish persons, controlling the same amount of capital,—the rates of insurance will indicate it; the soundness of banks will show it: the highways will be less secure: the schools will feel it; the children will bring home their little dose of the poison: the judge will sit less firmly on the bench, and his decisions be less upright; he has lost so much support and constraint,—which all need; and the pulpit will betray it, in a laxer rule of life. An apple-tree, if you take out every day for a number of days, a load of loam, and put in a load of sand about its roots,—will find it out. An apple-tree is a stupid kind of creature, but if this treatment be pursued for a short time, I think it would begin to mistrust something. And if you should take out of the powerful class engaged in trade a hundred good men, and put in a hundred bad, or, what is just the same thing, introduce a demoralizing institution, would not the dollar, which is not much stupider than an apple-tree, presently find it out? The value of a dollar is social, as it is created by society. Every man who removes into this city, with any purchasable talent or skill in him, gives to every man's labor in the city, a new worth. If a talent is anywhere born into the world, the community of nations is enriched; and, much more, with a new degree of probity. The expense of crime, one of the principal charges of every nation, is so far stopped. In Europe, crime is observed to increase or abate with the price of bread. If the Rothschilds at Paris do not accept bills, the people at Manchester, at Paisley,[24] at Birmingham, are forced into the highway, and landlords are shot down in Ireland. The police records attest it. The vibrations are presently felt in New York, New Orleans, and Chicago. Not much otherwise, the economical power touches the masses through the political lords. Rothschild refuses the Russian loan, and there is peace, and the harvests are saved. He takes it, and there is war, and an agitation through a large portion of mankind, with every hideous result, ending in revolution, and a new order.

Wealth brings with it its own checks and balances. The basis of political economy is non-interference. The only safe rule is found in the self-adjusting meter of demand and supply. Do not legislate. Meddle, and you snap the sinews with your sumptuary laws.[25] Give no bounties: make equal laws: secure life and property, and you need not give alms. Open the doors of opportunity to talent and virtue, and they will do themselves justice, and property will not be in bad hands. In a free and just commonwealth, property rushes from the idle and imbecile, to the industrious, brave, and persevering.

The laws of nature play through trade, as a toy-battery exhibits the effects of electricity. The level of the sea is not more surely kept, than is the equilibrium of value in society, by the demand and supply: and artifice or legislation punishes itself, by reactions, gluts, and bankruptcies. The sublime laws play indifferently through atoms and galaxies. Whoever knows what happens in the getting and spending of a loaf of bread and a pint of beer; that no wishing will change the rigorous limits of pints and penny loaves; that, for all that is consumed, so much less remains in the basket and pot; but what is gone out of these is not wasted, but well spent, if it nourish his body, and enable him to finish his task;—knows all of political economy that the budgets of empires can teach him. The interest of petty economy is this symbolization of the great economy; the way in which a house, and a private man's methods, tally with the solar system, and the laws of give and take, throughout nature; and, however wary we are of the falsehoods and petty tricks which we suicidally play off on each other, every man has a certain satisfaction, whenever his dealing touches on the inevitable facts; when he sees that things themselves dictate the price, as they always tend to do, and, in large manufactures, are seen to do. Your paper is not fine or coarse enough,—is too heavy, or too thin. The manufacturer says, he will furnish you with just that thickness or thinness you want; the pattern is quite indifferent to him; here is his schedule;—any variety of paper, as cheaper or dearer, with the prices annexed. A pound of paper costs so much, and you may have it made up in any pattern you fancy.

There is in all our dealings a self-regulation that supersedes chaffering.[26] You will rent a house, but must have it cheap. The owner can reduce the rent, but so he incapacitates himself from making proper repairs, and the tenant gets not the house he would have, but a worse one; besides, that a relation a little injurious is established between land-lord and tenant. You dismiss your laborer, saying, "Patrick, I shall send for you as soon as I cannot do without you." Patrick goes off contented, for he knows that the weeds will grow with the potatoes, the vines must be planted, next week, and, however unwilling you may be, the cantelopes, crook-necks, and cucumbers will send for him. Who but must wish that all labor and value should stand on the same simple and surly market? If it is the best of its kind, it will. We must have joiner, locksmith, planter, priest, poet, doctor, cook, weaver, ostler;[27] each in turn, through the year.

If a St. Michael's pear sells for a shilling, it costs a shilling to raise it. If, in Boston, the best securities offer twelve *per cent* for money, they have just six *per cent* of insecurity. You may not see that the fine pear costs you a shilling, but it costs the community so much. The shilling represents the number of enemies the pear has, and the amount of risk in ripening it. The price of coal shows the narrowness of the coal-field, and a compulsory confinement of the miners to a certain district. All salaries are reckoned on contingent, as well as on actual services. "If the wind were always southwest by west," said the skipper, "women might take ships to sea." One might say, that all things are of one price; that nothing is cheap or dear; and that the apparent disparities that strike us, are only a shopman's trick of concealing the damage in your bargain. A youth coming into the city from his native New Hampshire farm, with its hard fare still fresh in his remembrance, boards at a first-class hotel, and believes he must somehow have outwitted Dr. Franklin and Malthus,[28] for luxuries are cheap. But he pays for the one convenience of a better dinner, by the loss of some of the richest social and educational advantages. He has lost what guards! what incentives! He will perhaps find by and by, that he left the Muses at the door of the hotel, and found the Furies inside. Money often costs too much, and power and pleasure are not cheap. The ancient poet said, "the gods sell all things at a fair price."

There is an example of the compensations in the commercial history of this country. When the European wars threw the carrying-trade of the world, from 1800 to 1812, into American bottoms, a seizure was now and then made of an American ship. Of course, the loss was serious to the owner, but the country was indemnified; for we charged threepence a pound for carrying cotton, sixpence for tobacco, and so on; which paid for the risk and loss, and brought into the country an immense prosperity, early marriages, private wealth, the building of cities, and of states: and, after the war was over, we received compensation over and above, by treaty, for all the seizures. Well, the Americans grew rich and great. But the pay-day comes round. Britain, France, and Germany, which our extraordinary profits had impoverished, send out, attracted by the fame of our advantages, first their thousands, then their millions, of poor people, to share the crop. At first, we employ them, and increase our prosperity: but, in the artificial system of society and of protected labor, which we also have adopted and enlarged, there come presently checks and stoppages. Then we refuse to employ these poor men. But they will not so be answered. They go into the poor rates, and, though we refuse wages, we must now pay the same amount in the form of taxes. Again, it turns out that the largest proportion of crimes are committed by foreigners. The cost of the crime, and the expense of courts, and of prisons, we must bear, and the standing army of preventive police we must pay. The cost of education of the posterity of this great colony, I will not compute. But the gross amount of these costs will begin to pay back what we thought was a net gain from our transatlantic customers of 1800. It is vain to refuse this payment. We cannot get rid of these people, and we cannot get rid of their will to be supported. That has become an inevitable element of our politics; and, for their votes, each of the dominant parties courts and assists them to get it executed. Moreover, we have to pay, not what would have contented them at home, but what they have learned to think necessary here; so that opinion, fancy, and all manner of moral considerations complicate the problem.[29]

There are a few measures of economy which will bear to be named without disgust; for the subject is tender, and we may easily have too much of it; and therein resembles the hideous animalcules of which our bodies are built up,— which, offensive in the particular, yet compose valuable and effective masses.

Our nature and genius force us to respect ends, whilst we use means. We must use the means, and yet, in our most accurate using, somehow screen and cloak them, as we can only give them any beauty, by a reflection of the glory of the end. That is the good head, which serves the end, and commands the means. The rabble are corrupted by their means: the means are too strong for them, and they desert their end.

1. The first of these measures is that each man's expense must proceed from his character. As long as your genius buys, the investment is safe, though you spend like a monarch. Nature arms each man with some faculty which enables him to do easily some feat impossible to any other, and thus makes him necessary to society. This native determination guides his labor and his spending. He wants an equipment of means and tools proper to his talent. And to save on this point, were to neutralize the special strength and helpfulness of each mind. Do your work, respecting the excellence of the work, and not its acceptableness. This is so much economy, that, rightly read, it is the sum of economy. Profligacy consists not in spending years of time or chests of money,—but in spending them off the line of your career. The crime which bankrupts men and states, is, job-work;—declining from your main design, to serve a turn here or there. Nothing is beneath you, if it is in the direction of your life: nothing is great or desirable, if it is off from that. I think we are entitled here to draw a straight line, and say, that society can never prosper, but must always be bankrupt, until every man does that which he was created to do.

Spend for your expense, and retrench the expense which is not yours. Allston,[30] the painter, was wont to say, that he built a plain house, and filled it with plain furniture, because he would hold out no bribe to any to visit him, who had not similar tastes to his own. We are sympathetic, and, like children, want everything we see. But it is a large stride to independence,—when a man, in the discovery of his proper talent, has sunk the necessity for false expenses. As the betrothed maiden, by one secure affection, is relieved from a system of slaveries,—the daily inculcated necessity of pleasing all,—so the man who has found what he can do, can spend on that, and leave all other spending. Montaigne[31] said, "When he was a younger brother, he went brave in dress and equipage, but afterward his chateau and farms might answer for him." Let a man who belongs to the class of nobles, those, namely, who have found out that they can do something, relieve himself of all vague squandering on objects not his. Let the realist not mind appearances. Let him delegate to others the costly courtesies and decorations of social life. The virtues are economists, but some of the vices are also. Thus, next to humility, I have noticed that pride is a pretty good husband. A good pride is, as I reckon it, worth from five hundred to fifteen hundred a year. Pride is handsome, economical: pride eradicates so many vices, letting none subsist but itself, that it seems as if it were a great gain to exchange vanity for pride. Pride can go without domestics, without fine clothes, can live in a house with two rooms, can eat potato, purslane, beans, lyed corn,[32] can work on the soil, can travel afoot, can talk with poor men, or sit silent well-contented in fine saloons. But vanity costs money, labor, horses, men, women, health, and peace, and is still nothing at last, a long way leading nowhere.—Only one drawback; proud people are intolerably selfish, and the vain are gentle and giving.

Art is a jealous mistress, and, if a man have a genius for painting, poetry, music, architecture, or philosophy, he makes a bad husband, and an ill pro-vider, and should be wise in season, and not fetter himself with duties which will embitter his days, and spoil him for his proper work. We had in this region, twenty years ago, among our educated men, a sort of Arcadian[33] fanaticism, a passionate desire to go upon the land, and unite farming to intellectual pursuits. Many effected their purpose, and made the experiment, and some became downright ploughmen; but all were cured of their faith that scholarship and practical farming, (I mean, with one's own hands,)—could be united.

With brow bent, with firm intent, the pale scholar leaves his desk to draw a freer breath, and get a juster statement of his thought, in the garden-walk. He stoops to pull up a purslane, or a dock,[34] that is choking the young corn, and finds there are two: close behind the last, is a third; he reaches out his hand to a fourth; behind that, are four thousand and one. He is heated and untuned, and, by and by, wakes up from his idiot dream of chickweed and red-root, to remember his morning thought, and to find, that, with his adamantine purposes, he has been duped by a dandelion. A garden is like those pernicious machiner-ies we read of, every month, in the newspapers, which catch a man's coat-skirt or his hand, and draw in his arm, his leg, and his whole body to irresistible destruction. In an evil hour he pulled down his wall, and added a field to his homestead. No land is bad, but land is worse. If a man own land, the land owns him. Now let him leave home, if he dare. Every tree and graft, every hill of melons, row of corn, or quickset hedge, all he has done, and all he means to do, stand in his way, like duns,[35] when he would go out of his gate. The devotion to these vines and trees he finds poisonous. Long free walks, a circuit of miles, free his brain, and serve his body.[36] Long marches are no hardship to him. He believes he composes easily on the hills. But this pottering in a few square yards of garden is dispiriting and driveling. The smell of the plants has drugged him, and robbed him of energy. He finds a catalepsy[37] in his bones. He grows peevish and poor-spirited. The genius of reading and of gardening are antagonistic, like resinous and vitreous electricity. One is concentrative in sparks and shocks: the other is diffuse strength; so that each disqualifies its workman for the other's duties.

An engraver, whose hands must be of an exquisite delicacy of stroke, should not lay stone walls. Sir David Brewster[38] gives exact instructions for microscopic observation:—"Lie down on your back, and hold the single lens and object over your eye," *etc., etc.* How much more the seeker of abstract truth, who needs periods of isolation, and rapt concentration, and almost a going out of the body to think!

2. Spend after your genius, *and by system.* Nature goes by rule, not by sallies and saltations.[39] There must be system in the economies. Saving and unexpensiveness will not keep the most pathetic family from ruin, nor will bigger incomes make free spending safe. The secret of success lies never in the amount of money, but in the relation of income to outgo; as if, after expense has been fixed at a certain point, then new and steady rills of income, though never so small, being added, wealth begins. But in ordinary, as means increase, spending increases faster, so that, large incomes, in England and elsewhere, are found not to help matters;—the eating quality of debt does not relax its voracity. When the cholera is in the potato,[40] what is the use of planting larger crops? In England, the richest country in the universe, I was assured by shrewd observers, that great lords and ladies had no more guineas to give away than other people; that liberality with money is as rare, and as immediately famous a virtue as it is here. Want is a growing giant whom the coat of Have was never large enough to cover. I remember in Warwickshire, to have been shown a fair manor, still in the same name as in Shakespeare's time. The rent-roll, I was told, is some fourteen thousand pounds a year: but, when the second son of the late proprietor was born, the father was perplexed how to provide for him. The eldest son must inherit the manor; what to do with this supernumerary? He was advised to breed him for the Church, and to settle him in the rectorship, which was in the gift of the family; which was done. It is a general rule in that country, that bigger incomes do not help anybody. It is commonly observed, that a sudden wealth, like a prize drawn in a lottery, or a large bequest to a poor family, does not permanently enrich. They have served no apprenticeship to

wealth, and, with the rapid wealth, come rapid claims: which they do not know how to deny, and the treasure is quickly dissipated.

A system must be in every economy, or the best single expedients are of no avail. A farm is a good thing, when it begins and ends with itself, and does not need a salary, or a shop, to eke it out. Thus, the cattle are a main link in the chain-ring. If the non-conformist or aesthetic farmer leaves out the cattle, and does not also leave out the want which the cattle must supply, he must fill the gap by begging or stealing. When men now alive were born, the farm yielded everything that was consumed on it. The farm yielded no money, and the farmer got on without. If he fell sick, his neighbors came in to his aid: each gave a day's work; or a half day; or lent his yoke of oxen, or his horse, and kept his work even: hoed his potatoes, mowed his hay, reaped his rye; well knowing that no man could afford to hire labor, without selling his land. In autumn, a farmer could sell an ox or a hog, and get a little money to pay taxes withal. Now, the farmer buys almost all he consumes,—tin-ware, cloth, sugar, tea, coffee, fish, coal, railroad-tickets, and newspapers.

A master in each art is required, because the practice is never with still or dead subjects, but they change in your hands. You think farm-buildings and broad acres a solid property: but its value is flowing like water. It requires as much watching as if you were decanting wine from a cask. The farmer knows what to do with it, stops every leak, turns all the streamlets to one reservoir, and decants wine: but a blunderhead comes out of Cornhill, tries his hand, and it all leaks away. So is it with granite streets, or timber townships, as with fruit or flowers. Nor is any investment so permanent, that it can be allowed to remain without incessant watching, as the history of each attempt to lock up an inheritance through two generations for an unborn inheritor may show.

When Mr. Cockayne takes a cottage in the country, and will keep his cow, he thinks a cow is a creature that is fed on hay, and gives a pail of milk twice a day. But the cow that he buys gives milk for three months; then her bag dries up. What to do with a dry cow? who will buy her? Perhaps he bought also a yoke of oxen to do his work; but they get blown[41] and lame. What to do with blown and lame oxen? The farmer fats his, after the spring-work is done, and kills them in the fall. But how can Cockayne, who has no pastures, and leaves his cottage daily in the cars, at business hours, be bothered with fatting and killing oxen? He plants trees; but there must be crops, to keep the trees in ploughed land. What shall be the crops? He will have nothing to do with trees, but will have grass. After a year or two, the grass must be turned up and ploughed: now what crops? Credulous Cockayne!

3. Help comes in the custom of the country, and the rule of *Impera parendo*.[42] The rule is not to dictate, nor to insist on carrying out each of your schemes by ignorant willfulness, but to learn practically the secret spoken from all nature, that things themselves refuse to be mismanaged, and will show to the watchful their own law. Nobody need stir hand or foot. The custom of the country will do it all. I know not how to build or to plant; neither how to buy wood, nor what to do with the house-lot, the field, or the wood-lot, when bought. Never fear: it is all settled how it shall be, long beforehand, in the custom of the country, whether to sand, or whether to clay it, when to plough, and how to dress, whether to grass, or to corn; and you cannot help or hinder it. Nature has her own best mode of doing each thing, and she has somewhere told it plainly, if we will keep our eyes and ears open. If not, she will not be slow in undeceiving us, when we prefer our own way to hers. How often we must remember the art of the surgeon, which, in replacing the broken bone, contents itself with releasing the parts from false position; they fly into place by the action of the muscles. On this art of nature all our arts rely.

Of the two eminent engineers in the recent construction of railways in England, Mr. Brunel[43] went straight from terminus to terminus, through mountains, over streams, crossing highways, cutting ducal estates in two, and shooting through this man's cellar, and that man's attic window, and so arriving at his end, at great pleasure to geometers, but with cost to his company. Mr. Stephenson,[44] on the contrary, believing that the river knows the way, followed his valley, as implicitly as our Western Railroad follows the Westfield River, and turned out to be the safest and cheapest engineer. We say the cows laid out Boston. Well, there are worse surveyors. Every pedestrian in our pastures has frequent occasion to thank the cows for cutting the best path through the thicket, and over the hills: and travelers and Indians know the value of a buffalo-trail, which is sure to be the easiest possible pass through the ridge.

When a citizen, fresh from Dock-square, or Milk-street,[45] comes out and buys land in the country, his first thought is to a fine outlook from his windows: his library must command a western view: a sunset every day, bathing the shoulder of Blue Hills, Wachusett, and the peaks of Monadnock and Uncanoonuc.[46] What, thirty acres, and all this magnificence for fifteen hundred dollars! It would be cheap at fifty thousand. He proceeds at once, his eyes dim with tears of joy, to fix the spot for his corner-stone. But the man who is to level the ground, thinks it will take many hundred loads of gravel to fill the hollow to the road. The stone-mason who should build the well thinks he shall have to dig forty feet: the baker doubts he shall never like to drive up to the door: the practical neighbor cavils[47] at the position of the barn; and the citizen comes to know that his predecessor the farmer built the house in the right spot for the sun and wind, the spring, and water-drainage, and the convenience to the pasture, the garden, the field, and the road. So Dock-square yields the point, and things have their own way. Use has made the farmer wise, and the foolish citizen learns to take his counsel. From step to step he comes at last to surrender at discretion. The farmer affects to take his orders; but the citizen says, You may ask me as often as you will, and in what ingenious forms, for an opinion concerning the mode of building my wall, or sinking my well, or laying out my acre, but the ball will rebound to you. These are matters on which I neither know, nor need to know anything. These are questions which you and not I shall answer.

Not less, within doors, a system settles itself paramount and tyrannical over master and mistress, servant and child, cousin and acquaintance. 'Tis in vain that genius or virtue or energy of character strive and cry against it. This is fate. And 'tis very well that the poor husband reads in a book of a new way of living, and resolves to adopt it at home: let him go home and try it, if he dare.

4. Another point of economy is to look for seed of the same kind as you sow: and not to hope to buy one kind with another kind. Friendship buys friendship; justice, justice; military merit, military success. Good husbandry finds wife, children, and household. The good merchant large gains, ships, stocks, and money. The good poet fame, and literary credit; but not either, the other. Yet there is commonly a confusion of expectations on these points. Hotspur lives for the moment; praises himself for it; and despises Furlong, that he does not. Hotspur, of course, is poor; and Furlong a good provider. The odd circumstance is, that Hotspur thinks it a superiority in himself, this improvidence, which ought to be rewarded with Furlong's lands.

I have not at all completed my design. But we must not leave the topic, without casting one glance into the interior recesses. It is a doctrine of philosophy, that man is a being of degrees; that there is nothing in the world, which is not repeated in his body; his body being a sort of miniature or summary of the world: then that there is nothing in his body, which is not repeated as in a celestial sphere in his mind: then, there is nothing in his brain, which is not repeated in a higher sphere, in his moral system.

5. Now these things are so in Nature. All things ascend, and the royal rule of economy is, that it should ascend also, or, whatever we do must always have a higher aim. Thus it is a maxim, that money is another kind of blood. *Pecunia alter sanguis*: or, the estate of a man is only a larger kind of body, and admits of regimen analogous to his bodily circulations. So there is no maxim of the merchant, *e.g.*, "Best use of money is to pay debts;" "Every business by itself;" "Best time is present time;" "The right investment is in tools of your trade;" or the like, which does not admit of an extended sense. The counting-room maxims liberally expounded are laws of the Universe. The merchant's economy is a coarse symbol of the soul's economy. It is, to spend for power, and not for pleasure. It is to invest income; that is to say, to take up particulars into generals; days into integral eras,—literary, emotive, practical, of its life, and still to ascend in its investment. The merchant has but one rule, *absorb and invest*: he is to be capitalist: the scraps and filings must be gathered back into the crucible; the gas and smoke must be burned, and earnings must not go to increase expense, but to capital again. Well, the man must be capitalist. Will he spend his income, or will he invest? His body and every organ is under the same law. His body is a jar, in which the liquor of life is stored. Will he spend for pleasure? The way to ruin is short and facile. Will he not spend, but hoard for power? It passes through the sacred fermentations, by that law of Nature whereby everything climbs to higher platforms, and bodily vigor becomes mental and moral vigor. The bread he eats is first strength and animal spirits: it becomes, in higher laboratories, imagery and thought; and in still higher results, courage and endurance. This is the right compound interest; this is capital doubled, quadrupled, centupled; man raised to his highest power.

The true thrift is always to spend on the higher plane; to invest and invest, with keener avarice, that he may spend in spiritual creation, and not in augmenting animal existence. Nor is the man enriched, in repeating the old experiments of animal sensation, nor unless through new powers and ascending pleasures, he knows himself by the actual experience of higher good, to be already on the way to the highest.

IV

CULTURE

———•———

Can rules or tutors educate
The semigod whom we await?
He must be musical,
Tremulous, impressional,
Alive to gentle influence
Of landscape and of sky,
And tender to the spirit-touch
Of man's or maiden's eye:
But, to his native center fast,
Shall into Future fuse the Past,
And the world's flowing fates in his own mould
    recast.

CULTURE

The word of ambition at the present day is Culture. Whilst all the world is in pursuit of power, and of wealth as a means of power, culture corrects the theory of success. A man is the prisoner of his power. A topical memory makes him an almanac; a talent for debate, a disputant; skill to get money makes him a miser, that is, a beggar. Culture reduces these inflammations by invoking the aid of other powers against the dominant talent, and by appealing to the rank of powers. It watches success. For performance, Nature has no mercy, and sacrifices the performer to get it done; makes a dropsy or a tympany[1] of him. If she wants a thumb, she makes one at the cost of arms and legs, and any excess of power in one part is usually paid for at once by some defect in a contiguous part.

Our efficiency depends so much on our concentration, that Nature usually in the instances where a marked man is sent into the world, overloads him with bias, sacrificing his symmetry to his working power. It is said a man can write but one book; and if a man have a defect, it is apt to leave its impression on all his performances. If she creates a policeman like Fouché, he is made up of suspicions and of plots to circumvent them. "The air," said Fouché, "is full of poniards." The physician Sanctorius spent his life in a pair of scales, weighing his food. Lord Coke[2] valued Chaucer highly, because the Canon Yeman's Tale illustrates the statute *Hen. IV. Chap.* 4, against alchemy. I saw a man who believed the principal mischiefs in the English state were derived from the devotion to musical concerts. A freemason, not long since, set out to explain to this country that the principal cause of the success of General Washington was the aid he derived from the freemasons.

But worse than the harping on one string, Nature has secured individualism, by giving the private person a high conceit of his weight in the system. The pest of society is egotists. There are dull and bright, sacred and profane, coarse and fine egotists. 'Tis a disease that, like influenza, falls on all constitutions. In the distemper known to physicians as *chorea*,[3] the patient sometimes turns round, and continues to spin slowly on one spot. Is egotism a metaphysical variety of this malady? The man runs round a ring formed by his own talent, falls into an admiration of it, and loses relation to the world. It is a tendency in all minds. One of its annoying forms, is a craving for sympathy. The sufferers parade their miseries, tear the lint from their bruises, reveal their indictable crimes, that you may pity them. They like sickness, because physical pain will extort some show of interest from the bystanders, as we have seen children, who, finding themselves of no account when grown people come in, will cough till they choke, to draw attention.

This distemper is the scourge of talent,—of artists, inventors, and philosophers. Eminent spiritualists shall have an incapacity of putting their act or word aloof from them, and seeing it bravely for the nothing it is. Beware of the man who says, "I am on the eve of a revelation." It is speedily punished, inasmuch as this habit invites men to humor it, and by treating the patient tenderly, to shut him up in a narrower selfism, and exclude him from the great world of God's cheerful fallible men and women. Let us rather be insulted, whilst we are insultable. Religious literature has eminent examples, and if we run over our private list of poets, critics, philanthropists, and philosophers, we shall find them infected with this dropsy and elephantiasis, which we ought to have tapped.

This goiter[4] of egotism is so frequent among notable persons that we must infer some strong necessity in nature which it subserves; such as we see in the sexual attraction. The preservation of the species was a point of such necessity that Nature has secured it at all hazards by immensely overloading the passion, at the risk of perpetual crime and disorder. So egotism has its root in the cardinal necessity by which each individual persists to be what he is.

This individuality is not only not inconsistent with culture, but is the basis of it. Every valuable nature is there in its own right, and the student we speak to must have a mother-wit invincible by his culture, which uses all books, arts, facilities, and elegancies of intercourse, but is never subdued and lost in them. He only is a well-made man who has a good determination. And the end of culture is not to destroy this, God forbid! but to train away all impediment and mixture, and leave nothing but pure power. Our student must have a style and determination, and be a master in his own specialty. But, having this, he must put it behind him. He must have a catholicity, a power to see with a free and disengaged look every object. Yet is this private interest and self so overcharged that, if a man seeks a companion who can look at objects for their own sake, and without affection or self-reference, he will find the fewest who will give him that satisfaction; whilst most men are afflicted with a coldness, an incuriosity, as soon as any object does not connect with their self-love. Though they talk of the object before them, they are thinking of themselves, and their vanity is laying little traps for your admiration.

But after a man has discovered that there are limits to the interest which his private history has for mankind, he still converses with his family, or a few companions,—perhaps with half a dozen personalities that are famous in his neighborhood. In Boston, the question of life is the names of some eight or ten men. Have you seen Mr. Allston, Doctor Channing, Mr. Adams, Mr. Webster, Mr. Greenough?[5] Have you heard Everett, Garrison, Father Taylor,[6] Theodore Parker?[7] Have you talked with Messieurs Turbinewheel, Summitlevel, and Lacofrupees? Then you may as well die. In New York, the question is of some other eight, or ten, or twenty. Have you seen a few lawyers, merchants, and brokers,—two or three scholars, two or three capitalists, two or three editors of newspapers? New York is a sucked orange. All conversation is at an end, when we have discharged ourselves of a dozen personalities, domestic or imported, which make up our American existence. Nor do we expect anybody to be other than a faint copy of these heroes.

Life is very narrow. Bring any club or company of intelligent men together again after ten years, and if the presence of some penetrating and calming genius could dispose them to frankness, what a confession of insanities would come up! The "causes" to which we have sacrificed, Tariff or Democracy, Whiggism or Abolition, Temperance or Socialism, would show like roots of bitterness and dragons of wrath: and our talents are as mischievous as if each had been seized upon by some bird of prey, which had whisked him away from fortune, from truth, from the dear society of the poets, some zeal, some bias, and only when he was now gray and nerveless, was it relaxing its claws, and he awaking to sober perceptions.

Culture is the suggestion from certain best thoughts, that a man has a range of affinities, through which he can modulate the violence of any master-tones that have a droning preponderance in his scale, and succor him against himself. Culture redresses his balance, puts him among his equals and superiors, revives the delicious sense of sympathy, and warns him of the dangers of solitude and repulsion.

'Tis not a compliment but a disparagement to consult a man only on horses, or on steam, or on theaters, or on eating, or on books, and, whenever he appears, considerately to turn the conversation to the bantling[8] he is known to

fondle. In the Norse heaven of our forefathers, Thor's house had five hundred
and forty floors; and man's house has five hundred and forty floors. His excellence is facility of adaptation and of transition through many related points, to
wide contrasts and extremes. Culture kills his exaggeration, his conceit of his
village or his city. We must leave our pets at home, when we go into the street,
and meet men on broad grounds of good meaning and good sense. No performance is worth loss of geniality. 'Tis a cruel price we pay for certain fancy goods
called fine arts and philosophy. In the Norse legend, Allfadir did not get a drink
of Mimir's spring (the fountain of wisdom,) until he left his eye in pledge. And
here is a pedant that cannot unfold his wrinkles, nor conceal his wrath at interruption by the best, if their conversation do not fit his impertinency,—here is he
to afflict us with his personalities. 'Tis incident to scholars that each of them
fancies he is pointedly odious in his community. Draw him out of this limbo of
irritability. Cleanse with healthy blood his parchment skin. You restore to him
his eyes which he left in pledge at Mimir's spring. If you are the victim of your
doing, who cares what you do? We can spare your opera, your gazetteer, your
chemic analysis, your history, your syllogisms. Your man of genius pays dear
for his distinction. His head runs up into a spire, and instead of a healthy man,
merry and wise, he is some mad dominie.[9] Nature is reckless of the individual.
When she has points to carry, she carries them. To wade in marshes and
sea-margins is the destiny of certain birds, and they are so accurately made for
this that they are imprisoned in those places. Each animal out of its *habitat*
would starve. To the physician, each man, each woman, is an amplification of
one organ. A soldier, a locksmith, a bank-clerk, and a dancer could not
exchange functions. And thus we are victims of adaptation.

The antidotes against this organic egotism, are, the range and variety of attractions, as gained by acquaintance with the world, with men of merit, with
classes of society, with travel, with eminent persons, and with the high resources of philosophy, art, and religion: books, travel, society, solitude.

The hardiest skeptic who has seen a horse broken, a pointer trained, or, who
has visited a menagerie, or the exhibition of the Industrious Fleas, will not deny
the validity of education. "A boy," says Plato,[10] "is the most vicious of all wild
beasts;" and, in the same spirit, the old English poet Gascoigne[11] says, "a boy is
better unborn than untaught." The city breeds one kind of speech and manners;
the back-country a different style; the sea, another; the army, a fourth. We
know that an army which can be confided in, may be formed by discipline;
that, by systematic discipline all men may be made heroes: Marshal Lannes[12]

said to a French officer, "Know, Colonel, that none but a poltroon[13] will boast that he never was afraid." A great part of courage is the courage of having done the thing before. And, in all human action, those faculties will be strong which are used. Robert Owen[14] said, "Give me a tiger, and I will educate him." 'Tis inhuman to want faith in the power of education, since to meliorate, is the law of nature; and men are valued precisely as they exert onward or meliorating force. On the other hand, poltroonery[15] is the acknowledging an inferiority to be incurable.

Incapacity of melioration is the only mortal distemper. There are people who can never understand a trope,[16] or any second or expanded sense given to your words, or any humor; but remain literalists, after hearing the music, and poetry, and rhetoric, and wit, of seventy or eighty years. They are past the help of surgeon or clergy. But even these can understand pitchforks and the cry of fire! and I have noticed in some of this class a marked dislike of earthquakes.

Let us make our education brave and preventive. Politics is an after-work, a poor patching. We are always a little late. The evil is done, the law is passed, and we begin the up-hill agitation for repeal of that of which we ought to have prevented the enacting. We shall one day learn to supersede politics by education. What we call our root-and-branch reforms of slavery, war, gambling, intemperance, is only medicating the symptoms. We must begin higher up, namely, in Education.

Our arts and tools give to him who can handle them much the same advantage over the novice, as if you extended his life, ten, fifty, or a hundred years. And I think it the part of good sense to provide every fine soul with such culture that it shall not, at thirty or forty years, have to say, 'This which I might do is made hopeless through my want of weapons.'

But it is conceded that much of our training fails of effect; that all success is hazardous and rare; that a large part of our cost and pains is thrown away. Nature takes the matter into her own hands, and, though we must not omit any jot of our system, we can seldom be sure that it has availed much, or that as much good would not have accrued from a different system.

Books, as containing the finest records of human wit, must always enter into our notion of culture. The best heads that ever existed, Pericles, Plato, Julius Caesar, Shakespeare, Goethe, Milton,[17] were well-read, universally educated men, and quite too wise to undervalue letters. Their opinion has weight, because they had means of knowing the opposite opinion. We look that a great man should be a good reader, or, in proportion to the spontaneous power should be the assimilating power. Good criticism is very rare, and always precious. I am always happy to meet persons who perceive the transcendent superiority of Shakespeare over all other writers. I like people who like Plato. Because this love does not consist with self-conceit.

But books are good only as far as a boy is ready for them. He sometimes gets ready very slowly. You send your child to the schoolmaster, but 'tis the schoolboys who educate him. You send him to the Latin class, but much of his tuition comes, on his way to school, from the shop-windows. You like the strict rules and the long terms; and he finds his best leading in a by-way of his own, and refuses any companions but of his choosing. He hates the grammar and *Gradus*,[18] and loves guns, fishing-rods, horses, and boats. Well, the boy is right; and you are not fit to direct his bringing up, if your theory leaves out his gymnastic training. Archery, cricket, gun and fishing-rod, horse and boat, are all educators, liberalizers; and so are dancing, dress, and the street-talk; and,— provided only the boy has resources, and is of a noble and ingenuous strain,— these will not serve him less than the books. He learns chess, whist, dancing, and theatricals. The father observes that another boy has learned algebra and geometry in the same time. But the first boy has acquired much more than these poor games along with them. He is infatuated for weeks with whist and chess; but presently will find out, as you did, that when he rises from the game too long played, he is vacant and forlorn, and despises himself. Thenceforward it takes place with other things, and has its due weight in his experience. These minor skills and accomplishments, for example, dancing, are tickets of admission to the dress-circle of mankind, and the being master of them enables the youth to judge intelligently of much, on which, otherwise, he would give a pedantic squint. Landor[19] said, "I have suffered more from my bad dancing, than from all the misfortunes and miseries of my life put together." Provided always the boy is teachable, (for we are not proposing to make a statue out of punk,) football, cricket, archery, swimming, skating, climbing, fencing, riding, are lessons in the art of power, which it is his main business to learn;—riding, specially, of which Lord Herbert of Cherbury[20] said, "a good rider on a good horse is as much above himself and others as the world can make him." Besides, the gun, fishing-rod, boat, and horse, constitute, among all who use them, secret freemasonries. They are as if they belonged to one club.

There is also a negative value in these arts. Their chief use to the youth, is, not amusement, but to be known for what they are, and not to remain to him occasions of heart-burn. We are full of superstitions. Each class fixes its eyes on the advantages it has not; the refined, on rude strength; the democrat, on birth and breeding. One of the benefits of a college education is, to show the boy its little avail. I knew a leading man in a leading city, who, having set his heart on an education at the university, and missed it, could never quite feel himself the equal of his own brothers who had gone thither. His easy superiority to multitudes of professional men could never quite countervail to him this imaginary defect. Balls, riding, wine-parties, and billiards, pass to a poor boy for something fine and romantic, which they are not; and a free admission to them on an equal footing, if it were possible, only once or twice, would be worth ten times its cost, by undeceiving him.

I am not much an advocate for traveling, and I observe that men run away to other countries, because they are not good in their own, and run back to their own, because they pass for nothing in the new places. For the most part, only the light characters travel. Who are you that have no task to keep you at home? I have been quoted as saying captious[21] things about travel; but I mean to do justice. I think, there is a restlessness in our people, which argues want of character. All educated Americans, first or last, go to Europe;—perhaps, because it is their mental home, as the invalid habits of this country might suggest. An eminent teacher of girls said, "the idea of a girl's education, is, whatever qualifies them for going to Europe." Can we never extract this tapeworm of Europe from the brain of our countrymen? One sees very well what their fate must be. He that does not fill a place at home, cannot abroad. He only goes there to hide his insignificance in a larger crowd. You do not think you will find anything there which you have not seen at home? The stuff of all countries is just the same. Do you suppose, there is any country where they do not scald milk pans, and swaddle the infants, and burn the brushwood, and broil the fish? What is true anywhere is true everywhere. And let him go where he will, he can only find so much beauty or worth as he carries.

Of course, for some men, travel may be useful. Naturalists, discoverers, and sailors are born. Some men are made for couriers, exchangers, envoys, missionaries, bearers of dispatches, as others are for farmers and workingmen. And if the man is of a light and social turn, and Nature has aimed to make a legged and winged creature, framed for locomotion, we must follow her hint, and furnish him with that breeding which gives currency, as sedulously[22] as with that which gives worth. But let us not be pedantic, but allow to travel its full effect. The boy grown up on the farm, which he has never left, is said in the country to have had *no chance*, and boys and men of that condition look upon

work on a railroad, or drudgery in a city, as opportunity. Poor country boys of
Vermont and Connecticut formerly owed what knowledge they had, to their
peddling trips to the Southern States. California and the Pacific Coast is now
the university of this class, as Virginia was in old times. 'To have *some chance*'
is their word. And the phrase 'to know the world,' or to travel, is synonymous
with all men's ideas of advantage and superiority. No doubt, to a man of sense,
travel offers advantages. As many languages as he has, as many friends, as
many arts and trades, so many times is he a man. A foreign country is a point of
comparison, wherefrom to judge his own. One use of travel, is, to recommend
the books and works of home,—we go to Europe to be Americanized;[23] and
another, to find men. For, as Nature has put fruits apart in latitudes, a new fruit
in every degree, so knowledge and fine moral quality she lodges in distant men.
And thus, of the six or seven teachers whom each man wants among his
contemporaries, it often happens that one or two of them live on the other side
of the world.

Moreover, there is in every constitution a certain solstice,[24] when the stars
stand still in our inward firmament, and when there is required some foreign
force, some diversion or alterative to prevent stagnation. And, as a medical
remedy, travel seems one of the best. Just as a man witnessing the admirable
effect of ether to lull pain, and meditating on the contingencies of wounds,
cancers, lockjaws, rejoices in Dr. Jackson's[25] benign discovery, so a man who
looks at Paris, at Naples, or at London, says, 'If I should be driven from my
own home, here, at least, my thoughts can be consoled by the most prodigal
amusement and occupation which the human race in ages could contrive and
accumulate.'

Akin to the benefit of foreign travel, the aesthetic value of railroads is to
unite the advantages of town and country life, neither of which we can spare. A
man should live in or near a large town, because, let his own genius be what it
may, it will repel quite as much of agreeable and valuable talent as it draws,
and, in a city, the total attraction of all the citizens is sure to conquer, first or
last, every repulsion, and drag the most improbable hermit within its walls
some day in the year. In town, he can find the swimming-school, the gymna-
sium, the dancing-master, the shooting-gallery, opera, theater, and panorama;
the chemist's shop, the museum of natural history; the gallery of fine arts; the
national orators, in their turn; foreign travelers, the libraries, and his club. In the
country, he can find solitude and reading, manly labor, cheap living, and his old
shoes; moors for game, hills for geology, and groves for devotion. Aubrey

writes, "I have heard Thomas Hobbes[26] say, that, in the Earl of Devon's house, in Derbyshire, there was a good library and books enough for him, and his lordship stored the library with what books he thought fit to be bought. But the want of good conversation was a very great inconvenience, and, though he conceived he could order his thinking as well as another, yet he found a great defect. In the country, in long time, for want of good conversation, one's understanding and invention contract a moss on them, like an old paling[27] in an orchard."[28]

Cities give us collision. 'Tis said, London and New York take the nonsense out of a man. A great part of our education is sympathetic and social. Boys and girls who have been brought up with well-informed and superior people, show in their manners an inestimable grace. Fuller says that "William, Earl of Nassau,[29] won a subject from the King of Spain, every time he put off his hat." You cannot have one well-bred man, without a whole society of such. They keep each other up to any high point. Especially women;—it requires a great many cultivated women,—saloons of bright, elegant, reading women, accustomed to ease and refinement, to spectacles, pictures, sculpture, poetry, and to elegant society, in order that you should have one Madame de Staël.[30] The head of a commercial house, or a leading lawyer or politician is brought into daily contact with troops of men from all parts of the country, and those too the driving-wheels, the business men of each section, and one can hardly suggest for an apprehensive man a more searching culture. Besides, we must remember the high social possibilities of a million of men. The best bribe which London offers today to the imagination is that in such a vast variety of people and conditions, one can believe there is room for persons of romantic character to exist, and that the poet, the mystic, and the hero may hope to confront their counterparts.

I wish cities could teach their best lesson,—of quiet manners. It is the foible especially of American youth,—pretension. The mark of the man of the world is absence of pretension. He does not make a speech; he takes a low business-tone, avoids all brag, is nobody, dresses plainly, promises not at all, performs much, speaks in monosyllables, hugs his fact. He calls his employment by its lowest name, and so takes from evil tongues their sharpest weapon. His conversation clings to the weather and the news, yet he allows himself to be surprised into thought, and the unlocking of his learning and philosophy. How the imagination is piqued by anecdotes of some great man passing incognito, as a king in gray clothes,—of Napoleon affecting a plain suit at his glittering levee;[31] of Burns, or Scott, or Beethoven, or Wellington, or Goethe, or any container of transcendent power, passing for nobody; of Epaminondas,[32] "who never says anything, but will listen eternally;" of Goethe, who preferred trifling subjects and common expressions in intercourse with strangers, worse rather than better clothes, and to appear a little more capricious than he was. There are advantages in the old hat and box-coat.[33] I have heard that throughout this country, a certain respect is paid to good broadcloth; but dress makes a little restraint: men will not commit themselves. But the box-coat is like wine; it unlocks the tongue, and men say what they think. An old poet says,

> "Go far and go sparing,
> For you'll find it certain,
> The poorer and the baser you appear,
> The more you'll look through still."[34]

Not much otherwise Milnes[35] writes, in the "Lay of the Humble,"

> "To me men are for what they are,
> They wear no masks with me."

'Tis odd that our people should have—not water on the brain,—but a little gas there. A shrewd foreigner said of the Americans that "whatever they say has a little the air of a speech." Yet one of the traits down in the books as distinguishing the Anglo-Saxon, is, a trick of self-disparagement. To be sure, in old, dense countries, among a million of good coats, a fine coat comes to be no distinction, and you find humorists. In an English party, a man with no marked manners or features, with a face like red dough, unexpectedly discloses wit, learning, a wide range of topics, and personal familiarity with good men in all parts of the world, until you think you have fallen upon some illustrious personage. Can it be that the American forest has refreshed some weeds of old Pietish barbarism just ready to die out,—the love of the scarlet feather, of beads, and tinsel? The Italians are fond of red clothes, peacock plumes, and embroidery; and I remember one rainy morning in the city of Palermo, the street was in a blaze with scarlet umbrellas. The English have a plain taste. The equipages of the grandees are plain. A gorgeous livery indicates new and awkward city wealth. Mr. Pitt, like Mr. Pym,[36] thought the title of *Mister* good against any king in Europe. They have piqued themselves on governing the whole world in the poor, plain, dark Committee-room which the House of Commons sat in, before the fire.

Whilst we want cities as the centers where the best things are found, cities degrade us by magnifying trifles. The countryman finds the town a chop-house, a barber's shop. He has lost the lines of grandeur of the horizon, hills and plains, and with them, sobriety and elevation. He has come among a supple, glib-tongued tribe, who live for show, servile to public opinion. Life is dragged down to a fracas of pitiful cares and disasters. You say the gods ought to respect a life whose objects are their own; but in cities they have betrayed you to a cloud of insignificant annoyances:

"Mirmidons, race féconde,
Mirmidons,
Enfin nous commandons;
Jupiter livre le monde
Aux mirmidons, aux mirmidons." [37]

'Tis heavy odds
Against the gods,
When they will match with myrmidons.
We spawning, spawning myrmidons,
Our turn today! we take command,
Jove gives the globe into the hand
Of myrmidons, of myrmidons. [38]

What is odious but noise, and people who scream and bewail? people whose vane points always east, who live to dine, who send for the doctor, who coddle themselves, who toast their feet on the register, who intrigue to secure a padded chair, and a corner out of the draught. Suffer them once to begin the enumeration of their infirmities, and the sun will go down on the unfinished tale. Let these triflers put us out of conceit with petty comforts. To a man at work, the frost is but a color: the rain, the wind, he forgot them when he came in. Let us learn to live coarsely, dress plainly, and lie hard. The least habit of dominion over the palate has certain good effects not easily estimated. Neither will we be driven into a quiddling abstemiousness. 'Tis a superstition to insist on a special diet. All is made at last of the same chemical atoms.

A man in pursuit of greatness feels no little wants. How can you mind diet, bed, dress, or salutes or compliments, or the figure you make in company, or wealth, or even the bringing things to pass, when you think how paltry are the machinery and the workers? Wordsworth[39] was praised to me, in Westmoreland, for having afforded to his country neighbors an example of a modest household where comfort and culture were secured, without display. And a tender boy who wears his rusty cap and outgrown coat, that he may secure the coveted place in college, and the right in the library, is educated to some purpose. There is a great deal of self-denial and manliness in poor and middle-class houses, in town and country, that has not got into literature, and never will, but that keeps the earth sweet; that saves on superfluities, and spends on essentials; that goes rusty, and educates the boy; that sells the horse, but builds the school; works early and late, takes two looms in the factory, three looms, six looms, but pays off the mortgage on the paternal farm, and then goes back cheerfully to work again.

We can ill spare the commanding social benefits of cities; they must be used; yet cautiously, and haughtily,—and will yield their best values to him who best can do without them. Keep the town for occasions, but the habits should be formed to retirement. Solitude, the safeguard of mediocrity, is to genius the stern friend, the cold, obscure shelter where moult the wings which will bear it farther than suns and stars. He who should inspire and lead his race must be defended from traveling with the souls of other men, from living, breathing, reading, and writing in the daily, time-worn yoke of their opinions. "In the morning,—solitude;" said Pythagoras; that Nature may speak to the imagination, as she does never in company, and that her favorite may make acquaintance with those divine strengths which disclose themselves to serious and abstracted thought. 'Tis very certain that Plato, Plotinus, Archimedes, Hermes,[40] Newton, Milton, Wordsworth, did not live in a crowd, but descended into it from time to time as benefactors: and the wise instructor will press this point of securing to the young soul in the disposition of time and the arrangements of living, periods and habits of solitude. The high advantage of university-life is often the mere mechanical one, I may call it, of a separate chamber and fire,—which parents will allow the boy without hesitation at Cambridge, but do not think needful at home. We say solitude, to mark the character of the tone of thought; but if it can be shared between two or more than two, it is happier, and not less noble. "We four," wrote Neander to his sacred friends, "will enjoy at Halle the inward blessedness of a *civitas Dei*,[41] whose foundations are forever friendship. The more I know you, the more I dissatisfy and must dissatisfy all my wonted companions. Their very presence stupefies me. The common understanding withdraws itself from the one center of all existence."

Solitude takes off the pressure of present importunities that more catholic and humane relations may appear. The saint and poet seek privacy to ends the most public and universal: and it is the secret of culture, to interest the man more in his public, than in his private quality. Here is a new poem, which elicits a good many comments in the journals, and in conversation. From these it is easy, at last, to eliminate the verdict which readers passed upon it; and that is, in the main, unfavorable. The poet, as a craftsman, is only interested in the praise accorded to him, and not in the censure, though it be just. And the poor little poet hearkens only to that, and rejects the censure, as proving incapacity in the critic. But the poet *cultivated* becomes a stockholder in both companies, —say Mr. Curfew,—in the Curfew stock, and in the *humanity* stock;—and, in the last, exults as much in the demonstration of the unsoundness of Curfew, as his interest in the former gives him pleasure in the currency of Curfew. For, the depreciation of his Curfew stock only shows the immense values of the humanity stock. As soon as he sides with his critic against himself, with joy, he is a cultivated man.[42]

We must have an intellectual quality in all property and in all action, or they are nought. I must have children, I must have events, I must have a social state and history, or my thinking and speaking want body or basis. But to give these accessories any value, I must know them as contingent and rather showy possessions, which pass for more to the people than to me. We see this abstraction in scholars, as a matter of course: but what a charm it adds when observed in practical men. Bonaparte, like Caesar, was intellectual, and could look at every object for itself, without affection. Though an egotist *à l'outrance*,[43] he could criticize a play, a building, a character, on universal grounds, and give a just opinion. A man known to us only as a celebrity in politics or in trade, gains largely in our esteem if we discover that he has some intellectual taste or skill; as when we learn of Lord Fairfax, the Long Parliament's general, his passion for antiquarian studies; or of the French regicide Carnot,[44] his sublime genius in mathematics; or of a living banker, his success in poetry; or of a partisan journalist, his devotion to ornithology. So, if in traveling in the dreary wildernesses of Arkansas or Texas, we should observe on the next seat a man reading Horace, or Martial, or Calderon,[45] we should wish to hug him. In callings that require roughest energy, soldiers, sea-captains, and civil engineers sometimes betray a fine insight, if only through a certain gentleness when off duty; a good-natured admission that there are illusions, and who shall say that he is not their sport? We only vary the phrase, not the doctrine, when we say, that culture opens the sense of beauty. A man is a beggar who only lives to the useful, and, however he may serve as a pin or rivet in the social machine, cannot be said to have arrived at self-possession. I suffer, every day, from the want of perception of beauty in people. They do not know the charm with which all moments and objects can be embellished, the charm of manners, of self-command, of benevolence. Repose and cheerfulness are the badge of the gentleman,—repose in energy. The Greek battle-pieces are calm; the heroes, in whatever violent actions engaged, retain a serene aspect; as we say of Niagara, that it falls without speed. A cheerful, intelligent face is the end of culture, and success enough. For it indicates the purpose of Nature and wisdom attained.

When our higher faculties are in activity, we are domesticated, and awkwardness and discomfort give place to natural and agreeable movements. It is noticed, that the consideration of the great periods and spaces of astronomy induces a dignity of mind, and an indifference to death. The influence of fine scenery, the presence of mountains, appeases our irritations and elevates our friendships. Even a high dome, and the expansive interior of a cathedral, have a sensible effect on manners. I have heard that stiff people lose something of their awkwardness under high ceilings, and in spacious halls. I think, sculpture and painting have an effect to teach us manners, and abolish hurry.

But, over all, culture must reinforce from higher influx the empirical skills of eloquence, or of politics, or of trade, and the useful arts. There is a certain loftiness of thought and power to marshal and adjust particulars, which can only come from an insight of their whole connection. The orator who has once seen things in their divine order, will never quite lose sight of this, and will come to affairs as from a higher ground, and, though he will say nothing of philosophy, he will have a certain mastery in dealing with them, and an incapableness of being dazzled or frighted, which will distinguish his handling from that of attorneys and factors. A man who stands on a good footing with the heads of parties at Washington, reads the rumors of the newspapers, and the guesses of provincial politicians, with a key to the right and wrong in each statement, and sees well enough where all this will end. Archimedes will look through your Connecticut machine, at a glance, and judge of its fitness. And much more, a wise man who knows not only what Plato, but what Saint John [46] can show him, can easily raise the affair he deals with, to a certain majesty. Plato says, Pericles owed this elevation to the lessons of Anaxagoras.[47] Burke descended from a higher sphere when he would influence human affairs. Franklin, Adams,[48] Jefferson, Washington, stood on a fine humanity, before which the brawls of modern senates are but pot-house politics.

But there are higher secrets of culture, which are not for the apprentices, but for proficients. These are lessons only for the brave. We must know our friends

under ugly masks. The calamities are our friends. Ben Jonson[49] specifies in his
address to the Muse:—

> "Get him the time's long grudge, the court's ill-will,
> And, reconciled, keep him suspected still,
> Make him lose all his friends, and, what is worse,
> almost all ways to any better course;
> With me thou leav'st a better Muse than thee,
> And which thou brought'st me, blessed Poverty."

We wish to learn philosophy by rote, and play at heroism. But the wiser God
says, Take the shame, the poverty, and the penal solitude, that belong to truth-
speaking. Try the rough water as well as the smooth. Rough water can teach
lessons worth knowing. When the state is unquiet, personal qualities are more
than ever decisive. Fear not a revolution which will constrain you to live five
years in one. Don't be so tender at making an enemy now and then. Be willing
to go to Coventry[50] sometimes, and let the populace bestow on you their coldest
contempts. The finished man of the world must eat of every apple once. He
must hold his hatreds also at arm's length, and not remember spite. He has
neither friends nor enemies, but values men only as channels of power.

He who aims high, must dread an easy home and popular manners. Heaven
sometimes hedges a rare character about with ungainliness and odium, as the
burr that protects the fruit. If there is any great and good thing in store for you,
it will not come at the first or the second call, nor in the shape of fashion, ease,
and city drawing-rooms. Popularity is for dolls. "Steep and craggy," said Porphyry,[51] "is the path of the gods." Open your Marcus Antoninus.[52] In the
opinion of the ancients, he was the great man who scorned to shine, and who
contested the frowns of fortune. They preferred the noble vessel too late for the
tide, contending with winds and waves, dismantled and unrigged, to her companion borne into harbor with colors flying and guns firing. There is none of
the social goods that may not be purchased too dear, and mere amiableness
must not take rank with high aims and self-subsistency.

Bettine[53] replies to Goethe's mother, who chides her disregard of dress,—
"If I cannot do as I have a mind, in our poor Frankfurt, I shall not carry things
far." And the youth must rate at its true mark the inconceivable levity of local
opinion. The longer we live, the more we must endure the elementary existence
of men and women; and every brave heart must treat society as a child, and
never allow it to dictate.

"All that class of the severe and restrictive virtues," said Burke, "are almost too costly for humanity." Who wishes to be severe? Who wishes to resist the eminent and polite, in behalf of the poor, and low, and impolite? and who that dares do it, can keep his temper sweet, his frolic spirits? The high virtues are not debonair, but have their redress in being illustrious at last. What forests of laurel we bring, and the tears of mankind, to those who stood firm against the opinion of their contemporaries! The measure of a master is his success in bringing all men round to his opinion twenty years later.

Let me say here, that culture cannot begin too early. In talking with scholars, I observe that they lost on ruder companions those years of boyhood which alone could give imaginative literature a religious and infinite quality in their esteem. I find, too, that the chance for appreciation is much increased by being the son of an appreciator, and that these boys who now grow up are caught not only years too late, but two or three births too late, to make the best scholars of. And I think it a presentable motive to a scholar, that, as, in an old community, a well-born proprietor is usually found, after the first heats of youth, to be a careful husband, and to feel a habitual desire that the estate shall suffer no harm by his administration, but shall be delivered down to the next heir in as good condition as he received it;—so, a considerate man will reckon himself a subject of that secular melioration[54] by which mankind is mollified, cured, and refined, and will shun every expenditure of his forces on pleasure or gain, which will jeopardize this social and secular accumulation.

The fossil strata show us that Nature began with rudimental forms, and rose to the more complex, as fast as the earth was fit for their dwelling-place; and that the lower perish, as the higher appear. Very few of our race can be said to be yet finished men. We still carry sticking to us some remains of the preceding inferior quadruped organization. We call these millions men; but they are not yet men. Half-engaged in the soil, pawing to get free, man needs all the music that can be brought to disengage him. If Love, red Love, with tears and joy; if Want with his scourge; if War with his cannonade; if Christianity with its charity; if Trade with its money; if Art with its portfolios; if Science with her telegraphs through the deeps of space and time; can set his dull nerves throbbing, and by loud taps on the tough chrysalis,[55] can break its walls, and let the new creature emerge erect and free,—make way, and sing paean! The age of the quadruped is to go out,—the age of the brain and of the heart is to come in. The time will come when the evil forms we have known can no more be organized. Man's culture can spare nothing, wants all the material. He is to convert all impediments into instruments, all enemies into power. The formidable mischief will only make the more useful slave. And if one shall read the future of the race hinted in the organic effort of Nature to mount and meliorate, and the corresponding impulse to the Better in the human being, we shall dare affirm that there is nothing he will not overcome and convert, until at last culture shall absorb the chaos and gehenna.[56] He will convert the Furies into Muses, and the hells into benefit.

V

BEHAVIOR

—•—

Grace, Beauty, and Caprice
Build this golden portal;
Graceful women, chosen men
Dazzle every mortal:
Their sweet and lofty countenance
His enchanting food;
He need not go to them, their forms
Beset his solitude.
He looketh seldom in their face,
His eyes explore the ground,
The green grass is a looking-glass
Whereon their traits are found.
Little he says to them,
So dances his heart in his breast,
Their tranquil mien bereaveth him
Of wit, of words, of rest.
Too weak to win, too fond to shun
The tyrants of his doom,
The much deceived Endymion
slips behind a tomb.

BEHAVIOR

The soul which animates Nature is not less significantly published in the figure, movement, and gesture of animated bodies, than in its last vehicle of articulate speech. This silent and subtle language is Manners; not *what*, but *how*. Life expresses. A statue has no tongue, and needs none. Good tableaux[1] do not need declamation. Nature tells every secret once. Yes, but in man she tells it all the time, by form, attitude, gesture, mien,[2] face, and parts of the face, and by the whole action of the machine. The visible carriage or action of the individual, as resulting from his organization and his will combined, we call manners. What are they but thought entering the hands and feet, controlling the movements of the body, the speech and behavior?

There is always a best way of doing everything, if it be to boil an egg. Manners are the happy ways of doing things; each once a stroke of genius or of love,—now repeated and hardened into usage. They form at last a rich varnish, with which the routine of life is washed, and its details adorned. If they are superficial, so are the dew-drops which give such a depth to the morning meadows. Manners are very communicable: men catch them from each other. Consuelo,[3] in the romance, boasts of the lessons she had given the nobles in manners, on the stage; and, in real life, Talma[4] taught Napoleon the arts of behavior. Genius invents fine manners, which the baron and the baroness copy very fast, and, by the advantage of a palace, better the instruction. They stereotype the lesson they have learned into a mode.

The power of manners is incessant,—an element as unconcealable as fire. The nobility cannot in any country be disguised, and no more in a republic or a democracy, than in a kingdom. No man can resist their influence. There are certain manners which are learned in good society, of that force, that, if a person have them, he or she must be considered, and is everywhere welcome, though without beauty, or wealth, or genius. Give a boy address and accomplishments, and you give him the mastery of palaces and fortunes where he goes. He has not the trouble of earning or owning them: they solicit him to enter and possess. We send girls of a timid, retreating disposition to the boarding-school, to the riding-school, to the ballroom, or wheresoever they can come into acquaintance and nearness of leading persons of their own sex; where they might learn address, and see it near at hand. The power of a woman of fashion to lead, and also to daunt and repel, derives from their belief that she knows resources and behaviors not known to them; but when these have mastered her secret, they learn to confront her, and recover their self-possession.

Every day bears witness to their gentle rule. People who would obtrude, now do not obtrude. The mediocre circle learns to demand that which belongs to a high state of nature or of culture. Your manners are always under examination, and by committees little suspected,—a police in citizens' clothes,—but are awarding or denying you very high prizes when you least think of it.

We talk much of utilities,—but 'tis our manners that associate us. In hours of business, we go to him who knows, or has, or does this or that which we want, and we do not let our taste or feeling stand in the way. But this activity over, we return to the indolent state, and wish for those we can be at ease with; those who will go where we go, whose manners do not offend us, whose social tone chimes with ours. When we reflect on their persuasive and cheering force; how they recommend, prepare, and draw people together; how, in all clubs, manners make the members; how manners make the fortune of the ambitious youth; that, for the most part, his manners marry him, and, for the most part, he marries manners; when we think what keys they are, and to what secrets; what high lessons and inspiring tokens of character they convey; and what divination is required in us, for the reading of this fine telegraph, we see what range the subject has, and what relations to convenience, power, and beauty.

Their first service is very low,—when they are the minor morals: but 'tis the beginning of civility,—to make us, I mean, endurable to each other. We prize them for their rough-plastic, abstergent[5] force; to get people out of the quadruped state; to get them washed, clothed, and set up on end; to slough their animal husks and habits; compel them to be clean; overawe their spite and meanness, teach them to stifle the base, and choose the generous expression, and make them know how much happier the generous behaviors are.

Bad behavior the laws cannot reach. Society is infested with rude, cynical, restless, and frivolous persons who prey upon the rest, and whom, a public opinion concentrated into good manners, forms accepted by the sense of all, can reach:—the contradictors and railers at public and private tables, who are like terriers, who conceive it the duty of a dog of honor to growl at any passer-by, and do the honors of the house by barking him out of sight:—I have seen men who neigh like a horse when you contradict them, or say something which they do not understand:—then the overbold, who make their own invitation to your hearth; the persevering talker, who gives you his society in large, saturating doses; the pitiers of themselves,—a perilous class; the frivolous Asmodeus,[6] who relies on you to find him in ropes of sand to twist; the monotones; in short, every stripe of absurdity;—these are social inflictions which the magistrate cannot cure or defend you from, and which must be intrusted to the restraining force of custom, and proverbs, and familiar rules of behavior impressed on young people in their school-days.

In the hotels on the banks of the Mississippi, they print, or used to print, among the rules of the house, that "no gentleman can be permitted to come to the public table without his coat;" and in the same country, in the pews of the churches, little placards plead with the worshipper against the fury of expectoration. Charles Dickens self-sacrificingly undertook the reformation of our American manners in unspeakable particulars.[7] I think the lesson was not quite lost; that it held bad manners up, so that the churls could see the deformity. Unhappily, the book had its own deformities. It ought not to need to print in a reading-room a caution to strangers not to speak loud; nor to persons who look over fine engravings, that they should be handled like cobwebs and butterflies' wings; nor to persons who look at marble statues, that they shall not smite them with canes. But, even in the perfect civilization of this city, such cautions are not quite needless in the Athenaeum and City Library.

Manners are factitious,[8] and grow out of circumstance as well as out of character. If you look at the pictures of patricians and of peasants, of different periods and countries, you will see how well they match the same classes in our towns. The modern aristocrat not only is well drawn in Titian's Venetian Doges, and in Roman coins and statues, but also in the pictures which Commodore Perry[9] brought home of dignitaries in Japan. Broad lands and great interests not only arrive to such heads as can manage them, but form manners of power. A keen eye, too, will see nice gradations of rank, or see in the manners the degree of homage the party is wont to receive. A prince who is accustomed every day to be courted and deferred to by the highest grandees, acquires a corresponding expectation, and a becoming mode of receiving and replying to this homage.

There are always exceptional people and modes. English grandees affect to be farmers. Claverhouse is a fop,[10] and, under the finish of dress, and levity of behavior, hides the terror of his war. But Nature and Destiny are honest, and never fail to leave their mark, to hang out a sign for each and for every quality. It is much to conquer one's face, and perhaps the ambitious youth thinks he has got the whole secret when he has learned, that disengaged manners are commanding. Don't be deceived by a facile exterior. Tender men sometimes have strong wills. We had, in Massachusetts, an old statesman, who had sat all his life in courts and in chairs of state, without overcoming an extreme irritability of face, voice, and bearing: when he spoke, his voice would not serve him; it cracked, it broke, it wheezed, it piped;—little cared he; he knew that it had got to pipe, or wheeze, or screech his argument and his indignation. When he sat down, after speaking, he seemed in a sort of fit, and held on to his chair with both hands: but underneath all this irritability, was a puissant[11] will, firm, and advancing, and a memory in which lay in order and method like geologic strata every fact of his history, and under the control of his will.

Manners are partly factitious, but, mainly, there must be capacity for culture in the blood. Else all culture is vain. The obstinate prejudice in favor of blood, which lies at the base of the feudal and monarchical fabrics of the old world, has some reason in common experience. Every man,—mathematician, artist, soldier, or merchant,—looks with confidence for some traits and talents in his own child, which he would not dare to presume in the child of a stranger. The Orientalists are very orthodox on this point. "Take a thorn-bush," said the Emir Abdel-Kader,[12] "and sprinkle it for a whole year with water;—it will yield nothing but thorns. Take a date-tree, leave it without culture, and it will always produce dates. Nobility is the date-tree, and the Arab populace is a bush of thorns."

A main fact in the history of manners is the wonderful expressiveness of the human body. If it were made of glass, or of air, and the thoughts were written on steel tablets within, it could not publish more truly its meaning than now. Wise men read very sharply all your private history in your look and gait and behavior. The whole economy of nature is bent on expression. The tell-tale body is all tongues. Men are like Geneva watches with crystal faces which expose the whole movement. They carry the liquor of life flowing up and down in these beautiful bottles, and announcing to the curious how it is with them. The face and eyes reveal what the spirit is doing, how old it is, what aims it has. The eyes indicate the antiquity of the soul, or, through how many forms it has already ascended. It almost violates the proprieties, if we say above the breath here, what the confessing eyes do not hesitate to utter to every street passenger.

Man cannot fix his eye on the sun, and so far seems imperfect. In Siberia, a late traveler found men who could see the satellites of Jupiter with their un-armed eye. In some respects the animals excel us. The birds have a longer sight, beside the advantage by their wings of a higher observatory. A cow can bid her calf, by secret signal, probably of the eye, to run away, or to lie down and hide itself. The jockeys say of certain horses, that "they look over the whole ground." The out-door life, and hunting, and labor, give equal vigor to the human eye. A farmer looks out at you as strong as the horse; his eyebeam is like the stroke of a staff. An eye can threaten like a loaded and leveled gun, or can insult like hissing or kicking; or, in its altered mood, by beams of kindness, it can make the heart dance with joy.

The eye obeys exactly the action of the mind. When a thought strikes us, the eyes fix, and remain gazing at a distance; in enumerating the names of persons or of countries, as France, Germany, Spain, Turkey, the eyes wink at each new name. There is no nicety of learning sought by the mind, which the eyes do not vie in acquiring. "An artist," said Michelangelo, "must have his measuring tools not in the hand, but in the eye;" and there is no end to the catalogue of its performances, whether in indolent vision (that of health and beauty,) or in strained vision, (that of art and labor.)

Eyes are bold as lions,—roving, running, leaping, here and there, far and near. They speak all languages. They wait for no introduction; they are no Englishmen; ask no leave of age, or rank; they respect neither poverty nor riches, neither learning nor power, nor virtue, nor sex, but intrude, and come again, and go through and through you, in a moment of time. What inundation of life and thought is discharged from one soul into another, through them! The glance is natural magic. The mysterious communication established across a house between two entire strangers, moves all the springs of wonder. The communication by the glance is in the greatest part not subject to the control of the will. It is the bodily symbol of identity of nature. We look into the eyes to know if this other form is another self, and the eyes will not lie, but make a faithful confession what inhabitant is there. The revelations are sometimes terri-fic. The confession of a low, usurping devil is there made, and the observer shall seem to feel the stirring of owls, and bats, and horned hoofs, where he looked for innocence and simplicity. 'Tis remarkable, too, that the spirit that appears at the windows of the house does at once invest himself in a new form of his own, to the mind of the beholder.

The eyes of men converse as much as their tongues, with the advantage, that the ocular dialect needs no dictionary, but is understood all the world over. When the eyes say one thing, and the tongue another, a practiced man relies on the language of the first. If the man is off his center, the eyes show it. You can read in the eyes of your companion, whether your argument hits him, though his tongue will not confess it. There is a look by which a man shows he is going to say a good thing, and a look when he has said it. Vain and forgotten are all the fine offers and offices of hospitality, if there is no holiday in the eye. How many furtive[13] inclinations avowed by the eye, though dissembled by the lips! One comes away from a company, in which, it may easily happen, he has said nothing, and no important remark has been addressed to him, and yet, if in sympathy with the society, he shall not have a sense of this fact, such a stream of life has been flowing into him, and out from him, through the eyes. There are eyes, to be sure, that give no more admission into the man than blueberries. Others are liquid and deep,—wells that a man might fall into;—others are aggressive and devouring, seem to call out the police, take all too much notice, and require crowded Broadways, and the security of millions, to protect individuals against them. The military eye I meet, now darkly sparkling under clerical, now under rustic brows. 'Tis the city of Lacedaemon;[14] 'tis a stack of bayonets. There are asking eyes, asserting eyes, prowling eyes; and eyes full of fate,—some of good, and some of sinister omen. The alleged power to charm down insanity, or ferocity in beasts, is a power behind the eye. It must be a victory achieved in the will, before it can be signified in the eye. 'Tis very certain that each man carries in his eye the exact indication of his rank in the immense scale of men, and we are always learning to read it. A complete man should need no auxiliaries to his personal presence. Whoever looked on him would consent to his will, being certified that his aims were generous and universal. The reason why men do not obey us, is because they see the mud at the bottom of our eye.

If the organ of sight is such a vehicle of power, the other features have their own. A man finds room in the few square inches of the face for the traits of all his ancestors; for the expression of all his history, and his wants. The sculptor, and Winckelmann, and Lavater,[15] will tell you how significant a feature is the nose; how its forms express strength or weakness of will, and good or bad temper. The nose of Julius Caesar, of Dante, and of Pitt, suggest "the terrors of the beak." What refinement, and what limitations, the teeth betray! "Beware you don't laugh," said the wise mother, "for then you show all your faults."

Balzac[16] left in manuscript a chapter, which he called *"Théorie de la démarche,"*[17] in which he says: "The look, the voice, the respiration, and the attitude or walk, are identical. But, as it has not been given to man, the power to stand guard, at once, over these four different simultaneous expressions of his thought, watch that one which speaks out the truth, and you will know the whole man."

Palaces interest us mainly in the exhibition of manners, which, in the idle and expensive society dwelling in them, are raised to a high art. The maxim of courts is, that manner is power. A calm and resolute bearing, a polished speech, an embellishment of trifles, and the art of hiding all uncomfortable feeling, are essential to the courtier: and Saint-Simon, and Cardinal de Retz, and Roederer,[18] and an encyclopedia of *Mémoires*, will instruct you, if you wish, in those potent secrets. Thus, it is a point of pride with kings, to remember faces and names. It is reported of one prince that his head had the air of leaning downwards, in order not to humble the crowd. There are people who come in ever like a child with a piece of good news. It was said of the late Lord Holland,[19] that he always came down to breakfast with the air of a man who had just met with some signal good-fortune. In *"Notre Dame,"* the grandee took his place on the dais, with the look of one who is thinking of something else. But we must not peep and eavesdrop at palace-doors.

Fine manners need the support of fine manners in others. A scholar may be a well-bred man, or he may not. The enthusiast is introduced to polished scholars in society, and is chilled and silenced by finding himself not in their element. They all have somewhat which he has not, and, it seems, ought to have. But if he finds the scholar apart from his companions, it is then the enthusiast's turn, and the scholar has no defense, but must deal on his terms. Now they must fight the battle out on their private strengths. What is the talent of that character so common,—the successful man of the world,—in all marts, senates, and drawing-rooms? Manners: manners of power; sense to see his advantage, and manners up to it. See him approach his man. He knows that troops behave as they are handled at first;—that is his cheap secret; just what happens to every two persons who meet on any affair,—one instantly perceives that he has the key of the situation, that his will comprehends the other's will, as the cat does the mouse; and he has only to use courtesy, and furnish good-natured reasons to his victim to cover up the chain, lest he be shamed into resistance.

The theater in which this science of manners has a formal importance is not with us a court, but dress-circles, wherein, after the close of the day's business, men and women meet at leisure, for mutual entertainment, in ornamented drawing-rooms. Of course, it has every variety of attraction and merit; but, to earnest persons, to youths or maidens who have great objects at heart, we cannot extol it highly. A well-dressed, talkative company, where each is bent to amuse the other,—yet the high-born Turk who came hither fancied that every woman seemed to be suffering for a chair; that all the talkers were brained and exhausted by the deoxygenated air: it spoiled the best persons: it put all on stilts. Yet here are the secret biographies written and read. The aspect of that man is repulsive; I do not wish to deal with him. The other is irritable, shy, and on his guard. The youth looks humble and manly: I choose him. Look on this woman. There is not beauty, nor brilliant sayings, nor distinguished power to serve you; but all see her gladly; her whole air and impression are healthful. Here come the sentimentalists, and the invalids. Here is Elise, who caught cold in coming into the world, and has always increased it since. Here are creep-mouse manners; and thievish manners. "Look at Northcote," said Fuseli;[20] "he looks like a rat that has seen a cat." In the shallow company, easily excited, easily tired, here is the columnar Bernard: the Alleghenies do not express more repose than his behavior. Here are the sweet following eyes of Cecile: it seemed always that she demanded the heart. Nothing can be more excellent in kind than the Corinthian grace of Gertrude's manners, and yet Blanche, who has no manners, has better manners than she; for the movements of Blanche are the sallies of a spirit which is sufficient for the moment, and she can afford to express every thought by instant action.

Manners have been somewhat cynically defined to be a contrivance of wise men to keep fools at a distance. Fashion is shrewd to detect those who do not belong to her train, and seldom wastes her attentions. Society is very swift in its instincts, and, if you do not belong to it, resists and sneers at you; or quietly drops you. The first weapon enrages the party attacked; the second is still more effective, but is not to be resisted, as the date of the transaction is not easily found. People grow up and grow old under this infliction, and never suspect the truth, ascribing the solitude which acts on them very injuriously, to any cause but the right one.

The basis of good manners is self-reliance. Necessity is the law of all who are not self-possessed. Those who are not self-possessed, obtrude, and pain us. Some men appear to feel that they belong to a Pariah[21] caste. They fear to offend, they bend and apologize, and walk through life with a timid step. As we sometimes dream that we are in a well-dressed company without any coat, so Godfrey acts ever as if he suffered from some mortifying circumstance. The hero should find himself at home, wherever he is; should impart comfort by his own security and good-nature to all beholders. The hero is suffered to be himself. A person of strong mind comes to perceive that for him an immunity is secured so long as he renders to society that service which is native and proper to him,—an immunity from all the observances, yea, and duties, which society so tyrannically imposes on the rank and file of its members. "Euripides," says Aspasia, "has not the fine manners of Sophocles;[22] but,"—she adds good-humoredly, "the movers and masters of our souls have surely a right to throw out their limbs as carelessly as they please, on the world that belongs to them, and before the creatures they have animated."[23]

Manners require time, as nothing is more vulgar than haste. Friendship should be surrounded with ceremonies and respects, and not crushed into corners. Friendship requires more time than poor busy men can usually command. Here comes to me Roland, with a delicacy of sentiment leading and inwrapping him like a divine cloud or holy ghost. 'Tis a great destitution to both that this should not be entertained with large leisures, but contrarywise should be balked by importunate affairs.

But through this lustrous varnish, the reality is ever shining. 'Tis hard to keep the *what* from breaking through this pretty painting of the *how*. The core will come to the surface. Strong will and keen perception overpower old manners, and create new; and the thought of the present moment has a greater value than all the past. In persons of character, we do not remark manners, because of their instantaneousness. We are surprised by the thing done, out of all power to watch the way of it. Yet nothing is more charming than to recognize the great style which runs through the actions of such. People masquerade before us in their fortunes, titles, offices, and connections, as academic or civil presidents, or senators, or professors, or great lawyers, and impose on the frivolous, and a good deal on each other, by these fames. At least, it is a point of prudent good manners to treat these reputations tenderly, as if they were merited. But the sad realist knows these fellows at a glance, and they know him; as when in Paris the chief of the police enters a ballroom, so many diamonded pretenders shrink and make themselves as inconspicuous as they can, or give him a supplicating look as they pass. "I had received," said a sibyl, "I had received at birth the fatal gift of penetration:"—and these Cassandras[24] are always born.

Manners impress as they indicate real power. A man who is sure of his point, carries a broad and contented expression, which everybody reads. And you cannot rightly train one to an air and manner, except by making him the kind of man of whom that manner is the natural expression. Nature forever puts a premium on reality. What is done for effect, is seen to be done for effect; what is done for love, is felt to be done for love. A man inspires affection and honor, because he was not lying in wait for these. The things of a man for which we visit him, were done in the dark and the cold. A little integrity is better than any career. So deep are the sources of this surface-action, that even the size of your companion seems to vary with his freedom of thought. Not only is he larger, when at ease, and his thoughts generous, but everything around him becomes variable with expression. No carpenter's rule, no rod and chain, will measure the dimensions of any house or house-lot: go into the house: if the proprietor is constrained and deferring, 'tis of no importance how large his house, how beautiful his grounds,—you quickly come to the end of all: but if the man is self-possessed, happy, and at home, his house is deep-founded, indefinitely large and interesting, the roof and dome buoyant as the sky. Under the humblest roof, the commonest person in plain clothes sits there massive, cheerful, yet formidable like the Egyptian colossi.[25]

Neither Aristotle, nor Leibniz, nor Junius, nor Champollion[26] has set down the grammar-rules of this dialect, older than Sanskrit;[27] but they who cannot yet read English, can read this. Men take each other's measure, when they meet for the first time,—and every time they meet. How do they get this rapid knowledge, even before they speak, of each other's power and dispositions? One would say, that the persuasion of their speech is not in what they say,—or, that men do not convince by their argument,—but by their personality, by who they are, and what they said and did heretofore. A man already strong is listened to, and everything he says is applauded. Another opposes him with sound argument, but the argument is scouted, until by and by it gets into the mind of some weighty person; then it begins to tell on the community.

Self-reliance is the basis of behavior, as it is the guaranty that the powers are not squandered in too much demonstration. In this country, where school education is universal, we have a superficial culture, and a profusion of reading and writing and expression. We parade our nobilities in poems and orations, instead of working them up into happiness. There is a whisper out of the ages to him who can understand it,—'whatever is known to thyself alone, has always very great value.' There is some reason to believe, that, when a man does not write his poetry, it escapes by other vents through him, instead of the one vent of writing; clings to his form and manners, whilst poets have often nothing poetical about them except their verses. Jacobi[28] said, that "when a man has fully expressed his thought, he has somewhat less possession of it." One would say, the rule is,—What a man is irresistibly urged to say, helps him and us. In explaining his thought to others, he explains it to himself: but when he opens it for show, it corrupts him.

Society is the stage on which manners are shown; novels are their literature. Novels are the journal or record of manners; and the new importance of these books derives from the fact, that the novelist begins to penetrate the surface, and treat this part of life more worthily. The novels used to be all alike, and had a quite vulgar tone. The novels used to lead us on to a foolish interest in the fortunes of the boy and girl they described. The boy was to be raised from a humble to a high position. He was in want of a wife and a castle, and the object of the story was to supply him with one or both. We watched sympathetically, step by step, his climbing, until, at last, the point is gained, the wedding day is fixed, and we follow the gala procession home to the castle, when the doors are slammed in our face, and the poor reader is left outside in the cold, not enriched by so much as an idea, or a virtuous impulse.

But the victories of character are instant, and victories for all. Its greatness enlarges all. We are fortified by every heroic anecdote. The novels are as useful as Bibles, if they teach you the secret, that the best of life is conversation, and the greatest success is confidence, or perfect understanding between sincere people. 'Tis a French definition of friendship, *rien que s'entendre*, good understanding. The highest compact we can make with our fellow, is,—'Let there be truth between us two forevermore.' That is the charm in all good novels, as it is the charm in all good histories, that the heroes mutually understand, from the first, and deal loyally, and with a profound trust in each other. It is sublime to feel and say of another, I need never meet, or speak, or write to him: we need not reinforce ourselves, or send tokens of remembrance: I rely on him as on myself: if he did thus or thus, I know it was right.

In all the superior people I have met, I notice directness, truth spoken more truly, as if everything of obstruction, of malformation, had been trained away. What have they to conceal? What have they to exhibit? Between simple and noble persons, there is always a quick intelligence: they recognize at sight, and meet on a better ground than the talents and skills they may chance to possess, namely, on sincerity and uprightness. For, it is not what talents or genius a man has, but how he is to his talents, that constitutes friendship and character. The man that stands by himself, the universe stands by him also. It is related of the monk Basle, that, being excommunicated by the Pope, he was, at his death, sent in charge of an angel to find a fit place of suffering in hell; but, such was the eloquence and good-humor of the monk, that, wherever he went he was received gladly, and civilly treated, even by the most uncivil angels: and, when he came to discourse with them, instead of contradicting or forcing him, they took his part, and adopted his manners: and even good angels came from far, to see him, and take up their abode with him. The angel that was sent to find a place of torment for him, attempted to remove him to a worse pit, but with no better success; for such was the contented spirit of the monk, that he found something to praise in every place and company, though in hell, and made a kind of heaven of it. At last the escorting angel returned with his prisoner to them that sent him, saying, that no phlegethon[29] could be found that would burn him; for that, in whatever condition, Basle remained incorrigibly Basle. The legend says, his sentence was remitted, and he was allowed to go into heaven, and was canonized as a saint.

There is a stroke of magnanimity in the correspondence of Bonaparte with his brother Joseph, when the latter was King of Spain, and complained that he missed in Napoleon's letters the affectionate tone which had marked their childish correspondence. "I am sorry," replies Napoleon, "you think you shall find your brother again only in the Elysian Fields.[30] It is natural, that at forty, he should not feel towards you as he did at twelve. But his feelings towards you have greater truth and strength. His friendship has the features of his mind."

How much we forgive to those who yield us the rare spectacle of heroic manners! We will pardon them the want of books, of arts, and even of the gentler virtues. How tenaciously we remember them! Here is a lesson which I brought along with me in boyhood from the Latin School, and which ranks with the best of Roman anecdotes. Marcus Scaurus[31] was accused by Quintus Varius Hispanus, that he had excited the allies to take arms against the Republic. But he, full of firmness and gravity, defended himself in this manner: "Quintus Varius Hispanus alleges that Marcus Scaurus, President of the Senate, excited the allies to arms: Marcus Scaurus, President of the Senate, denies it. There is no witness. Which do you believe, Romans?" "*Utri creditis,*

Quirites?" When he had said these words, he was absolved by the assembly of the people.

I have seen manners that make a similar impression with personal beauty; that give the like exhilaration, and refine us like that; and, in memorable experiences, they are suddenly better than beauty, and make that superfluous and ugly. But they must be marked by fine perception, the acquaintance with real beauty. They must always show self-control: you shall not be facile, apologetic, or leaky, but king over your word; and every gesture and action shall indicate power at rest. Then they must be inspired by the good heart. There is no beautifier of complexion, or form, or behavior, like the wish to scatter joy and not pain around us. 'Tis good to give a stranger a meal, or a night's lodging. 'Tis better to be hospitable to his good meaning and thought, and give courage to a companion. We must be as courteous to a man as we are to a picture, which we are willing to give the advantage of a good light. Special precepts are not to be thought of: the talent of well-doing contains them all. Every hour will show a duty as paramount as that of my whim just now; and yet I will write it,—that there is one topic peremptorily forbidden to all well-bred, to all rational mortals, namely, their distempers. If you have not slept, or if you have slept, or if you have headache, or sciatica, or leprosy, or thunder-stroke, I beseech you, by all angels, to hold your peace, and not pollute the morning, to which all the housemates bring serene and pleasant thoughts, by corruption and groans. Come out of the azure. Love the day. Do not leave the sky out of your landscape. The oldest and the most deserving person should come very modestly into any newly awaked company, respecting the divine communications, out of which all must be presumed to have newly come. An old man who added an elevating culture to a large experience of life, said to me, "When you come into the room, I think I will study how to make humanity beautiful to you."

As respects the delicate question of culture, I do not think that any other than negative rules can be laid down. For positive rules, for suggestion, Nature alone inspires it. Who dare assume to guide a youth, a maid, to perfect manners?—the golden mean is so delicate, difficult,—say frankly, unattainable. What finest hands would not be clumsy to sketch the genial precepts of the young girl's demeanor? The chances seem infinite against success; and yet success is continually attained. There must not be secondariness, and 'tis a thousand to one that her air and manner will at once betray that she is not primary, but that there is some other one or many of her class, to whom she habitually postpones herself. But Nature lifts her easily, and without knowing it, over these impossibilities, and we are continually surprised with graces and felicities not only unteachable, but undescribable.

VI

WORSHIP

———•———

This is he, who, felled by foes,
Sprung harmless up, refreshed by blows:
He to captivity was sold,
But him no prison-bars would hold:
Though they sealed him in a rock,
Mountain chains he can unlock:
Thrown to lions for their meat,
The crouching lion kissed his feet:
Bound to the stake, no flames appalled,
But arched o'er him an honoring vault.
This is he men miscall Fate,
Threading dark ways, arriving late,
But ever coming in time to crown
The truth, and hurl wrongdoers down.
He is the oldest, and best known,
More near than aught thou call'st thy own,
Yet, greeted in another's eyes,
Disconcerts with glad surprise.
This is Jove, who, deaf to prayers,
Floods with blessings unawares.
Draw, if thou canst, the mystic line,
Severing rightly his from thine,
Which is human, which divine.

WORSHIP

Some of my friends have complained, when the preceding papers were read, that we discussed Fate, Power, and Wealth, on too low a platform; gave too much line to the evil spirit of the times; too many cakes to Cerberus;[1] that we ran Cudworth's[2] risk of making, by excess of candor, the argument of atheism so strong, that he could not answer it. I have no fears of being forced in my own despite to play, as we say, the devil's attorney. I have no infirmity of faith; no belief that it is of much importance what I or any man may say: I am sure that a certain truth will be said through me, though I should be dumb, or though I should try to say the reverse. Nor do I fear skepticism for any good soul. A just thinker will allow full swing to his skepticism. I dip my pen in the blackest ink, because I am not afraid of falling into my inkpot. I have no sympathy with a poor man I knew, who, when suicides abounded, told me he dared not look at his razor. We are of different opinions at different hours, but we always may be said to be at heart on the side of truth.

I see not why we should give ourselves such sanctified airs. If the Divine Providence has hid from men neither disease, nor deformity, nor corrupt society, but has stated itself out in passions, in war, in trade, in the love of power and pleasure, in hunger and need, in tyrannies, literatures, and arts,—let us not be so nice that we cannot write these facts down coarsely as they stand, or doubt but there is a counter-statement as ponderous, which we can arrive at, and which, being put, will make all square. The solar system has no anxiety about its reputation, and the credit of truth and honesty is as safe; nor have I any fear that a skeptical bias can be given by leaning hard on the sides of fate, of practical power, or of trade, which the doctrine of Faith cannot down-weigh. The strength of that principle is not measured in ounces and pounds: it tyrannizes at the center of Nature. We may well give skepticism as much line as we can. The spirit will return, and fill us. It drives the drivers. It counterbalances any accumulations of power.

"Heaven kindly gave our blood a moral flow."

We are born loyal. The whole creation is made of hooks and eyes, of bitumen, of sticking-plaster, and whether your community is made in Jerusalem or in

California, of saints or of wreckers, it coheres in a perfect ball. Men as naturally make a state, or a church, as caterpillars a web. If they were more refined, it would be less formal, it would be nervous, like that of the Shakers, who, from long habit of thinking and feeling together, it is said, are affected in the same way, at the same time, to work and to play, and as they go with perfect sympathy to their tasks in the field or shop, so are they inclined for a ride or a journey at the same instant, and the horses come up with the family carriage unbespoken to the door.

We are born believing. A man bears beliefs, as a tree bears apples. A self-poise belongs to every particle; and a rectitude to every mind, and is the Nemesis and protector of every society. I and my neighbors have been bred in the notion, that, unless we came soon to some good church,—Calvinism, or Behmenism, or Romanism, or Mormonism,[3]—there would be a universal thaw and dissolution. No Isaiah or Jeremy has arrived. Nothing can exceed the anarchy that has followed in our skies. The stern old faiths have all pulverized. 'Tis a whole population of gentlemen and ladies out in search of religions. 'Tis as flat anarchy in our ecclesiastic realms, as that which existed in Massachusetts, in the Revolution, or which prevails now on the slope of the Rocky Mountains or Pike's Peak. Yet we make shift to live. Men are loyal. Nature has self-poise in all her works; certain proportions in which oxygen and azote[4] combine, and, not less a harmony in faculties, a fitness in the spring and the regulator.

The decline of the influence of Calvin, or Fénelon, or Wesley,[5] or Channing, need give us no uneasiness. The builder of heaven has not so ill constructed his creature as that the religion, that is, the public nature, should fall out: the public and the private element, like north and south, like inside and outside, like centrifugal and centripetal, adhere to every soul, and cannot be subdued, except the soul is dissipated. God builds his temple in the heart on the ruins of churches and religions.

In the last chapters, we treated some particulars of the question of culture. But the whole state of man is a state of culture; and its flowering and completion may be described as Religion, or Worship. There is always some religion, some hope and fear extended into the invisible,—from the blind boding which nails a horseshoe to the mast or the threshold, up to the song of the Elders in the Apocalypse.[6] But the religion cannot rise above the state of the votary.[7] Heaven always bears some proportion to earth. The god of the cannibals will be a cannibal, of the crusaders a crusader, and of the merchants a merchant. In all ages, souls out of time, extraordinary, prophetic, are born, who are rather related to the system of the world, than to their particular age and locality. These announce absolute truths, which, with whatever reverence received, are speedily dragged down into a savage interpretation. The interior tribes of our Indians, and some of the Pacific islanders, flog their gods, when things take an unfavorable turn. The Greek poets did not hesitate to let loose their petulant[8] wit on their deities also. Laomedon,[9] in his anger at Neptune and Apollo, who had built Troy for him, and demanded their price, does not hesitate to menace them that he will cut their ears off.[10] Among our Norse forefathers, King Olaf's[11] mode of converting Eyvind to Christianity was to put a pan of glowing coals on his belly, which burst asunder. "Wilt thou now, Eyvind, believe in Christ?" asks Olaf, in excellent faith. Another argument was an adder put into the mouth of the reluctant disciple Rand, who refused to believe.

Christianity, in the romantic ages, signified European culture,—the grafted or meliorated tree in a crab forest. And to marry a pagan wife or husband, was to marry Beast, and voluntarily to take a step backwards towards the baboon.

> "Hengist had verament
> A daughter both fair and gent,
> But she was heathen Sarazine,
> And Vortigern for love fine
> Her took to fere[12] and to wife,
> And was cursed in all his life;
> For he let Christian wed heathen,
> And mixed our blood as flesh and mathen."[13]

What Gothic mixtures the Christian creed drew from the pagan sources, Richard of Devizes's chronicle of Richard I.'s crusade,[14] in the twelfth century, may show. King Richard taunts God with forsaking him: "O fie! O how unwilling should I be to forsake thee, in so forlorn and dreadful a position, were I thy lord and advocate, as thou art mine. In sooth, my standards will in future be despised, not through my fault, but through thine: in sooth, not through any cowardice of my warfare, art thou thyself, my king and my God conquered, this day, and not Richard thy vassal." The religion of the early English poets is anomalous, so devout and so blasphemous, in the same breath. Such is Chaucer's extraordinary confusion of heaven and earth in the picture of Dido.

> "She was so fair,
> So young, so lusty, with her eyen glad,
> That if that God that heaven and earthe made
> Would have a love for beauty and goodness,

And womanhede,[15] truth, and seemliness,
Whom should he loven but this lady sweet?
There n' is no woman to him half so meet."

With these grossnesses, we complacently compare our own taste and decorum. We think and speak with more temperance and gradation,—but is not indifferentism as bad as superstition?

We live in a transition period, when the old faiths which comforted nations, and not only so, but made nations, seem to have spent their force. I do not find the religions of men at this moment very creditable to them, but either childish and insignificant, or unmanly and effeminating. The fatal trait is the divorce between religion and morality. Here are know-nothing religions, or churches that proscribe intellect; scortatory[16] religions; slave-holding and slave-trading religions; and, even in the decent populations, idolatries wherein the whiteness of the ritual covers scarlet indulgence. The lover of the old religion complains that our contemporaries, scholars as well as merchants, succumb to a great despair,—have corrupted into a timorous conservatism, and believe in nothing. In our large cities, the population is godless, materialized,—no bond, no fellow-feeling, no enthusiasm. These are not men, but hungers, thirsts, fevers, and appetites walking. How is it people manage to live on,—so aimless as they are? After their peppercorn aims are gained, it seems as if the lime in their bones alone held them together, and not any worthy purpose. There is no faith in the intellectual, none in the moral universe. There is faith in chemistry, in meat, and wine, in wealth, in machinery, in the steam-engine, galvanic battery, turbine-wheels, sewing machines, and in public opinion, but not in divine causes. A silent revolution has loosed the tension of the old religious sects, and, in place of the gravity and permanence of those societies of opinion, they run into freak and extravagance. In creeds never was such levity; witness the heathenisms in Christianity, the periodic "revivals," the Millennium mathematics, the peacock ritualism, the retrogression to Popery, the maundering[17] of Mormons, the squalor of Mesmerism,[18] the deliration of rappings, the rat and mouse revelation, thumps in table-drawers, and black art. The architecture, the music, the prayer, partake of the madness: the arts sink into shift and make-believe. Not knowing what to do, we ape our ancestors; the churches stagger backward to the mummeries[19] of the dark ages. By the irresistible maturing of the general mind, the Christian traditions have lost their hold. The dogma of the mystic offices of Christ being dropped, and he standing on his genius as a moral teacher, 'tis impossible to maintain the old emphasis of his personality; and it recedes, as all persons must, before the sublimity of the moral laws.[20] From this change, and in the momentary absence of any religious genius that could offset the immense material activity, there is a feeling that religion is gone. When Paul Leroux offered his article *"Dieu"* to the conductor of a leading French journal, he replied, *"La question de Dieu manque d'actualité."*[21] In Italy, Mr. Gladstone[22] said of the late King of Naples, "it has been a proverb, that he has erected the negation of God into a system of government."[23] In this country, the like stupefaction was in the air, and the phrase "higher law" became a political jibe.[24] What proof of infidelity, like the toleration and propagandism of slavery? What, like the direction of education? What, like the facility of conversion? What, like the externality of churches that once sucked the roots of right and wrong, and now have perished away till they are a speck of whitewash on the wall? What proof of skepticism like the base rate at which the highest mental and moral gifts are held? Let a man attain the highest and broadest culture that any American has possessed, then let him die by sea-storm, railroad collision, or other accident, and all America will acquiesce that the best thing has happened to him;[25] that, after the education has gone far, such is the expensiveness of America, that the best use to put a fine person to, is, to drown him to save his board.

Another scar of this skepticism is the distrust in human virtue. It is believed by well-dressed proprietors that there is no more virtue than they possess; that the solid portion of society exist for the arts of comfort: that life is an affair to put somewhat between the upper and lower mandibles. How prompt the suggestion of a low motive! Certain patriots in England devoted themselves for years to creating a public opinion that should break down the corn-laws and establish free trade. 'Well,' says the man in the street, 'Cobden got a stipend out of it.' Kossuth fled hither across the ocean to try if he could rouse the New World to a sympathy with European liberty. 'Aye,' says New York, 'he made a handsome thing of it, enough to make him comfortable for life.'

See what allowance vice finds in the respectable and well-conditioned class. If a pickpocket intrude into the society of gentlemen, they exert what moral force they have, and he finds himself uncomfortable, and glad to get away. But if an adventurer go through all the forms, procure himself to be elected to a post of trust, as of senator, or president,—though by the same arts as we detest in the house-thief,—the same gentlemen who agree to discountenance the private rogue, will be forward to show civilities and marks of respect to the public one: and no amount of evidence of his crimes will prevent them giving him ovations, complimentary dinners, opening their own houses to him, and priding themselves on his acquaintance. We were not deceived by the professions of the private adventurer,—the louder he talked of his honor, the faster we counted our spoons; but we appeal to the sanctified preamble of the messages and proclamations of the public sinner, as the proof of sincerity. It must be that they who pay this homage have said to themselves, On the whole, we don't know about this that you call honesty; a bird in the hand is better.

Even well-disposed, good sort of people are touched with the same infidelity, and for brave, straightforward action, use half-measures and compromises. Forgetful that a little measure is a great error, forgetful that a wise mechanic uses a sharp tool, they go on choosing the dead men of routine. But the official men can in nowise help you in any question of today, they deriving entirely from the old dead things. Only those can help in counsel or conduct who did not make a party pledge to defend this or that, but who were appointed by God Almighty, before they came into the world, to stand for this which they uphold.

It has been charged that a want of sincerity in the leading men is a vice general throughout American society. But the multitude of the sick shall not make us deny the existence of health. In spite of our imbecility and terrors, and "universal decay of religion," and etc. and etc., the moral sense reappears today with the same morning newness that has been from of old the fountain of beauty and strength. You say, there is no religion now. 'Tis like saying in rainy weather, there is no sun, when at that moment we are witnessing one of his superlative effects. The religion of the cultivated class now, to be sure, consists in an avoidance of acts and engagements which it was once their religion to assume. But this avoidance will yield spontaneous forms in their due hour. There is a principle which is the basis of things, which all speech aims to say, and all action to evolve, a simple, quiet, undescribed, undescribable presence, dwelling very peacefully in us, our rightful lord: we are not to do, but to let do; not to work, but to be worked upon; and to this homage there is a consent of all thoughtful and just men in all ages and conditions. To this sentiment belong vast and sudden enlargements of power. 'Tis remarkable that our faith in ecstasy consists with total inexperience of it. It is the order of the world to educate with accuracy the senses and the understanding; and the enginery[26] at work to draw out these powers in priority, no doubt, has its office. But we are never without a hint that these powers are mediate and servile, and that we are one day to deal with real being,—essences with essences. Even the fury of material activity has some results friendly to moral health. The energetic action of the times develops individualism, and the religious appear isolated. I esteem this a step in the right direction. Heaven deals with us on no representative system. Souls are not saved in bundles. The Spirit saith to the man, 'How is it with thee? thee personally? is it well? is it ill?' For a great nature, it is a happiness to escape a religious training,—religion of character is so apt to be invaded. Religion must always be a crab fruit: it cannot be grafted and keep its wild beauty. "I have seen," said a traveler who had known the extremes of society, "I have seen human nature in all its forms, it is everywhere the same, but the wilder it is, the more virtuous."

We say, the old forms of religion decay, and that a skepticism devastates the community. I do not think it can be cured or stayed by any modification of theologic creeds, much less by theologic discipline. The cure for false theology is mother-wit. Forget your books and traditions, and obey your moral perceptions at this hour. That which is signified by the words "moral" and "spiritual," is a lasting essence, and, with whatever illusions we have loaded them, will certainly bring back the words, age after age, to their ancient meaning. I know no words that mean so much. In our definitions, we grope after the *spiritual* by describing it as invisible. The true meaning of *spiritual* is *real*; that law which executes itself, which works without means, and which cannot be conceived as not existing. Men talk of "mere morality,"—which is much as if one should say, 'poor God, with nobody to help him.' I find the omnipresence and the almightiness in the reaction of every atom in Nature. I can best indicate by examples those reactions by which every part of Nature replies to the purpose of the actor,—beneficently to the good, penally to the bad. Let us replace sentimentalism by realism, and dare to uncover those simple and terrible laws which, be they seen or unseen, pervade and govern.

Every man takes care that his neighbor shall not cheat him. But a day comes when he begins to care that he do not cheat his neighbor. Then all goes well. He has changed his market-cart into a chariot of the sun. What a day dawns, when we have taken to heart the doctrine of faith! to prefer, as a better investment, being to doing; being to seeming; logic to rhythm and to display; the year to the day; the life to the year; character to performance;—and have come to know, that justice will be done us; and, if our genius is slow, the term will be long.

'Tis certain that worship stands in some commanding relation to the health of man, and to his highest powers, so as to be, in some manner, the source of intellect. All the great ages have been ages of belief. I mean, when there was any extraordinary power of performance, when great national movements began, when arts appeared, when heroes existed, when poems were made, the human soul was in earnest, and had fixed its thoughts on spiritual verities, with as strict a grasp as that of the hands on the sword, or the pencil, or the trowel. It is true that genius takes its rise out of the mountains of rectitude; that all beauty and power which men covet, are somehow born out of that Alpine district; that any extraordinary degree of beauty in man or woman involves a moral charm. Thus, I think, we very slowly admit in another man a higher degree of moral sentiment than our own,—a finer conscience, more impressionable, or, which marks minuter degrees; an ear to hear acuter notes of right and wrong, than we can. I think we listen suspiciously and very slowly to any evidence to that point. But, once satisfied of such superiority, we set no limit to our expectation of his genius. For such persons are nearer to the secret of God than others; are bathed by sweeter waters; they hear notices, they see visions, where others are vacant. We believe that holiness confers a certain insight, because not by our private, but by our public force, can we share and know the nature of things.

There is an intimate interdependence of intellect and morals. Given the equality of two intellects,—which will form the most reliable judgments, the good, or the bad hearted? "The heart has its arguments, with which the understanding is not acquainted."[27] For the heart is at once aware of the state of health or disease, which is the controlling state, that is, of sanity or of insanity, prior, of course, to all question of the ingenuity of arguments, the amount of facts, or the elegance of rhetoric. So intimate is this alliance of mind and heart, that talent uniformly sinks with character. The bias of errors of principle carries away men into perilous courses, as soon as their will does not control their passion or talent. Hence the extraordinary blunders, and final wrong head, into which men spoiled by ambition usually fall. Hence the remedy for all blunders, the cure of blindness, the cure of crime, is love. "As much love, so much mind," said the Latin proverb. The superiority that has no superior; the redeemer and instructor of souls, as it is their primal essence, is love.

The moral must be the measure of health. If your eye is on the eternal, your intellect will grow, and your opinions and actions will have a beauty which no learning or combined advantages of other men can rival. The moment of your loss of faith, and acceptance of the lucrative standard, will be marked in the pause, or solstice of genius, the sequent retrogression, and the inevitable loss of attraction to other minds. The vulgar are sensible of the change in you, and of your descent, though they clap you on the back, and congratulate you on your increased common sense.[28]

Our recent culture has been in natural science. We have learned the manners of the sun and of the moon, of the rivers and the rains, of the mineral and elemental kingdoms, of plants and animals. Man has learned to weigh the sun, and its weight neither loses nor gains. The path of a star, the moment of an eclipse, can be determined to the fraction of a second. Well, to him the book of history, the book of love, the lures of passion, and the commandments of duty are opened: and the next lesson taught, is, the continuation of the inflexible law of matter into the subtle kingdom of will, and of thought; that, if, in sidereal ages, gravity and projection keep their craft, and the ball never loses its way in its wild path through space,—a secreter gravitation, a secreter projection, rule not less tyrannically in human history, and keep the balance of power from age to age unbroken. For, though the new element of freedom and an individual has been admitted, yet the primordial atoms are prefigured and predetermined to moral issues, are in search of justice, and ultimate right is done. Religion or worship is the attitude of those who see this unity, intimacy, and sincerity; who see that, against all appearances, the nature of things works for truth and right forever.[29]

'Tis a short sight to limit our faith in laws to those of gravity, of chemistry, of botany, and so forth. Those laws do not stop where our eyes lose them, but push the same geometry and chemistry up into the invisible plane of social and rational life, so that, look where we will, in a boy's game, or in the strifes of races, a perfect reaction, a perpetual judgment keeps watch and ward. And this appears in a class of facts which concerns all men, within and above their creeds.

Shallow men believe in luck, believe in circumstances: It was somebody's name, or he happened to be there at the time, or, it was so then, and another day it would have been otherwise. Strong men believe in cause and effect. The man was born to do it, and his father was born to be the father of him and of this deed, and, by looking narrowly, you shall see there was no luck in the matter, but it was all a problem in arithmetic, or an experiment in chemistry. The curve of the flight of the moth is preordained, and all things go by number, rule, and weight.

Skepticism is unbelief in cause and effect. A man does not see, that, as he eats, so he thinks: as he deals, so he is, and so he appears; he does not see, that his son is the son of his thoughts and of his actions; that fortunes are not exceptions but fruits; that relation and connection are not somewhere and sometimes, but everywhere and always; no miscellany, no exemption, no anomaly,—but method, and an even web; and what comes out, that was put in. As we are, so we do; and as we do, so is it done to us; we are the builders of our fortunes; cant and lying and the attempt to secure a good which does not belong to us, are, once for all, balked and vain. But, in the human mind, this tie of fate is made alive. The law is the basis of the human mind. In us, it is inspiration; out there in Nature, we see its fatal strength. We call it the moral sentiment.[30]

We owe to the Hindu Scriptures a definition of Law, which compares well with any in our Western books. "Law it is, which is without name, or color, or hands, or feet; which is smallest of the least, and largest of the large; all, and knowing all things; which hears without ears, sees without eyes, moves without feet, and seizes without hands."[31]

If any reader tax me with using vague and traditional phrases, let me suggest to him, by a few examples, what kind of a trust this is, and how real. Let me show him that the dice are loaded;[32] that the colors are fast, because they are the native colors of the fleece; that the globe is a battery, because every atom is a magnet; and that the police and sincerity of the Universe are secured by God's delegating his divinity to every particle; that there is no room for hypocrisy, no margin for choice.

The countryman leaving his native village, for the first time, and going abroad, finds all his habits broken up. In a new nation and language, his sect, as Quaker, or Lutheran, is lost. What! it is not then necessary to the order and existence of society? He misses this, and the commanding eye of his neighborhood, which held him to decorum. This is the peril of New York, of New Orleans, of London, of Paris, to young men. But after a little experience, he makes the discovery that there are no large cities,—none large enough to hide in; that the censors of action are as numerous and as near in Paris, as in Littleton or Portland; that the gossip is as prompt and vengeful. There is no concealment, and, for each offence, a several vengeance; that, reaction, or *nothing for nothing*, or, *things are as broad as they are long*, is not a rule for Littleton or Portland, but for the Universe.

We cannot spare the coarsest muniment[33] of virtue. We are disgusted by gossip; yet it is of importance to keep the angels in their proprieties. The smallest fly will draw blood, and gossip is a weapon impossible to exclude from the privatest, highest, selectest. Nature created a police of many ranks. God has delegated himself to a million deputies. From these low external penalties, the scale ascends. Next come the resentments, the fears, which injustice calls out; then, the false relations in which the offender is put to other men; and the reaction of his fault on himself, in the solitude and devastation of his mind.

You cannot hide any secret. If the artist succor his flagging spirits by opium or wine, his work will characterize itself as the effect of opium or wine. If you make a picture or a statue, it sets the beholder in that state of mind you had, when you made it. If you spend for show, on building, or gardening, or on pictures, or on equipages, it will so appear. We are all physiognomists and penetrators of character, and things themselves are detective. If you follow the suburban fashion in building a sumptuous-looking house for a little money, it will appear to all eyes as a cheap dear house. There is no privacy that cannot be penetrated. No secret can be kept in the civilized world. Society is a masked ball, where every one hides his real character, and reveals it by hiding. If a man wish to conceal anything he carries, those whom he meets know that he conceals somewhat, and usually know what he conceals. Is it otherwise if there be some belief or some purpose he would bury in his breast? 'Tis as hard to hide as fire. He is a strong man who can hold down his opinion. A man cannot utter two or three sentences, without disclosing to intelligent ears precisely where he stands in life and thought, namely, whether in the kingdom of the senses and the understanding, or, in that of ideas and imagination, in the realm of intuitions and duty. People seem not to see that their opinion of the world is also a confession of character. We can only see what we are, and if we misbehave we suspect others. The fame of Shakespeare or of Voltaire, of Thomas à Kempis,[34] or of Bonaparte, characterizes those who give it. As gas-light is found to be the best nocturnal police, so the universe protects itself by pitiless publicity.

Each must be armed—not necessarily with musket and pike. Happy, if, seeing these, he can feel that he has better muskets and pikes in his energy and constancy. To every creature is his own weapon, however skillfully concealed from himself, a good while. His work is sword and shield. Let him accuse none, let him injure none. The way to mend the bad world, is to create the right world. Here is a low political economy plotting to cut the throat of foreign competition, and establish our own;—excluding others by force, or making war on them; or, by cunning tariffs, giving preference to worse wares of ours. But the real and lasting victories are those of peace, and not of war. The way to conquer the foreign artisan, is, not to kill him, but to beat his work. And the Crystal Palaces[35] and World Fairs, with their committees and prizes on all kinds of industry, are the result of this feeling. The American workman who strikes ten blows with his hammer, whilst the foreign workman only strikes one, is as really vanquishing that foreigner, as if the blows were aimed at and told on his person. I look on that man as happy, who, when there is question of success, looks into his work for a reply, not into the market, not into opinion, not into patronage. In every variety of human employment, in the mechanical and in the fine arts, in navigation, in farming, in legislating, there are among the numbers who do their task perfunctorily, as we say, or just to pass, and as badly as they dare,—there are the working-men, on whom the burden of the business falls,—those who love work, and love to see it rightly done, who finish their task for its own sake; and the state and the world is happy, that has the most of such finishers. The world will always do justice at last to such finishers: it cannot otherwise. He who has acquired the ability, may wait securely the occasion of making it felt and appreciated, and know that it will not loiter. Men talk as if victory were something fortunate. Work is victory. Wherever work is done, victory is obtained. There is no chance, and no blanks.[36] You want but one verdict: if you have your own, you are secure of the rest. And yet, if witnesses are wanted, witnesses are near. There was never a man born so wise or good, but one or more companions came into the world with him, who delight in his faculty, and report it. I cannot see without awe, that no man thinks alone, and no man acts alone, but the divine assessors who came up with him into life,—now under one disguise, now under another,—like a police in citizens' clothes, walk with him, step for step, through all the kingdom of time.

This reaction, this sincerity is the property of all things. To make our word or act sublime, we must make it real. It is our system that counts, not the single word or unsupported action. Use what language you will, you can never say anything but what you are. What I am, and what I think, is conveyed to you, in spite of my efforts to hold it back. What I am has been secretly conveyed from me to another, whilst I was vainly making up my mind to tell him it. He has heard from me what I never spoke.

As men get on in life, they acquire a love for sincerity, and somewhat less solicitude to be lulled or amused. In the progress of the character, there is an increasing faith in the moral sentiment, and a decreasing faith in propositions. Young people admire talents, and particular excellences. As we grow older, we value total powers and effects, as the spirit, or quality of the man. We have another sight, and a new standard; an insight which disregards what is done *for* the eye, and pierces to the doer; an ear which hears not what men say, but hears what they do not say.

There was a wise, devout man who is called, in the Catholic Church, St. Philip Neri,[37] of whom many anecdotes touching his discernment and benevolence are told at Naples and Rome. Among the nuns in a convent not far from Rome, one had appeared, who laid claim to certain rare gifts of inspiration and prophecy, and the abbess advised the Holy Father, at Rome, of the wonderful powers shown by her novice. The Pope did not well know what to make of these new claims, and Philip coming in from a journey, one day, he consulted him. Philip undertook to visit the nun, and ascertain her character. He threw himself on his mule, all travel-soiled as he was, and hastened through the mud and mire to the distant convent. He told the abbess the wishes of his Holiness, and begged her to summon the nun without delay. The nun was sent for, and, as soon as she came into the apartment, Philip stretched out his leg all bespattered with mud, and desired her to draw off his boots. The young nun, who had become the object of much attention and respect, drew back with anger, and refused the office: Philip ran out of doors, mounted his mule, and returned instantly to the Pope; "Give yourself no uneasiness, Holy Father, any longer: here is no miracle, for here is no humility."

We need not much mind what people please to say, but what they must say; what their natures say, though their busy, artful, Yankee understandings try to hold back, and choke that word, and to articulate something different. If we will sit quietly,—what they ought to say is said, with their will, or against their will. We do not care for you, let us pretend what we will:—we are always looking through you to the dim dictator behind you. Whilst your habit or whim chatters, we civilly and impatiently wait until that wise superior shall speak again. Even children are not deceived by the false reasons which their parents give in answer to their questions, whether touching natural facts, or religion, or persons. When the parent, instead of thinking how it really is, puts them off with a traditional or a hypocritical answer, the children perceive that it is traditional or hypocritical. To a sound constitution the defect of another is at once manifest: and the marks of it are only concealed from us by our own dislocation. An anatomical observer remarks, that the sympathies of the chest, abdomen, and pelvis, tell at last on the face, and on all its features. Not only does our beauty waste, but it leaves word how it went to waste. Physiognomy and phrenology are not new sciences, but declarations of the soul that it is aware of certain new sources of information. And now sciences of broader scope are starting up behind these. And so for ourselves, it is really of little importance what blunders in statement we make, so only we make no willful departures from the truth. How a man's truth comes to mind, long after we have forgotten all his words! How it comes to us in silent hours, that truth is our only armor in all passages of life and death! Wit is cheap, and anger is cheap; but if you cannot argue or explain yourself to the other party, cleave to the truth against me, against thee, and you gain a station from which you cannot be dislodged. The other party will forget the words that you spoke, but the part you took continues to plead for you.

Why should I hasten to solve every riddle which life offers me? I am well assured that the Questioner, who brings me so many problems, will bring the answers also in due time. Very rich, very potent, very cheerful Giver that he is, he shall have it all his own way, for me. Why should I give up my thought, because I cannot answer an objection to it? Consider only, whether it remains in my life the same it was. That only which we have within, can we see without. If we meet no gods, it is because we harbor none. If there is grandeur in you, you will find grandeur in porters and sweeps. He only is rightly immortal, to whom all things are immortal. I have read somewhere, that none is accomplished, so long as any are incomplete; that the happiness of one cannot consist with the misery of any other.

The Buddhists say, "No seed will die:" every seed will grow. Where is the service which can escape its remuneration? What is vulgar, and the essence of all vulgarity, but the avarice of reward? 'Tis the difference of artisan and artist, of talent and genius, of sinner and saint. The man whose eyes are nailed not on the nature of his act, but on the wages, whether it be money, or office, or fame,—is almost equally low. He is great, whose eyes are opened to see that the reward of actions cannot be escaped, because he is transformed into his action, and taketh its nature, which bears its own fruit, like every other tree. A great man cannot be hindered of the effect of his act, because it is immediate. The genius of life is friendly to the noble, and in the dark brings them friends from far. Fear God, and where you go, men shall think they walk in hallowed cathedrals.

And so I look on those sentiments which make the glory of the human being, love, humility, faith, as being also the intimacy of Divinity in the atoms; and, that, as soon as the man is right, assurances and previsions emanate from the interior of his body and his mind; as, when flowers reach their ripeness, incense exhales from them, and, as a beautiful atmosphere is generated from the planet by the averaged emanations from all its rocks and soils.

Thus man is made equal to every event. He can face danger for the right. A poor, tender, painful body, he can run into flame or bullets or pestilence, with duty for his guide. He feels the insurance of a just employment. I am not afraid of accident, as long as I am in my place. It is strange that superior persons should not feel that they have some better resistance against cholera, than avoiding green peas and salads. Life is hardly respectable,—is it? if it has no generous, guaranteeing task, no duties or affections, that constitute a necessity of existing. Every man's task is his life-preserver. The conviction that his work is dear to God and cannot be spared, defends him. The lightning-rod that disarms the cloud of its threat is his body in its duty. A high aim reacts on the means, on the days, on the organs of the body. A high aim is curative, as well as arnica.[38] "Napoleon," says Goethe, "visited those sick of the plague, in order to prove that the man who could vanquish fear, could vanquish the plague also; and he was right. 'Tis incredible what force the will has in such cases: it penetrates the body, and puts it in a state of activity, which repels all hurtful influences; whilst fear invites them."[39]

It is related of William of Orange,[40] that, whilst he was besieging a town on the continent, a gentleman sent to him on public business came to his camp, and, learning that the King was before the walls, he ventured to go where he was. He found him directing the operation of his gunners, and, having explained his errand, and received his answer, the King said, "Do you not know, sir, that every moment you spend here is at the risk of your life?" "I run no more risk," replied the gentleman, "than your Majesty." "Yes," said the King, "but my duty brings me here, and yours does not." In a few minutes, a cannon-ball fell on the spot, and the gentleman was killed.

Thus can the faithful student reverse all the warnings of his early instinct, under the guidance of a deeper instinct. He learns to welcome misfortune, learns that adversity is the prosperity of the great. He learns the greatness of humility. He shall work in the dark, work against failure, pain, and ill-will. If he is insulted, he can be insulted; all his affair is not to insult. Hafiz writes,

At the last day, men shall wear
On their heads the dust,
As ensign and as ornament
Of their lowly trust.

The moral equalizes all; enriches, empowers all. It is the coin which buys all, and which all find in their pocket. Under the whip of the driver, the slave shall feel his equality with saints and heroes. In the greatest destitution and calamity, it surprises man with a feeling of elasticity which makes nothing of loss.

I recall some traits of a remarkable person whose life and discourse betrayed many inspirations of this sentiment. Benedict was always great in the present time. He had hoarded nothing from the past, neither in his cabinets, neither in his memory. He had no designs on the future, neither for what he should do to men, nor for what men should do for him. He said, 'I am never beaten until I know that I am beaten. I meet powerful brutal people to whom I have no skill to reply. They think they have defeated me. It is so published in society, in the journals; I am defeated in this fashion, in all men's sight, perhaps on a dozen different lines. My ledger may show that I am in debt, cannot yet make my ends meet, and vanquish the enemy so. My race may not be prospering: we are sick, ugly, obscure, unpopular. My children may be worsted. I seem to fail in my friends and clients, too. That is to say, in all the encounters that have yet chanced, I have not been weaponed for that particular occasion, and have been historically beaten; and yet, I know, all the time, that I have never been beaten; have never yet fought, shall certainly fight, when my hour comes, and shall beat.' "A man," says the Vishnu Sarma,[41] "who having well compared his own strength or weakness with that of others, after all doth not know the difference, is easily overcome by his enemies."

'I spent,' he said, 'ten months in the country. Thick-starred Orion was my only companion. Wherever a squirrel or a bee can go with security, I can go. I ate whatever was set before me; I touched ivy and dogwood. When I went abroad, I kept company with every man on the road, for I knew that my evil and my good did not come from these, but from the Spirit, whose servant I was. For I could not stoop to be a circumstance, as they did, who put their life into their fortune and their company. I would not degrade myself by casting about in my memory for a thought, nor by waiting for one. If the thought come, I would give it entertainment. It should, as it ought, go into my hands and feet; but if it come not spontaneously, it comes not rightly at all. If it can spare me, I am sure I can spare it. It shall be the same with my friends. I will never woo the loveliest. I will not ask any friendship or favor. When I come to my own, we shall both know it. Nothing will be to be asked or to be granted.' Benedict went out to seek his friend, and met him on the way; but he expressed no surprise at any coincidences. On the other hand, if he called at the door of his friend, and he was not at home, he did not go again; concluding that he had misinterpreted the intimations.

He had the whim not to make an apology to the same individual whom he had wronged. For this, he said, was a piece of personal vanity; but he would correct his conduct in that respect in which he had faulted, to the next person he should meet. Thus, he said, universal justice was satisfied.

Mira came to ask what she should do with the poor Genesee woman who had hired herself to work for her, at a shilling a day, and, now sickening, was like to be bedridden on her hands. Should she keep her, or should she dismiss her? But Benedict said, 'Why ask? One thing will clear itself as the thing to be done, and not another, when the hour comes. Is it a question, whether to put her into the street? Just as much whether to thrust the little Jenny on your arm into the street. The milk and meal you give the beggar, will fatten Jenny. Thrust the woman out, and you thrust your babe out of doors, whether it so seem to you or not.'

In the Shakers, so called, I find one piece of belief, in the doctrine which they faithfully hold, that encourages them to open their doors to every wayfaring man who proposes to come among them; for, they say, the Spirit will presently manifest to the man himself, and to the society, what manner of person he is, and whether he belongs among them. They do not receive him, they do not reject him. And not in vain have they worn their clay coat, and drudged in their fields, and shuffled in their Bruin dance, from year to year, if they have truly learned thus much wisdom.

Honor him whose life is perpetual victory; him, who, by sympathy with the invisible and real, finds support in labor, instead of praise; who does not shine, and would rather not. With eyes open, he makes the choice of virtue, which outrages the virtuous; of religion, which churches stop their discords to burn and exterminate; for the highest virtue is always against the law.

Miracle comes to the miraculous, not to the arithmetician. Talent and success interest me but moderately. The great class, they who affect our imagination, the men who could not make their hands meet around their objects, the rapt, the lost, the fools of ideas,—they suggest what they cannot execute. They speak to the ages, and are heard from afar. The Spirit does not love cripples and malformations. If there ever was a good man, be certain, there was another, and will be more.

And so in relation to that future hour, that specter clothed with beauty at our curtain by night, at our table by day,—the apprehension, the assurance of a coming change. The race of mankind have always offered at least this implied thanks for the gift of existence,—namely, the terror of its being taken away; the insatiable curiosity and appetite for its continuation. The whole revelation that is vouchsafed us, is, the gentle trust, which, in our experience we find, will cover also with flowers the slopes of this chasm.

Of immortality, the soul, when well employed, is incurious. It is so well, that it is sure it will be well. It asks no questions of the Supreme Power. The son of Antiochus asked his father, when he would join battle? "Dost thou fear," replied the King, "that thou only in all the army wilt not hear the trumpet?" 'Tis a higher thing to confide, that, if it is best we should live, we shall live,—'tis higher to have this conviction, than to have the lease of indefinite centuries and millenniums and eons. Higher than the question of our duration is the question of our deserving. Immortality will come to such as are fit for it, and he who would be a great soul in future, must be a great soul now. It is a doctrine too great to rest on any legend, that is, on any man's experience but our own. It must be proved, if at all, from our own activity and designs, which imply an interminable future for their play.

What is called religion effeminates and demoralizes. Such as you are, the gods themselves could not help you. Men are too often unfit to live, from their obvious inequality to their own necessities, or, they suffer from politics, or bad neighbors, or from sickness, and they would gladly know that they were to be dismissed from the duties of life. But the wise instinct asks, 'How will death help them?' These are not dismissed when they die. You shall not wish for death out of pusillanimity.[42] The weight of the Universe is pressed down on the shoulders of each moral agent to hold him to his task. The only path of escape known in all the worlds of God is performance. You must do your work, before you shall be released. And as far as it is a question of fact respecting the government of the Universe, Marcus Antoninus summed the whole in a word, "It is pleasant to die, if there be gods; and sad to live, if there be none."[43]

And so I think that the last lesson of life, the choral song which rises from all elements and all angels, is, a voluntary obedience, a necessitated freedom.[44] Man is made of the same atoms as the world is, he shares the same impressions, predispositions, and destiny. When his mind is illuminated, when his heart is kind, he throws himself joyfully into the sublime order, and does, with knowledge, what the stones do by structure.

The religion which is to guide and fulfill the present and coming ages, whatever else it be, must be intellectual. The scientific mind must have a faith which is science. "There are two things," said Muhammad, "which I abhor, the learned in his infidelities, and the fool in his devotions." Our times are impatient of both, and specially of the last. Let us have nothing now which is not its own evidence. There is surely enough for the heart and imagination in the religion itself. Let us not be pestered with assertions and half-truths, with emotions and snuffle.

There will be a new church founded on moral science, at first cold and naked, a babe in a manger again, the algebra and mathematics of ethical law, the church of men to come, without shawms, or psaltery, or sackbut;[45] but it will have heaven and earth for its beams and rafters; science for symbol and illustration; it will fast enough gather beauty, music, picture, poetry. Was never stoicism so stern and exigent as this shall be. It shall send man home to his central solitude, shame these social, supplicating manners, and make him know that much of the time he must have himself to his friend. He shall expect no cooperation, he shall walk with no companion. The nameless Thought, the nameless Power, the super-personal Heart,—he shall repose alone on that. He needs only his own verdict. No good fame can help, no bad fame can hurt him. The Laws are his consolers, the good Laws themselves are alive, they know if he have kept them, they animate him with the leading of great duty, and an endless horizon. Honor and fortune exist to him who always recognizes the neighborhood of the great, always feels himself in the presence of high causes.

VII

CONSIDERATIONS BY THE WAY

—•—

Hear what British Merlin sung,
Of keenest eye and truest tongue.
Say not, the chiefs who first arrive
Usurp the seats for which all strive;
The forefathers this land who found
Failed to plant the vantage-ground;
Ever from one who comes to-morrow
Men wait their good and truth to borrow.
But wilt thou measure all thy road,
See thou lift the lightest load.
Who has little, to him who has less, can spare,
And thou, Cyndyllan's son! beware
Ponderous gold and stuffs to bear,
To falter ere thou thy task fulfil,—
Only the light-armed climb the hill.
The richest of all lords is Use,
And ruddy Health the loftiest Muse.
Live in the sunshine, swim the sea,
Drink the wild air's salubrity:
Where the star Canope shines in May,
Shepherds are thankful, and nations gay.
The music that can deepest reach,
And cure all ill, is cordial speech:
Mask thy wisdom with delight,
Toy with the bow, yet hit the white.
Of all wit's uses, the main one
Is to live well with who has none.
Cleave to thine acre; the round year
Will fetch all fruits and virtues here:

Fool and foe may harmless roam,
Loved and lovers bide at home.
A day for toil, an hour for sport,
But for a friend is life too short.

CONSIDERATIONS BY THE WAY

Although this garrulity[1] of advising is born with us, I confess that life is rather a subject of wonder, than of didactics. So much fate, so much irresistible dictation from temperament and unknown inspiration enters into it, that we doubt we can say anything out of our own experience whereby to help each other. All the professions are timid and expectant agencies. The priest is glad if his prayers or his sermon meet the condition of any soul; if of two, if of ten, 'tis a signal success. But he walked to the church without any assurance that he knew the distemper, or could heal it. The physician prescribes hesitatingly out of his few resources, the same tonic or sedative to this new and peculiar constitution, which he has applied with various success to a hundred men before. If the patient mends, he is glad and surprised.[2] The lawyer advises the client, and tells his story to the jury, and leaves it with them, and is as gay and as much relieved as the client, if it turns out that he has a verdict. The judge weighs the arguments, and puts a brave face on the matter, and, since there must be a decision, decides as he can, and hopes he has done justice, and given satisfaction to the community; but is only an advocate after all. And so is all life a timid and unskillful spectator. We do what we must, and call it by the best names. We like very well to be praised for our action, but our conscience says, "Not unto us."[3] 'Tis little we can do for each other. We accompany the youth with sympathy, and manifold old sayings of the wise, to the gate of the arena, but 'tis certain that not by strength of ours, or of the old sayings, but only on strength of his own, unknown to us or to any, he must stand or fall. That by which a man conquers in any passage, is a profound secret to every other being in the world, and it is only as he turns his back on us and on all men, and draws on this most private wisdom, that any good can come to him. What we have, therefore, to say of life, is rather description, or if you please, celebration, than available rules.

Yet vigor is contagious, and whatever makes us either think or feel strongly, adds to our power, and enlarges our field of action. We have a debt to every great heart, to every fine genius; to those who have put life and fortune on the cast of an act of justice; to those who have added new sciences; to those who have refined life by elegant pursuits. 'Tis the fine souls who serve us, and not what is called fine society. Fine society is only a self-protection against the vulgarities of the street and the tavern. Fine society, in the common acceptation, has neither ideas nor aims. It renders the service of a perfumery, or a laundry, not of a farm or factory. 'Tis an exclusion and a precinct. Sydney Smith[4] said, "A few yards in London cement or dissolve friendship." It is an unprincipled decorum; an affair of clean linen and coaches, of gloves, cards, and elegance in trifles. There are other measures of self-respect for a man, than the number of clean shirts he puts on every day. Society wishes to be amused. I do not wish to be amused. I wish that life should not be cheap, but sacred. I wish the days to be as centuries, loaded, fragrant. Now we reckon them as bank-days, by some debt which is to be paid us, or which we are to pay, or some pleasure we are to taste. Is all we have to do to draw the breath in, and blow it out again? Porphyry's definition is better; "Life is that which holds matter together." The babe in arms is a channel through which the energies we call fate, love, and reason, visibly stream. See what a cometary train of auxiliaries man carries with him, of animals, plants, stones, gases, and imponderable elements. Let us infer his ends from this pomp of means. Mirabeau[5] said, "Why should we feel our-selves to be men, unless it be to succeed in everything, everywhere. You must say of nothing, *That is beneath me*, nor feel that anything can be out of your power. Nothing is impossible to the man who can will. *Is that necessary? That shall be*:—this is the only law of success." Whoever said it, this is in the right key. But this is not the tone and genius of the men in the street. In the streets, we grow cynical. The men we meet are coarse and torpid.[6] The finest wits have their sediment. What quantities of fribbles,[7] paupers, invalids, epicures, anti-quaries, politicians, thieves, and triflers of both sexes, might be advantageously spared! Mankind divides itself into two classes,—benefactors and malefactors. The second class is vast, the first a handful. A person seldom falls sick, but the bystanders are animated with a faint hope that he will die:—quantities of poor lives; of distressing invalids; of cases for a gun. Franklin said, "Mankind are very superficial and dastardly: they begin upon a thing, but, meeting with a dif-ficulty, they fly from it discouraged: but they have capacities, if they would employ them." Shall we then judge a country by the majority, or by the minor-ity? By the minority, surely. 'Tis pedantry[8] to estimate nations by the census, or by square miles of land, or other than by their importance to the mind of the time.

Leave this hypocritical prating[9] about the masses. Masses are rude, lame, unmade, pernicious in their demands and influence, and need not to be flattered but to be schooled. I wish not to concede anything to them, but to tame, drill, divide, and break them up, and draw individuals out of them. The worst of charity is, that the lives you are asked to preserve are not worth preserving. Masses! the calamity is the masses. I do not wish any mass at all, but honest men only, lovely, sweet, accomplished women only, and no shovel-handed, narrow-brained, gin-drinking million stockingers[10] or lazzaroni[11] at all. If government knew how, I should like to see it check, not multiply the population. When it reaches its true law of action, every man that is born will be hailed as essential. Away with this hurrah of masses, and let us have the considerate vote of single men spoken on their honor and their conscience. In old Egypt, it was established law, that the vote of a prophet be reckoned equal to a hundred hands. I think it was much under-estimated. "Clay and clay differ in dignity," as we discover by our preferences every day. What a vicious practice is this of our politicians at Washington pairing off! as if one man who votes wrong, going away, could excuse you, who mean to vote right, for going away; or, as if your presence did not tell in more ways than in your vote. Suppose the three hundred heroes at Thermopylae[12] had paired off with three hundred Persians: would it have been all the same to Greece, and to history? Napoleon was called by his men *Cent Mille*.[13] Add honesty to him, and they might have called him Hundred Million.

Nature makes fifty poor melons for one that is good, and shakes down a tree full of gnarled, wormy, unripe crabs, before you can find a dozen dessert apples; and she scatters nations of naked Indians, and nations of clothed Christians, with two or three good heads among them. Nature works very hard, and only hits the white once in a million throws. In mankind, she is contented if she yields one master in a century. The more difficulty there is in creating good men, the more they are used when they come. I once counted in a little neighborhood, and found that every able-bodied man had, say from twelve to fifteen persons dependent on him for material aid,—to whom he is to be for spoon and jug, for backer and sponsor, for nursery and hospital, and many functions beside: nor does it seem to make much difference whether he is bachelor or patriarch; if he do not violently decline the duties that fall to him, this amount of helpfulness will in one way or another be brought home to him. This is the tax which his abilities pay. The good men are employed for private centers of use, and for larger influence. All revelations, whether of mechanical or intellectual or moral science, are made not to communities, but to single persons. All the marked events of our day, all the cities, all the colonizations, may be traced back to their origin in a private brain. All the feats which make our civility were the thoughts of a few good heads.

Meantime, this spawning productivity is not noxious or needless. You would say, this rabble of nations might be spared. But no, they are all counted and depended on. Fate keeps everything alive so long as the smallest thread of public necessity holds it on to the tree. The coxcomb[14] and bully and thief class are allowed as proletaries, every one of their vices being the excess or acridity[15] of a virtue. The mass are animal, in pupilage,[16] and near chimpanzee. But the units, whereof this mass is composed are neuters, every one of which may be grown to a queen-bee. The rule is, we are used as brute atoms, until we think: then, we use all the rest. Nature turns all malfeasance to good. Nature provided for real needs. No sane man at last distrusts himself. His existence is a perfect answer to all sentimental cavils. If he is, he is wanted, and has the precise properties that are required. That we are here, is proof we ought to be here. We have as good right, and the same sort of right to be here, as Cape Cod or Sandy Hook have to be there.

To say then, the majority are wicked, means no malice, no bad heart in the observer, but, simply, that the majority are unripe, and have not yet come to themselves, do not yet know their opinion. *That*, if they knew it, is an oracle for them and for all. But in the passing moment, the quadruped interest is very prone to prevail: and this beast-force, whilst it makes the discipline of the world, the school of heroes, the glory of martyrs, has provoked, in every age, the satire of wits, and the tears of good men. They find the journals, the clubs, the governments, the churches, to be in the interest, and the pay of the devil. And wise men have met this obstruction in their times, like Socrates, with his famous irony; like Bacon, with life-long dissimulation; like Erasmus, with his book "The Praise of Folly;" like Rabelais, with his satire rending the nations. "They were the fools who cried against me, you will say," wrote the Chevalier de Boufflers[17] to Grimm; "aye, but the fools have the advantage of numbers, and 'tis that which decides. 'Tis of no use for us to make war with them; we shall not weaken them; they will always be the masters. There will not be a practice or a usage introduced, of which they are not the authors."

In front of these sinister facts, the first lesson of history is the good of evil. Good is a good doctor, but Bad is sometimes a better. 'Tis the oppressions of William the Norman, savage forest-laws, and crushing despotism, that made possible the inspirations of *Magna Charta* under John. Edward I.[18] wanted money, armies, castles, and as much as he could get. It was necessary to call the people together by shorter, swifter ways,—and the House of Commons arose. To obtain subsidies, he paid in privileges. In the twenty-fourth year of his reign, he decreed, "that no tax should be levied without consent of Lords and Commons;"—which is the basis of the English Constitution. Plutarch affirms that the cruel wars which followed the march of Alexander, introduced the civility, language, and arts of Greece into the savage East; introduced marriage; built seventy cities; and united hostile nations under one government. The barbarians who broke up the Roman empire did not arrive a day too soon. Schiller[19] says, the Thirty Years' War made Germany a nation. Rough, selfish despots serve men immensely, as Henry VIII. in the contest with the Pope; as the infatuations no less than the wisdom of Cromwell;[20] as the ferocity of the Russian czars; as the fanaticism of the French regicides of 1789. The frost which kills the harvest of a year, saves the harvests of a century, by destroying the weevil or the locust. Wars, fires, plagues, break up immovable routine, clear the ground of rotten races and dens of distemper, and open a fair field to new men. There is a tendency in things to right themselves, and the war or revolution or bankruptcy that shatters a rotten system, allows things to take a new and natural order. The sharpest evils are bent into that periodicity which makes the errors of planets, and the fevers and distempers of men, self-limiting. Nature is upheld by antagonism. Passions, resistance, danger, are educators. We acquire the strength we have overcome. Without war, no soldier; without enemies, no hero. The sun were insipid,[21] if the universe were not opaque. And the glory of character is in affronting the horrors of depravity, to draw thence new nobilities of power: as Art lives and thrills in new use and combining of contrasts, and mining into the dark evermore for blacker pits of night. What would painter do, or what would poet or saint, but for crucifixions and hells? And evermore in the world is this marvelous balance of beauty and disgust, magnificence and rats. Not Antoninus,[22] but a poor washer-woman said, "The more trouble, the more lion; that's my principle."

I do not think very respectfully of the designs or the doings of the people who went to California, in 1849. It was a rush and a scramble of needy adventurers, and, in the western country, a general jail-delivery of all the rowdies of the rivers. Some of them went with honest purposes, some with very bad ones, and all of them with the very commonplace wish to find a short way to wealth. But Nature watches over all, and turns this malfeasance to good. California gets peopled and subdued,—civilized in this immoral way,—and, on this fiction, a real prosperity is rooted and grown. 'Tis a decoy-duck; 'tis tubs thrown to amuse the whale: but real ducks, and whales that yield oil, are caught. And, out of Sabine rapes,[23] and out of robbers' forays, real Romes and their heroisms come in fullness of time.

In America, the geography is sublime, but the men are not: the inventions are excellent, but the inventors one is sometimes ashamed of. The agencies by which events so grand as the opening of California, of Texas, of Oregon, and the junction of the two oceans, are effected, are paltry,—coarse selfishness, fraud, and conspiracy: and most of the great results of history are brought about by discreditable means.

The benefaction derived in Illinois, and the great West, from railroads is inestimable, and vastly exceeding any intentional philanthropy on record. What is the benefit done by a good King Alfred, or by a Howard, or Pestalozzi, or Elizabeth Fry, or Florence Nightingale,[24] or any lover, less or larger, compared with the involuntary blessing wrought on nations by the selfish capitalists who built the Illinois, Michigan, and the network of the Mississippi valley roads, which have evoked not only all the wealth of the soil, but the energy of millions of men. 'Tis a sentence of ancient wisdom, "that God hangs the greatest weights on the smallest wires."

What happens thus to nations, befalls every day in private houses. When the friends of a gentleman brought to his notice the follies of his sons, with many hints of their danger, he replied, that he knew so much mischief when he was a boy, and had turned out on the whole so successfully, that he was not alarmed by the dissipation of boys; 'twas dangerous water, but, he thought, they would soon touch bottom, and then swim to the top. This is bold practice, and there are many failures to a good escape. Yet one would say, that a good understanding would suffice as well as moral sensibility to keep one erect; the gratifications of the passions are so quickly seen to be damaging, and,—what men like least,—seriously lowering them in social rank. Then all talent sinks with character.

"*Croyez moi, l'erreur aussi a son mérite,*" said Voltaire.[25] We see those who surmount, by dint of some egotism or infatuation, obstacles from which the prudent recoil. The right partisan is a heady narrow man, who, because he does not see many things, sees some one thing with heat and exaggeration, and, if he falls among other narrow men, or on objects which have a brief importance, as some trade or politics of the hour, he prefers it to the universe, and seems inspired, and a godsend to those who wish to magnify the matter, and carry a point. Better, certainly, if we could secure the strength and fire which rude, passionate men bring into society, quite clear of their vices. But who dares draw out the linchpin from the wagon-wheel? 'Tis so manifest, that there is no moral deformity, but is a good passion out of place; that there is no man who is not indebted to his foibles; that, according to the old oracle, "the Furies are the bonds of men;" that the poisons are our principal medicines, which kill the disease, and save the life. In the high prophetic phrase, *He causes the wrath of man to praise him,*[26] and twists and wrenches our evil to our good. Shakespeare wrote,—

"'Tis said, best men are molded of their faults;"[27]

and great educators and lawgivers, and especially generals, and leaders of colonies, mainly rely on this stuff, and esteem men of irregular and passional force the best timber. A man of sense and energy, the late head of the Farm School in Boston harbor, said to me, "I want none of your good boys,—give me the bad ones." And this is the reason, I suppose, why, as soon as the children are good, the mothers are scared, and think they are going to die. Mirabeau said, "There are none but men of strong passions capable of going to greatness; none but such capable of meriting the public gratitude." Passion, though a bad regulator, is a powerful spring. Any absorbing passion has the effect to deliver from the little coils and cares of every day: 'tis the heat which sets our human atoms spinning, overcomes the friction of crossing thresholds, and first addresses in society, and gives us a good start and speed, easy to continue, when once it is begun. In short, there is no man who is not at some time indebted to his vices, as no plant that is not fed from manures. We only insist that the man meliorate, and that the plant grow upward, and convert the base into the better nature.

The wise workman will not regret the poverty or the solitude which brought out his working talents. The youth is charmed with the fine air and accomplishments of the children of fortune. But all great men come out of the middle classes. 'Tis better for the head; 'tis better for the heart. Marcus Antoninus says, that Fronto[28] told him, "that the so-called high-born are for the most part heartless;" whilst nothing is so indicative of deepest culture as a tender consideration of the ignorant. Charles James Fox[29] said of England, "The history of this country proves, that we are not to expect from men in affluent circumstances the vigilance, energy, and exertion without which the House of Commons would lose its greatest force and weight. Human nature is prone to

indulgence, and the most meritorious public services have always been performed by persons in a condition of life removed from opulence." And yet
what we ask daily, is to be conventional. Supply, most kind gods! this defect in
my address, in my form, in my fortunes, which puts me a little out of the ring:
supply it, and let me be like the rest whom I admire, and on good terms with
them. But the wise gods say, No, we have better things for thee. By humilia-
tions, by defeats, by loss of sympathy, by gulfs of disparity, learn a wider truth
and humanity than that of a fine gentleman. A Fifth-Avenue landlord, a
West-End householder, is not the highest style of man: and, though good hearts
and sound minds are of no condition, yet he who is to be wise for many, must
not be protected. He must know the huts where poor men lie, and the chores
which poor men do. The first-class minds, Aesop, Socrates, Cervantes, Shakespeare, Franklin,[30] had the poor man's feeling and mortification. A rich man
was never insulted in his life: but this man must be stung. A rich man was
never in danger from cold, or hunger, or war, or ruffians, and you can see he
was not, from the moderation of his ideas. 'Tis a fatal disadvantage to be
cockered,[31] and to eat too much cake. What tests of manhood could he stand?
Take him out of his protections. He is a good book-keeper; or he is a shrewd
adviser in the insurance office: perhaps he could pass a college examination,
and take his degrees: perhaps he can give wise counsel in a court of law. Now
plant him down among farmers, firemen, Indians, and emigrants. Set a dog on
him: set a highwayman on him: try him with a course of mobs: send him to
Kansas,[32] to Pike's Peak, to Oregon: and, if he have true faculty, this may be
the element he wants, and he will come out of it with broader wisdom and
manly power. Aesop, Saadi, Cervantes, Regnard,[33] have been taken by corsairs,
left for dead, sold for slaves, and know the realities of human life.

Bad times have a scientific value. These are occasions a good learner would
not miss. As we go gladly to Faneuil Hall,[34] to be played upon by the stormy
winds and strong fingers of enraged patriotism, so is a fanatical persecution,
civil war, national bankruptcy, or revolution, more rich in the central tones than
languid years of prosperity. What had been, ever since our memory, solid
continent, yawns apart, and discloses its composition and genesis. We learn
geology the morning after the earthquake, on ghastly diagrams of cloven mountains, upheaved plains, and the dry bed of the sea.

In our life and culture, everything is worked up, and comes in use,—passion, war, revolt, bankruptcy, and not less, folly and blunders, insult, ennui,[35]
and bad company. Nature is a rag-merchant, who works up every shred and ort

and end into new creations; like a good chemist, whom I found, the other day, in his laboratory, converting his old shirts into pure white sugar. Life is a boundless privilege, and when you pay for your ticket, and get into the car, you have no guess what good company you shall find there. You buy much that is not rendered in the bill. Men achieve a certain greatness unawares, when working to another aim.

If now in this connection of discourse, we should venture on laying down the first obvious rules of life, I will not here repeat the first rule of economy, already propounded once and again, that every man shall maintain himself,—but I will say, get health. No labor, pains, temperance, poverty, nor exercise, that can gain it, must be grudged. For sickness is a cannibal which eats up all the life and youth it can lay hold of, and absorbs its own sons and daughters. I figure it as a pale, wailing, distracted phantom, absolutely selfish, heedless of what is good and great, attentive to its sensations, losing its soul, and afflicting other souls with meanness and mopings, and with ministration to its voracity of trifles. Dr. Johnson said severely, "Every man is a rascal as soon as he is sick." Drop the cant, and treat it sanely. In dealing with the drunken, we do not affect to be drunk. We must treat the sick with the same firmness, giving them, of course, every aid,—but withholding ourselves. I once asked a clergyman in a retired town, who were his companions? what men of ability he saw? he replied, that he spent his time with the sick and the dying. I said, he seemed to me to need quite other company, and all the more that he had this: for if people were sick and dying to any purpose, we would leave all and go to them, but, as far as I had observed, they were as frivolous as the rest, and sometimes much more frivolous. Let us engage our companions not to spare us. I knew a wise woman who said to her friends, "When I am old, rule me." And the best part of health is fine disposition. It is more essential than talent, even in the works of talent. Nothing will supply the want of sunshine to peaches, and, to make knowledge valuable, you must have the cheerfulness of wisdom. Whenever you are sincerely pleased, you are nourished. The joy of the spirit indicates its strength. All healthy things are sweet-tempered. Genius works in sport, and goodness smiles to the last; and, for the reason that whoever sees the law which distributes things, does not despond, but is animated to great desires and endeavors. He who desponds betrays that he has not seen it.

'Tis a Dutch proverb, that "paint costs nothing," such are its preserving qualities in damp climates. Well, sunshine costs less, yet is finer pigment. And so of cheerfulness, or a good temper, the more it is spent, the more of it remains. The latent heat of an ounce of wood or stone is inexhaustible. You may rub the same chip of pine to the point of kindling, a hundred times; and the power of happiness of any soul is not to be computed or drained. It is observed that a depression of spirits develops the germs of a plague in individuals and nations.

It is an old commendation of right behavior, "*Aliis laetus,—sapiens sibi*," which our English proverb translates, "Be merry *and* wise." I know how easy it is to men of the world to look grave and sneer at your sanguine youth, and its glittering dreams. But I find the gayest castles in the air that were ever piled, far better for comfort and for use, than the dungeons in the air that are daily dug and caverned out by grumbling, discontented people. I know those miserable fellows, and I hate them, who see a black star always riding through the light and colored clouds in the sky overhead: waves of light pass over and hide it for a moment, but the black star keeps fast in the zenith. But power dwells with cheerfulness; hope puts us in a working mood, whilst despair is no muse, and untunes the active powers. A man should make life and Nature happier to us, or he had better never been born. When the political economist reckons up the unproductive classes, he should put at the head this class of pitiers of themselves, cravers of sympathy, bewailing imaginary disasters. An old French verse runs, in my translation:—

"Some of your griefs you have cured,
    And the sharpest you still have survived;
But what torments of pain you endured
    From evils that never arrived!"

There are three wants which never can be satisfied: that of the rich, who wants something more; that of the sick, who wants something different; and that of the traveler, who says, 'Anywhere but here.' The Turkish cadi[36] said to Layard, "After the fashion of thy people, thou hast wandered from one place to another, until thou art happy and content in none." My countrymen are not less infatuated with the *rococo* toy of Italy. All America seems on the point of embarking for Europe. But we shall not always traverse seas and lands with light purposes, and for pleasure, as we say. One day we shall cast out the passion for Europe, by the passion for America. Culture will give gravity and domestic rest to those who now travel only as not knowing how else to spend money. Already, who provoke pity like that excellent family party just arriving in their well-appointed carriage, as far from home and any honest end as ever?

Each nation has asked successively, 'What are they here for?' until at last the party are shamefaced, and anticipate the question at the gates of each town.

Genial manners are good, and power of accommodation to any circumstance, but the high prize of life, the crowning fortune of a man is to be born with a bias to some pursuit, which finds him in employment and happiness,—whether it be to make baskets, or broadswords, or canals, or statutes, or songs. I doubt not this was the meaning of Socrates, when he pronounced artists the only truly wise, as being actually, not apparently so.

In childhood, we fancied ourselves walled in by the horizon, as by a glass bell, and doubted not, by distant travel, we should reach the baths of the descending sun and stars. On experiment, the horizon flies before us, and leaves us on an endless common, sheltered by no glass bell. Yet 'tis strange how tenaciously we cling to that bell-astronomy, of a protecting domestic horizon. I find the same illusion in the search after happiness, which I observe, every summer, recommenced in this neighborhood, soon after the pairing of the birds. The young people do not like the town, do not like the sea-shore, they will go inland; find a dear cottage deep in the mountains, secret as their hearts. They set forth on their travels in search of a home: they reach Berkshire;[37] they reach Vermont; they look at the farms;—good farms, high mountain-sides: but where is the seclusion? The farm is near this; 'tis near that; they have got far from Boston, but 'tis near Albany, or near Burlington, or near Montreal. They explore a farm, but the house is small, old, thin; discontented people lived there, and are gone:—there's too much sky, too much out-doors; too public. The youth aches for solitude. When he comes to the house, he passes through the house. That does not make the deep recess he sought. 'Ah! now, I perceive,' he says, 'it must be deep with persons; friends only can give depth.' Yes, but there is a great dearth, this year, of friends; hard to find, and hard to have when found: they are just going away: they too are in the whirl of the flitting world, and have engagements and necessities. They are just starting for Wisconsin; have letters from Bremen:—see you again, soon. Slow, slow to learn the lesson, that there is but one depth, but one interior, and that is—his purpose. When joy or calamity or genius shall show him it, then woods, then farms, then city shopmen and cab-drivers, indifferently with prophet or friend, will mirror back to him its unfathomable heaven, its populous solitude.

The uses of travel are occasional, and short; but the best fruit it finds, when it finds it, is conversation; and this is a main function of life. What a difference in the hospitality of minds! Inestimable is he to whom we can say what we cannot say to ourselves. Others are involuntarily hurtful to us, and bereave us of the power of thought, impound and imprison us. As, when there is sympathy, there needs but one wise man in a company, and all are wise,—so, a blockhead makes a blockhead of his companion. Wonderful power to benumb possesses this brother. When he comes into the office or public room, the society dissolves; one after another slips out, and the apartment is at his disposal. What is incurable but a frivolous habit? A fly is as untamable as a hyena. Yet folly in the sense of fun, fooling, or dawdling can easily be borne; as Talleyrand[38] said, "I find nonsense singularly refreshing;" but a virulent, aggressive fool taints the reason of a household. I have seen a whole family of quiet, sensible people unhinged and beside themselves, victims of such a rogue. For the steady wrongheadedness of one perverse person irritates the best: since we must withstand absurdity. But resistance only exasperates the acrid fool, who believes that Nature and gravitation are quite wrong, and he only is right. Hence all the dozen inmates are soon perverted, with whatever virtues and industries they have, into contradictors, accusers, explainers, and repairers of this one malefactor; like a boat about to be overset, or a carriage run away with,—not only the foolish pilot or driver, but everybody on board is forced to assume strange and ridiculous attitudes, to balance the vehicle and prevent the upsetting. For remedy, whilst the case is yet mild, I recommend phlegm and truth: let all the truth that is spoken or done be at the zero of indifferency, or truth itself will be folly. But, when the case is seated and malignant, the only safety is in amputation; as seamen say, you shall cut and run. How to live with unfit companions?—for, with such, life is for the most part spent: and experience teaches little better than our earliest instinct of self-defence, namely, not to engage, not to mix yourself in any manner with them; but let their madness spend itself unopposed;—you are you, and I am I.

Conversation is an art in which a man has all mankind for his competitors, for it is that which all are practising every day while they live. Our habit of thought,—take men as they rise,—is not satisfying; in the common experience, I fear, it is poor and squalid. The success which will content them, is, a bargain, a lucrative employment, an advantage gained over a competitor, a marriage, a patrimony, a legacy, and the like. With these objects, their conversation deals with surfaces: politics, trade, personal defects, exaggerated bad news, and the rain. This is forlorn, and they feel sore and sensitive. Now, if one comes who can illuminate this dark house with thoughts, show them their native riches, what gifts they have, how indispensable each is, what magical powers over nature and men; what access to poetry, religion, and the powers which constitute character; he wakes in them the feeling of worth, his suggestions require new ways of living, new books, new men, new arts and sciences,—then we come out of our egg-shell existence into the great dome, and see the zenith over and the nadir under us. Instead of the tanks and buckets of knowledge to which we are daily confined, we come down to the shore of the sea, and dip our hands in its miraculous waves. 'Tis wonderful the effect on the company. They are not the men they were. They have all been to California, and all have come back millionaires. There is no book and no pleasure in life comparable to it. Ask what is best in our experience, and we shall say, a few pieces of plain-dealing with wise people. Our conversation once and again has apprised us that we belong to better circles than we have yet beheld; that a mental power invites us, whose generalizations are more worth for joy and for effect than anything that is now called philosophy or literature. In excited conversation, we have glimpses of the Universe, hints of power native to the soul, far-darting lights and shadows of an Andes landscape, such as we can hardly attain in lone meditation. Here are oracles sometimes profusely given, to which the memory goes back in barren hours.

Add the consent of will and temperament, and there exists the covenant of friendship. Our chief want in life, is, somebody who shall make us do what we can. This is the service of a friend. With him we are easily great. There is a sublime attraction in him to whatever virtue is in us. How he flings wide the doors of existence! What questions we ask of him! what an understanding we have! how few words are needed! It is the only real society. An Eastern poet, Ali Ben Abu Taleb,[39] writes with sad truth,—

"He who has a thousand friends has not a friend to spare,
And he who has one enemy shall meet him everywhere."

But few writers have said anything better to this point than Hafiz, who indicates this relation as the test of mental health: "Thou learnest no secret until thou knowest friendship, since to the unsound no heavenly knowledge enters." Neither is life long enough for friendship. That is a serious and majestic affair, like a royal presence, or a religion, and not a postilion's dinner to be eaten on the run. There is a pudency[40] about friendship, as about love, and though fine souls never lose sight of it, yet they do not name it. With the first class of men our friendship or good understanding goes quite behind all accidents of estrangement, of condition, of reputation. And yet we do not provide for the greatest good of life. We take care of our health; we lay up money; we make our roof tight, and our clothing sufficient; but who provides wisely that he shall not be wanting in the best property of all,—friends? We know that all our training is to fit us for this, and we do not take the step towards it. How long shall we sit and wait for these benefactors?

It makes no difference, in looking back five years, how you have been dieted or dressed; whether you have been lodged on the first floor or the attic; whether you have had gardens and baths, good cattle and horses, have been carried in a neat equipage, or in a ridiculous truck: these things are forgotten so quickly, and leave no effect. But it counts much whether we have had good companions, in that time;—almost as much as what we have been doing. And see the overpowering importance of neighborhood in all association. As it is marriage, fit or unfit, that makes our home, so it is who lives near us of equal social degree,—a few people at convenient distance, no matter how bad company,—these, and these only, shall be your life's companions: and all those who are native, congenial, and by many an oath of the heart, sacramented to you, are gradually and totally lost. You cannot deal systematically with this fine element of society, and one may take a good deal of pains to bring people together, and to organize clubs and debating societies, and yet no result come of it. But it is certain that there is a great deal of good in us that does not know itself, and that a habit of union and competition brings people up and keeps them up to their highest point; that life would be twice or ten times life, if spent with wise and fruitful companions. The obvious inference is, a little useful deliberation and preconcert, when one goes to buy house and land.

But we live with people on other platforms; we live with dependents, not only with the young whom we are to teach all we know, and clothe with the advantages we have earned, but also with those who serve us directly, and for money. Yet the old rules hold good. Let not the tie be mercenary, though the service is measured by money. Make yourself necessary to somebody. Do not make life hard to any. This point is acquiring new importance in American social life. Our domestic service is usually a foolish fracas of unreasonable demand on one side, and shirking on the other. A man of wit was asked, in the train, what was his errand in the city? He replied, "I have been sent to procure an angel to do cooking." A lady complained to me, that, of her two maidens, one was absent-minded, and the other was absent-bodied. And the evil increases from the ignorance and hostility of every ship-load of the immigrant population swarming into houses and farms. Few people discern that it rests with the master or the mistress what service comes from the man or the maid;

that this identical hussy[41] was a tutelar[42] spirit in one house, and a harridan[43] in the other. All sensible people are selfish, and nature is tugging at every contract to make the terms of it fair. If you are proposing only your own, the other party must deal a little hardly by you. If you deal generously, the other, though selfish and unjust, will make an exception in your favor, and deal truly with you. When I asked an iron-master about the slag and cinder in railroad iron,—"Oh," he said, "there's always good iron to be had: if there's cinder in the iron, 'tis because there was cinder in the pay."

But why multiply these topics, and their illustrations, which are endless? Life brings to each his task, and, whatever art you select, algebra, planting, architecture, poems, commerce, politics,—all are attainable, even to the miraculous triumphs, on the same terms, of selecting that for which you are apt;— begin at the beginning, proceed in order, step by step. 'Tis as easy to twist iron anchors, and braid cannons, as to braid straw, to boil granite as to boil water, if you take all the steps in order. Wherever there is failure, there is some giddiness, some superstition about luck, some step omitted, which Nature never pardons. The happy conditions of life may be had on the same terms. Their attraction for you is the pledge that they are within your reach. Our prayers are prophets. There must be fidelity, and there must be adherence. How respectable the life that clings to its objects! Youthful aspirations are fine things, your theories and plans of life are fair and commendable:—but will you stick? Not one, I fear, in that Common full of people, or, in a thousand, but one: and, when you tax them with treachery, and remind them of their high resolutions, they have forgotten that they made a vow. The individuals are fugitive, and in the act of becoming something else, and irresponsible. The race is great, the ideal fair, but the men whiffling and unsure. The hero is he who is immovably centered. The main difference between people seems to be, that one man can come under obligations on which you can rely,—is obligable; and another is not. As he has not a law within him, there's nothing to tie him to.

'Tis inevitable to name particulars of virtue, and of condition, and to exaggerate them. But all rests at last on that integrity which dwarfs talent, and can spare it. Sanity consists in not being subdued by your means. Fancy prices are paid for position, and for the culture of talent, but to the grand interests, superficial success is of no account. The man,—it is his attitude,—not feats, but forces,—not on set days and public occasions, but, at all hours, and in repose alike as in energy, still formidable, and not to be disposed of. The populace says, with Horne Tooke,[44] "If you would be powerful, pretend to be powerful."

I prefer to say, with the old prophet, "Seekest thou great things? seek them not:"[45]—or, what was said of a Spanish prince, "The more you took from him, the greater he looked." *Plus on lui ôte, plus il est grand.*

The secret of culture is to learn that a few great points steadily reappear, alike in the poverty of the obscurest farm, and in the miscellany of metropolitan life, and that these few are alone to be regarded,—the escape from all false ties; courage to be what we are; and love of what is simple and beautiful; independence, and cheerful relation, these are the essentials,—these, and the wish to serve,—to add somewhat to the well-being of men.

VIII

BEAUTY

———•———

Was never form and never face
So sweet to SEYD as only grace
Which did not slumber like a stone
But hovered gleaming and was gone.
Beauty chased he everywhere,
In flame, in storm, in clouds of air.
He smote the lake to feed his eye
   With the beryl beam of the broken wave;
He flung in pebbles well to hear
   The moment's music which they gave.
Oft pealed for him a lofty tone
From nodding pole and belting zone.
He heard a voice none else could hear
From centered and from errant sphere.
The quaking earth did quake in rhyme,
Seas ebbed and flowed in epic chime.
In dens of passion, and pits of woe,
He saw strong Eros struggling through,
To sun the dark and solve the curse,
And beam to the bounds of the universe.
While thus to love he gave his days
In loyal worship, scorning praise,
How spread their lures for him, in vain,
Thieving Ambition and paltering Gain!
He thought it happier to be dead,
To die for Beauty, than live for bread.

BEAUTY

The spiral tendency of vegetation infects education also. Our books approach very slowly the things we most wish to know. What a parade we make of our science, and how far off, and at arm's length, it is from its objects! Our botany is all names, not powers: poets and romancers talk of herbs of grace and healing; but what does the botanist know of the virtues of his weeds? The geologist lays bare the strata, and can tell them all on his fingers: but does he know what effect passes into the man who builds his house in them? what effect on the race that inhabits a granite shelf? what on the inhabitants of marl[1] and of alluvium?[2]

We should go to the ornithologist with a new feeling, if he could teach us what the social birds say, when they sit in the autumn council, talking together in the trees. The want of sympathy makes his record a dull dictionary. His result is a dead bird. The bird is not in its ounces and inches, but in its relations to Nature; and the skin or skeleton you show me, is no more a heron, than a heap of ashes or a bottle of gases into which his body has been reduced, is Dante or Washington. The naturalist is led *from* the road by the whole distance of his fancied advance. The boy had juster views when he gazed at the shells on the beach, or the flowers in the meadow, unable to call them by their names, than the man in the pride of his nomenclature. Astrology interested us, for it tied man to the system. Instead of an isolated beggar, the farthest star felt him, and he felt the star. However rash and however falsified by pretenders and traders in it, the hint was true and divine, the soul's avowal of its large relations, and, that climate, century, remote natures, as well as near, are part of its biography. Chemistry takes to pieces, but it does not construct. Alchemy which sought to transmute one element into another, to prolong life, to arm with power,—that was in the right direction. All our science lacks a human side. The tenant is more than the house. Bugs and stamens and spores, on which we lavish so many years, are not finalities, and man, when his powers unfold in order, will take Nature along with him, and emit light into all her recesses. The human heart concerns us more than the poring into microscopes, and is larger than can be measured by the pompous figures of the astronomer.

We are just so frivolous and skeptical. Men hold themselves cheap and vile: and yet a man is a fagot of thunderbolts. All the elements pour through his system: he is the flood of the flood, and fire of the fire; he feels the antipodes and the pole, as drops of his blood: they are the extension of his personality. His duties are measured by that instrument he is; and a right and perfect man would be felt to the center of the Copernican system. 'Tis curious that we only believe as deep as we live. We do not think heroes can exert any more awful power than that surface-play which amuses us. A deep man believes in miracles, waits for them, believes in magic, believes that the orator will decompose his adversary; believes that the evil eye can wither, that the heart's blessing can heal; that love can exalt talent; can overcome all odds. From a great heart secret magnetisms flow incessantly to draw great events. But we prize very humble utilities, a prudent husband, a good son, a voter, a citizen, and deprecate any romance of character; and perhaps reckon only his money value,—his intellect, his affection, as a sort of bill of exchange, easily convertible into fine chambers, pictures, music, and wine.

The motive of science was the extension of man, on all sides, into Nature, till his hands should touch the stars, his eyes see through the earth, his ears understand the language of beast and bird, and the sense of the wind; and, through his sympathy, heaven and earth should talk with him. But that is not our science. These geologies, chemistries, astronomies, seem to make wise, but they leave us where they found us. The invention is of use to the inventor, of questionable help to any other. The formulas of science are like the papers in your pocket-book, of no value to any but the owner. Science in England, in America, is jealous of theory, hates the name of love and moral purpose. There's a revenge for this inhumanity. What manner of man does science make? The boy is not attracted. He says, I do not wish to be such a kind of man as my professor is. The collector has dried all the plants in his herbal, but he has lost weight and humor. He has got all snakes and lizards in his phials, but science has done for him also, and has put the man into a bottle. Our reliance on the physician is a kind of despair of ourselves. The clergy have bronchitis, which does not seem a certificate of spiritual health. Macready[3] thought it came of the *falsetto* of their voicing. An Indian prince, Tisso, one day riding in the forest, saw a herd of elk sporting. "See how happy," he said, "these browsing elks are! Why should not priests, lodged and fed comfortably in the temples, also amuse themselves?" Returning home, he imparted this reflection to the king. The king, on the next day, conferred the sovereignty on him, saying,

"Prince, administer this empire for seven days: at the termination of that period, I shall put thee to death." At the end of the seventh day, the king inquired, "From what cause hast thou become so emaciated?" He answered, "From the horror of death." The monarch rejoined: "Live, my child, and be wise. Thou hast ceased to take recreation, saying to thyself, in seven days I shall be put to death. These priests in the temple incessantly meditate on death; how can they enter into healthful diversions?" But the men of science or the doctors or the clergy are not victims of their pursuits, more than others. The miller, the lawyer, and the merchant, dedicate themselves to their own details, and do not come out men of more force. Have they divination, grand aims, hospitality of soul, and the equality to any event, which we demand in man, or only the reactions of the mill, of the wares, of the chicane?[4]

No object really interests us but man, and in man only his superiorities; and, though we are aware of a perfect law in Nature, it has fascination for us only through its relation to him, or, as it is rooted in the mind. At the birth of Winckelmann, more than a hundred years ago, side by side with this arid, departmental, *post mortem* science, rose an enthusiasm in the study of Beauty; and perhaps some sparks from it may yet light a conflagration in the other. Knowledge of men, knowledge of manners, the power of form, and our sensibility to personal influence, never go out of fashion. These are facts of a science which we study without book, whose teachers and subjects are always near us.

So inveterate is our habit of criticism that much of our knowledge in this direction belongs to the chapter of pathology. The crowd in the street oftener furnishes degradations than angels or redeemers: but they all prove the transparency. Every spirit makes its house; and we can give a shrewd guess from the house to the inhabitant. But not less does Nature furnish us with every sign of grace and goodness. The delicious faces of children, the beauty of school-girls, "the sweet seriousness of sixteen," the lofty air of well-born, well-bred boys, the passionate histories in the looks and manners of youth and early manhood, and the varied power in all that well-known company that escort us through life,—we know how these forms thrill, paralyze, provoke, inspire, and enlarge us.

Beauty is the form under which the intellect prefers to study the world. All privilege is that of beauty; for there are many beauties; as, of general nature, of the human face and form, of manners, of brain, or method, moral beauty, or beauty of the soul.

The ancients believed that a genius or demon took possession at birth of each mortal, to guide him; that these genii were sometimes seen as a flame of fire partly immersed in the bodies which they governed;—on an evil man, resting on his head; in a good man, mixed with his substance. They thought the same genius, at the death of its ward, entered a new-born child, and they pretended to guess the pilot, by the sailing of the ship. We recognize obscurely the same fact, though we give it our own names. We say, that every man is entitled to be valued by his best moment. We measure our friends so. We know, they have intervals of folly, whereof we take no heed, but wait the reappearings of the genius, which are sure and beautiful. On the other side, everybody knows people who appear beridden, and who, with all degrees of ability, never impress us with the air of free agency. They know it too, and peep with their eyes to see if you detect their sad plight. We fancy, could we pronounce the solving word, and disenchant them, the cloud would roll up, the little rider would be discovered and unseated, and they would regain their freedom. The remedy seems never to be far off, since the first step into thought lifts this mountain of necessity. Thought is the pent air-ball which can rive[5] the planet, and the beauty which certain objects have for him, is the friendly fire which expands the thought, and acquaints the prisoner that liberty and power await him.

The question of Beauty takes us out of surfaces, to thinking of the foundations of things. Goethe said, "The beautiful is a manifestation of secret laws of Nature, which, but for this appearance, had been forever concealed from us."[6] And the working of this deep instinct makes all the excitement—much of it superficial and absurd enough—about works of art, which leads armies of vain travelers every year to Italy, Greece, and Egypt. Every man values every acquisition he makes in the science of beauty, above his possessions. The most useful man in the most useful world, so long as only commodity was served, would remain unsatisfied. But, as fast as he sees beauty, life acquires a very high value.

I am warned by the ill fate of many philosophers not to attempt a definition of Beauty. I will rather enumerate a few of its qualities. We ascribe beauty to that which is simple; which has no superfluous parts; which exactly answers its end; which stands related to all things; which is the mean of many extremes. It is the most enduring quality, and the most ascending quality. We say, love is blind, and the figure of Cupid[7] is drawn with a bandage round his eyes. Blind: —yes, because he does not see what he does not like; but the sharpest-sighted hunter in the universe is Love, for finding what he seeks, and only that; and the mythologists tell us, that Vulcan was painted lame, and Cupid blind, to call attention to the fact, that one was all limbs, and the other, all eyes. In the true mythology, Love is an immortal child, and Beauty leads him as a guide: nor can we express a deeper sense than when we say, Beauty is the pilot of the young soul.

Beyond their sensuous delight, the forms and colors of Nature have a new charm for us in our perception, that not one ornament was added for ornament, but is a sign of some better health, or more excellent action. Elegance of form in bird or beast, or in the human figure, marks some excellence of structure: or beauty is only an invitation from what belongs to us. 'Tis a law of botany, that in plants, the same virtues follow the same forms. It is a rule of largest application, true in a plant, true in a loaf of bread, that in the construction of any fabric or organism, any real increase of fitness to its end, is an increase of beauty.

The lesson taught by the study of Greek and of Gothic art, of antique and of Pre-Raphaelite painting,[8] was worth all the research,—namely, that all beauty must be organic; that outside embellishment is deformity. It is the soundness of the bones that ultimates itself in a peach-bloom complexion: health of constitution that makes the sparkle and the power of the eye. 'Tis the adjustment of the size and of the joining of the sockets of the skeleton, that gives grace of outline and the finer grace of movement. The cat and the deer cannot move or sit inelegantly. The dancing-master can never teach a badly built man to walk well. The tint of the flower proceeds from its root, and the lusters of the sea-shell begin with its existence. Hence our taste in building rejects paint, and all shifts, and shows the original grain of the wood: refuses pilasters and columns that support nothing, and allows the real supporters of the house honestly to show themselves. Every necessary or organic action pleases the beholder. A man leading a horse to water, a farmer sowing seed, the labors of haymakers in the field, the carpenter building a ship, the smith at his forge, or, whatever useful labor, is becoming to the wise eye. But if it is done to be seen, it is mean. How beautiful are ships on the sea! but ships in the theater,—or ships kept for picturesque effect on Virginia Water, by George IV., and men hired to stand in fitting costumes at a penny an hour!—What a difference in effect between a battalion of troops marching to action, and one of our independent companies on a holiday! In the midst of a military show, and a festal procession gay with banners, I saw a boy seize an old tin pan that lay rusting under a wall, and poising it on the top of a stick, he set it turning, and made it describe the most elegant imaginable curves, and drew away attention from the decorated procession by this startling beauty.

Another text from the mythologists. The Greeks fabled that Venus was born
of the foam of the sea. Nothing interests us which is stark or bounded, but only
what streams with life, what is in act or endeavor to reach somewhat beyond.
The pleasure a palace or a temple gives the eye, is, that an order and method
has been communicated to stones, so that they speak and geometrize, become
tender or sublime with expression. Beauty is the moment of transition, as if the
form were just ready to flow into other forms. Any fixedness, heaping, or concentration on one feature,—a long nose, a sharp chin, a hump-back,—is the
reverse of the flowing, and therefore deformed. Beautiful as is the symmetry of
any form, if the form can move, we seek a more excellent symmetry. The interruption of equilibrium stimulates the eye to desire the restoration of symmetry,
and to watch the steps through which it is attained. This is the charm of running
water, sea-waves, the flight of birds, and the locomotion of animals. This is the
theory of dancing, to recover continually in changes the lost equilibrium, not by
abrupt and angular, but by gradual and curving movements. I have been told by
persons of experience in matters of taste, that the fashions follow a law of
gradation, and are never arbitrary. The new mode is always only a step onward
in the same direction as the last mode; and a cultivated eye is prepared for and
predicts the new fashion. This fact suggests the reason of all mistakes and
offence in our own modes. It is necessary in music, when you strike a discord,
to let down the ear by an intermediate note or two to the accord again: and
many a good experiment, born of good sense, and destined to succeed, fails,
only because it is offensively sudden. I suppose, the Parisian milliner who
dresses the world from her imperious[9] boudoir will know how to reconcile the
Bloomer costume[10] to the eye of mankind, and make it triumphant over Punch
himself, by interposing the just gradations. I need not say, how wide the same
law ranges; and how much it can be hoped to effect. All that is a little harshly
claimed by progressive parties, may easily come to be conceded without question, if this rule be observed. Thus the circumstances may be easily imagined,
in which woman may speak, vote, argue causes, legislate, and drive a coach,
and all the most naturally in the world, if only it come by degrees.[11] To this
streaming or flowing belongs the beauty that all circular movement has; as, the
circulation of waters, the circulation of the blood, the periodical motion of
planets, the annual wave of vegetation, the action and reaction of Nature: and,

if we follow it out, this demand in our thought for an ever-onward action, is the argument for the immortality.

One more text from the mythologists is to the same purpose,—*Beauty rides on a lion*. Beauty rests on necessities. The line of beauty is the result of perfect economy. The cell of the bee is built at that angle which gives the most strength with the least wax; the bone or the quill of the bird gives the most alar[12] strength, with the least weight. "It is the purgation of superfluities," said Michelangelo. There is not a particle to spare in natural structures. There is a compelling reason in the uses of the plant, for every novelty of color or form: and our art saves material, by more skillful arrangement, and reaches beauty by taking every superfluous ounce that can be spared from a wall, and keeping all its strength in the poetry of columns. In rhetoric, this art of omission is a chief secret of power, and, in general, it is proof of high culture, to say the greatest matters in the simplest way.[13]

Veracity first of all, and forever. *Rien de beau que le vrai*.[14] In all design, art lies in making your object prominent, but there is a prior art in choosing objects that are prominent. The fine arts have nothing casual, but spring from the instincts of the nations that created them.

Beauty is the quality which makes to endure. In a house that I know, I have noticed a block of spermaceti[15] lying about closets and mantel-pieces, for twenty years together, simply because the tallow-man gave it the form of a rabbit; and, I suppose, it may continue to be lugged about unchanged for a century. Let an artist scrawl a few lines or figures on the back of a letter, and that scrap of paper is rescued from danger, is put in portfolio, is framed and glazed, and, in proportion to the beauty of the lines drawn, will be kept for centuries. Burns writes a copy of verses, and sends them to a newspaper, and the human race take charge of them that they shall not perish.

As the flute is heard farther than the cart, see how surely a beautiful form strikes the fancy of men, and is copied and reproduced without end. How many copies are there of the Belvedere Apollo, the Venus, the Psyche, the Warwick Vase, the Parthenon, and the Temple of Vesta?[16] These are objects of tenderness to all. In our cities, an ugly building is soon removed, and is never repeated, but any beautiful building is copied and improved upon, so that all masons and carpenters work to repeat and preserve the agreeable forms, whilst the ugly ones die out.

The felicities of design in art, or in works of Nature, are shadows or forerunners of that beauty which reaches its perfection in the human form. All men are its lovers. Wherever it goes, it creates joy and hilarity, and everything is permitted to it. It reaches its height in woman. "To Eve," say the Mohammedans, "God gave two thirds of all beauty." A beautiful woman is a practical poet, taming her savage mate, planting tenderness, hope, and eloquence, in all whom she approaches. Some favors of condition must go with it, since a certain serenity is essential, but we love its reproofs and superiorities. Nature wishes that woman should attract man, yet she often cunningly moulds into her face a little sarcasm, which seems to say, 'Yes, I am willing to attract, but to attract a little better kind of a man than any I yet behold.' French *mémoires* of the fifteenth century celebrate the name of Pauline de Viguier, a virtuous and accomplished maiden, who so fired the enthusiasm of her contemporaries, by her enchanting form, that the citizens of her native city of Toulouse obtained the aid of the civil authorities to compel her to appear publicly on the balcony at least twice a week, and, as often as she showed herself, the crowd was dangerous to life. Not less, in England, in the last century, was the fame of the Gunnings, of whom, Elizabeth married the Duke of Hamilton; and Maria, the Earl of Coventry. Walpole[17] says, "the concourse was so great, when the Duchess of Hamilton was presented at court, on Friday, that even the noble crowd in the drawing-room clambered on chairs and tables to look at her. There are mobs at their doors to see them get into their chairs, and people go early to get places at the theaters, when it is known they will be there." "Such crowds," he adds, elsewhere, "flock to see the Duchess of Hamilton, that seven hundred people sat up all night, in and about an inn, in Yorkshire, to see her get into her post-chaise[18] next morning."

But why need we console ourselves with the fames of Helen of Argos, or Corinna, or Pauline of Toulouse, or the Duchess of Hamilton? We all know this magic very well, or can divine it. It does not hurt weak eyes to look into beautiful eyes never so long. Women stand related to beautiful Nature around us, and the enamored youth mixes their form with moon and stars, with woods and waters, and the pomp of summer. They heal us of awkwardness by their words and looks. We observe their intellectual influence on the most serious student. They refine and clear his mind; teach him to put a pleasing method into what is dry and difficult. We talk to them, and wish to be listened to; we fear to fatigue them, and acquire a facility of expression which passes from conversation into habit of style.

That Beauty is the normal state, is shown by the perpetual effort of Nature to attain it. Mirabeau had an ugly face on a handsome ground; and we see faces every day which have a good type, but have been marred in the casting: a proof that we are all entitled to beauty, should have been beautiful, if our ancestors had kept the laws,—as every lily and every rose is well. But our bodies do not fit us, but caricature and satirize us. Thus, short legs, which constrain us to short, mincing steps, are a kind of personal insult and contumely[19] to the owner; and long stilts, again, put him at perpetual disadvantage, and force him to stoop to the general level of mankind. Martial ridicules a gentleman of his day whose countenance resembled the face of a swimmer seen under water. Saadi describes a schoolmaster "so ugly and crabbed, that a sight of him would derange the ecstasies of the orthodox." Faces are rarely true to any ideal type, but are a record in sculpture of a thousand anecdotes of whim and folly. Portrait painters say that most faces and forms are irregular and unsymmetrical; have one eye blue, and one gray; the nose not straight; and one shoulder higher than another; the hair unequally distributed, etc. The man is physically as well as metaphysically a thing of shreds and patches, borrowed unequally from good and bad ancestors, and a misfit from the start.

A beautiful person, among the Greeks, was thought to betray by this sign some secret favor of the immortal gods: and we can pardon pride, when a woman possesses such a figure, that wherever she stands, or moves, or leaves a shadow on the wall, or sits for a portrait to the artist, she confers a favor on the world. And yet—it is not beauty that inspires the deepest passion. Beauty without grace is the hook without the bait. Beauty, without expression, tires. Abbé Ménage said of the President Le Bailleul,[20] "that he was fit for nothing but to sit for his portrait." A Greek epigram intimates that the force of love is not shown by the courting of beauty, but when the like desire is inflamed for one who is ill-favored. And petulant old gentlemen, who have chanced to suffer some intolerable weariness from pretty people, or who have seen cut flowers to some profusion, or who see, after a world of pains have been successfully taken for the costume, how the least mistake in sentiment takes all the beauty out of your clothes,—affirm, that the secret of ugliness consists not in irregularity, but in being uninteresting.

We love any forms, however ugly, from which great qualities shine. If command, eloquence, art, or invention, exist in the most deformed person, all the accidents that usually displease, please, and raise esteem and wonder higher. The great orator was an emaciated, insignificant person, but he was all brain. Cardinal De Retz says of De Bouillon, "With the physiognomy of an ox, he had the perspicacity of an eagle." It was said of Hooke,[21] the friend of Newton, "he is the most, and promises the least, of any man in England." "Since I am so ugly," said Du Guesclin,[22] "it behooves that I be bold." Sir Philip Sidney,[23] the darling of mankind, Ben Jonson tells us, "was no pleasant man in countenance, his face being spoiled with pimples, and of high blood, and long." Those who have ruled human destinies, like planets, for thousands of years, were not handsome men. If a man can raise a small city to be a great kingdom, can make bread cheap, can irrigate deserts, can join oceans by canals, can subdue steam, can organize victory, can lead the opinions of mankind, can enlarge knowledge, 'tis no matter whether his nose is parallel to his spine, as it ought to be, or whether he has a nose at all; whether his legs are straight, or whether his legs are amputated; his deformities will come to be reckoned ornamental, and advantageous on the whole. This is the triumph of expression, degrading beauty, charming us with a power so fine and friendly and intoxicating, that it makes admired persons insipid, and the thought of passing our lives with them insupportable. There are faces so fluid with expression, so flushed and rippled by the play of thought, that we can hardly find what the mere features really are. When the delicious beauty of lineaments[24] loses its power, it is because a more delicious beauty has appeared; that an interior and durable form has been disclosed. Still, Beauty rides on her lion, as before. Still, "it was for beauty that the world was made." The lives of the Italian artists, who established a despotism of genius amidst the dukes and kings and mobs of their stormy epoch, prove how loyal men in all times are to a finer brain, a finer method, than their own. If a man can cut such a head on his stone gate-post as shall draw and keep a crowd about it all day, by its beauty, good nature, and inscrutable meaning;—if a man can build a plain cottage with such symmetry, as to make all the fine palaces look cheap and vulgar; can take such advantage of Nature, that all her powers serve him; making use of geometry, instead of expense; tapping a mountain for his water-jet; causing the sun and moon to seem only the decorations of his estate; this is still the legitimate dominion of beauty.

The radiance of the human form, though sometimes astonishing, is only a burst of beauty for a few years or a few months, at the perfection of youth, and in most, rapidly declines. But we remain lovers of it, only transferring our interest to interior excellence. And it is not only admirable in singular and salient talents, but also in the world of manners.

But the sovereign attribute remains to be noted. Things are pretty, graceful, rich, elegant, handsome, but, until they speak to the imagination, not yet beautiful. This is the reason why beauty is still escaping out of all analysis. It is not yet possessed, it cannot be handled. Proclus[25] says, "it swims on the light of forms." It is properly not in the form, but in the mind. It instantly deserts possession, and flies to an object in the horizon. If I could put my hand on the north star, would it be as beautiful? The sea is lovely, but when we bathe in it, the beauty forsakes all the near water. For the imagination and senses cannot be gratified at the same time. Wordsworth rightly speaks of "a light that never was on sea or land,"[26] meaning, that it was supplied by the observer, and the Welsh bard warns his countrywomen, that

— "half of their charms with Cadwallon shall die."

The new virtue which constitutes a thing beautiful, is a certain cosmical quality, or, a power to suggest relation to the whole world, and so lift the object out of a pitiful individuality. Every natural feature,—sea, sky, rainbow, flowers, musical tone,—has in it somewhat which is not private, but universal, speaks of that central benefit which is the soul of Nature, and thereby is beautiful. And, in chosen men and women, I find somewhat in form, speech, and manners, which is not of their person and family, but of a humane, catholic, and spiritual character, and we love them as the sky. They have a largeness of suggestion, and their face and manners carry a certain grandeur, like time and justice.

The feat of the imagination is in showing the convertibility of every thing into every other thing. Facts which had never before left their stark common sense, suddenly figure as Eleusinian mysteries.[27] My boots and chair and candlestick are fairies in disguise, meteors and constellations. All the facts in Nature are nouns of the intellect, and make the grammar of the eternal language. Every word has a double, treble, or centuple use and meaning. What! has my stove and pepper-pot a false bottom! I cry you mercy, good shoe-box! I did not know you were a jewel-case. Chaff and dust begin to sparkle, and are clothed about with immortality. And there is a joy in perceiving the representative or symbolic character of a fact, which no bare fact or event can ever give. There are no days in life so memorable as those which vibrated to some stroke of the imagination.

The poets are quite right in decking their mistresses with the spoils of the landscape, flower-gardens, gems, rainbows, flushes of morning, and stars of night, since all beauty points at identity, and whatsoever thing does not express to me the sea and sky, day and night, is somewhat forbidden and wrong. Into every beautiful object, there enters somewhat immeasurable and divine, and just as much into form bounded by outlines, like mountains on the horizon, as into tones of music, or depths of space. Polarized light showed the secret architecture of bodies; and when the *second-sight* of the mind is opened, now one color or form or gesture, and now another, has a pungency, as if a more interior ray had been emitted, disclosing its deep holdings in the frame of things.

The laws of this translation we do not know, or why one feature or gesture enchants, why one word or syllable intoxicates, but the fact is familiar that the fine touch of the eye, or a grace of manners, or a phrase of poetry, plants wings at our shoulders; as if the Divinity, in his approaches, lifts away mountains of obstruction, and deigns to draw a truer line, which the mind knows and owns. This is that haughty force of beauty, "*vis superba formae*,"[28] which the poets praise,—under calm and precise outline, the immeasurable and divine: Beauty hiding all wisdom and power in its calm sky.

All high beauty has a moral element in it, and I find the antique sculpture as ethical as Marcus Antoninus: and the beauty ever in proportion to the depth of thought. Gross and obscure natures, however decorated, seem impure shambles; but character gives splendor to youth, and awe to wrinkled skin and gray hairs. An adorer of truth we cannot choose but obey, and the woman who has shared with us the moral sentiment,—her locks must appear to us sublime. Thus there is a climbing scale of culture, from the first agreeable sensation which a sparkling gem or a scarlet stain affords the eye, up through fair outlines and details of the landscape, features of the human face and form, signs and tokens of thought and character in manners, up to the ineffable mysteries of the intellect. Wherever we begin, thither our steps tend: an ascent from the joy of a horse in his trappings, up to the perception of Newton, that the globe on which we ride is only a larger apple falling from a larger tree; up to the perception of Plato, that globe and universe are rude and early expressions of an all-dissolving Unity,—the first stair on the scale to the temple of the Mind.

IX

ILLUSIONS

———•———

Flow, flow the waves hated,
Accursed, adored,
The waves of mutation:
No anchorage is.
Sleep is not, death is not;
Who seem to die live.
House you were born in,
Friends of your spring-time,
Old man and young maid,
Day's toil and its guerdon,
They are all vanishing,
Fleeing to fables,
Cannot be moored.
See the stars through them,
Through treacherous marbles.
Know, the stars yonder
The stars everlasting,
Are fugitive also,
And emulate, vaulted,
The lambent heat-lightning,
And fire-fly's flight.

When thou dost return
On the wave's circulation,
Beholding the shimmer,
The wild dissipation,
And, out of endeavor
To change and to flow,
The gas become solid,
And phantoms and nothings
Return to be things,
And endless imbroglio
Is law and the world,—
Then first shalt thou know,
That in the wild turmoil,
Horsed on the Proteus,
Thou ridest to power,
And to endurance.

ILLUSIONS

Some years ago, in company with an agreeable party, I spent a long summer day in exploring the Mammoth Cave in Kentucky.[1] We traversed, through spacious galleries affording a solid masonry foundation for the town and county overhead, the six or eight black miles from the mouth of the cavern to the innermost recess which tourists visit,—a niche or grotto made of one seamless stalactite, and called, I believe, Serena's Bower. I lost the light of one day. I saw high domes, and bottomless pits; heard the voice of unseen waterfalls; paddled three quarters of a mile in the deep Echo River, whose waters are peopled with the blind fish; crossed the streams "Lethe" and "Styx;" plied with music and guns the echoes in these alarming galleries; saw every form of stalagmite and stalactite in the sculptured and fretted chambers,—icicle, orange-flower, acanthus,[2] grapes, and snowball. We shot Bengal lights[3] into the vaults and groins of the sparry cathedrals, and examined all the masterpieces which the four combined engineers, water, limestone, gravitation, and time, could make in the dark.

The mysteries and scenery of the cave had the same dignity that belongs to all natural objects, and which shames the fine things to which we foppishly compare them. I remarked, especially, the mimetic habit, with which Nature, on new instruments, hums her old tunes, making night to mimic day, and chemistry to ape vegetation. But I then took notice, and still chiefly remember, that the best thing which the cave had to offer was an illusion. On arriving at what is called the "Star-Chamber," our lamps were taken from us by the guide, and extinguished or put aside, and, on looking upwards, I saw or seemed to see the night heaven thick with stars glimmering more or less brightly over our heads, and even what seemed a comet flaming among them. All the party were touched with astonishment and pleasure. Our musical friends sung with much feeling a pretty song, "The stars are in the quiet sky," and etc., and I sat down on the rocky floor to enjoy the serene picture. Some crystal specks in the black ceiling high overhead, reflecting the light of a half-hid lamp, yielded this magnificent effect.

I own, I did not like the cave so well for eking out its sublimities with this theatrical trick. But I have had many experiences like it, before and since; and we must be content to be pleased without too curiously analyzing the occasions. Our conversation with Nature is not just what it seems. The cloud-rack, the sunrise and sunset glories, rainbows, and northern lights are not quite so spheral as our childhood thought them; and the part our organization plays in them is too large. The senses interfere everywhere, and mix their own structure with all they report of. Once, we fancied the earth a plane, and stationary. In admiring the sunset, we do not yet deduct the rounding, coordinating, pictorial powers of the eye.

The same interference from our organization creates the most of our pleasure and pain. Our first mistake is the belief that the circumstance gives the joy which we give to the circumstance. Life is an ecstasy. Life is sweet as nitrous oxide; and the fisherman dripping all day over a cold pond, the switchman at the railway intersection, the farmer in the field, the Negro in the rice-swamp, the fop in the street, the hunter in the woods, the barrister with the jury, the belle at the ball, all ascribe a certain pleasure to their employment, which they themselves give it. Health and appetite impart the sweetness to sugar, bread, and meat. We fancy that our civilization has got on far, but we still come back to our primers.

We live by our imaginations, by our admirations, by our sentiments. The child walks amid heaps of illusions, which he does not like to have disturbed. The boy, how sweet to him is his fancy! how dear the story of barons and battles! What a hero he is, whilst he feeds on his heroes! What a debt is his to imaginative books! He has no better friend or influence, than Scott, Shakespeare, Plutarch, and Homer. The man lives to other objects, but who dare affirm that they are more real? Even the prose of the streets is full of refractions. In the life of the dreariest alderman, fancy enters into all details, and colors them with rosy hue. He imitates the air and actions of people whom he admires, and is raised in his own eyes. He pays a debt quicker to a rich man than to a poor man. He wishes the bow and compliment of some leader in the state, or in society; weighs what he says; perhaps he never comes nearer to him for that, but dies at last better contented for this amusement of his eyes and his fancy.

The world rolls, the din of life is never hushed. In London, in Paris, in Boston, in San Francisco, the carnival, the masquerade is at its height. Nobody drops his domino.[4] The unities, the fictions of the piece it would be an impertinence to break. The chapter of fascinations is very long. Great is paint; nay, God is the painter; and we rightly accuse the critic who destroys too many illusions. Society does not love its unmaskers. It was wittily, if somewhat bitterly, said by D'Alembert, *"qu'un état de vapeur était un état très fâcheux, parce-qu'il nous faisait voir les choses comme elles sont."*[5] I find men victims of illusion in all parts of life. Children, youths, adults, and old men, all are led by one bawble or another. Yoganidra, the goddess of illusion, Proteus, or Momus, or Gylfi's Mocking,—for the Power has many names,—is stronger than the Titans, stronger than Apollo.[6] Few have overheard the gods, or surprised their secret. Life is a succession of lessons which must be lived to be understood. All is riddle, and the key to a riddle is another riddle. There are as many pillows of illusion as flakes in a snow-storm. We wake from one dream into another dream. The toys, to be sure, are various, and are graduated in refinement to the quality of the dupe. The intellectual man requires a fine bait; the sots are easily amused. But everybody is drugged with his own frenzy, and the pageant marches at all hours, with music and banner and badge.

Amid the joyous troop who give in to the charivari,[7] comes now and then a sad-eyed boy, whose eyes lack the requisite refractions to clothe the show in due glory, and who is afflicted with a tendency to trace home the glittering miscellany of fruits and flowers to one root. Science is a search after identity, and the scientific whim is lurking in all corners. At the State Fair, a friend of mine complained that all the varieties of fancy pears in our orchards seem to have been selected by somebody who had a whim for a particular kind of pear, and only cultivated such as had that perfume; they were all alike. And I remember the quarrel of another youth with the confectioners, that, when he racked his wit to choose the best comfits in the shops, in all the endless varieties of sweetmeat he could only find three flavors, or two. What then? Pears and cakes are good for something; and because you, unluckily, have an eye or nose too keen, why need you spoil the comfort which the rest of us find in them? I knew a humorist, who, in a good deal of rattle, had a grain or two of sense. He shocked the company by maintaining that the attributes of God were two,— power and risibility;[8] and that it was the duty of every pious man to keep up the comedy. And I have known gentlemen of great stake in the community, but whose sympathies were cold,—presidents of colleges, and governors, and senators,—who held themselves bound to sign every temperance pledge, and act with Bible societies, and missions, and peace-makers, and cry *Hist-a-boy!* [9] to every good dog. We must not carry comity[10] too far, but we all have kind impulses in this direction. When the boys come into my yard for leave to gather horse-chestnuts, I own I enter into Nature's game, and affect to grant the permission reluctantly, fearing that any moment they will find out the imposture of that showy chaff.[11] But this tenderness is quite unnecessary; the enchantments are laid on very thick. Their young life is thatched with them. Bare and grim to tears is the lot of the children in the hovel I saw yesterday; yet not the less they hung it round with frippery[12] romance, like the children of the happiest fortune, and talked of "the dear cottage where so many joyful hours had flown." Well, this thatching of hovels is the custom of the country. Women, more than all, are the element and kingdom of illusion. Being fascinated, they fascinate. They see through Claude-Lorraines. And how dare any one, if he could, pluck away the *coulisses*,[13] stage effects, and ceremonies, by which they live? Too pathetic, too pitiable, is the region of affection, and its atmosphere always liable to *mirage*.

We are not very much to blame for our bad marriages. We live amid hallucinations; and this especial trap is laid to trip up our feet with, and all are tripped up first or last. But the mighty Mother who had been so sly with us, as if she felt that she owed us some indemnity, insinuates into the Pandora-box[14] of marriage some deep and serious benefits, and some great joys. We find a delight in the beauty and happiness of children, that makes the heart too big for the body. In the worst-assorted connections there is ever some mixture of true marriage. Teague[15] and his jade get some just relations of mutual respect, kindly observation, and fostering of each other, learn something, and would carry themselves wiselier, if they were now to begin.

'Tis fine for us to point at one or another fine madman, as if there were any exempts. The scholar in his library is none. I, who have all my life heard any number of orations and debates, read poems and miscellaneous books, conversed with many geniuses, am still the victim of any new page; and, if Marmaduke, or Hugh, or Moosehead, or any other, invent a new style or mythology, I fancy that the world will be all brave and right, if dressed in these colors, which I had not thought of. Then at once I will daub with this new paint; but it will not stick. 'Tis like the cement which the peddler sells at the door; he makes broken crockery hold with it, but you can never buy of him a bit of the cement which will make it hold when he is gone.

Men who make themselves felt in the world avail themselves of a certain fate in their constitution, which they know how to use. But they never deeply interest us, unless they lift a corner of the curtain, or betray never so slightly their penetration of what is behind it. 'Tis the charm of practical men, that outside of their practicality are a certain poetry and play, as if they led the good horse Power by the bridle, and preferred to walk, though they can ride so fiercely. Bonaparte is intellectual, as well as Caesar; and the best soldiers, sea-captains, and railway men have a gentleness, when off duty; a good-natured admission that there are illusions, and who shall say that he is not their sport? We stigmatize the cast-iron fellows, who cannot so detach themselves, as "dragon-ridden," "thunder-stricken," and fools of fate, with whatever powers endowed.

Since our tuition is through emblems and indirections, 'tis well to know that there is method in it, a fixed scale, and rank above rank in the phantasms. We begin low with coarse masks, and rise to the most subtle and beautiful. The red men told Columbus, "they had an herb which took away fatigue;" but he found the illusion of "arriving from the east at the Indies" more composing to his lofty spirit than any tobacco. Is not our faith in the impenetrability of matter more sedative than narcotics? You play with jackstraws,[16] balls, bowls, horse and gun, estates and politics; but there are finer games before you. Is not time a pretty toy? Life will show you masks that are worth all your carnivals. Yonder mountain must migrate into your mind. The fine star-dust and nebulous blur in Orion, "the portentous year of Mizar and Alcor,"[17] must come down and be dealt with in your household thought. What if you shall come to discern that the play and playground of all this pompous history are radiations from yourself, and that the sun borrows his beams? What terrible questions we are learning to ask! The former men believed in magic, by which temples, cities, and men were swallowed up, and all trace of them gone. We are coming on the secret of a magic which sweeps out of men's minds all vestige of theism and beliefs which they and their fathers held and were framed upon.

There are deceptions of the senses, deceptions of the passions, and the structural, beneficent illusions of sentiment and of the intellect. There is the illusion of love, which attributes to the beloved person all which that person shares with his or her family, sex, age, or condition, nay, with the human mind itself. 'Tis these which the lover loves, and Anna Matilda gets the credit of them. As if one shut up always in a tower, with one window, through which the face of heaven and earth could be seen, should fancy that all the marvels he beheld belonged to that window. There is the illusion of time, which is very deep; who has disposed of it? or come to the conviction that what seems the *succession* of thought is only the distribution of wholes into causal series? The intellect sees that every atom carries the whole of Nature; that the mind opens to omnipotence; that, in the endless striving and ascents, the metamorphosis is entire, so that the soul doth not know itself in its own act, when that act is perfected. There is illusion that shall deceive even the elect. There is illusion that shall deceive even the performer of the miracle. Though he make his body, he denies that he makes it. Though the world exist from thought, thought is daunted in presence of the world. One after the other we accept the mental laws, still resisting those which follow, which however must be accepted. But all our concessions only compel us to new profusion. And what avails it that science has come to treat space and time as simply forms of thought, and the material world as hypothetical, and withal our pretension of *property* and even of self-hood are fading with the rest, if, at last, even our thoughts are not finalities; but the incessant flowing and ascension reach these also, and each thought which yesterday was a finality, today is yielding to a larger generalization?

With such volatile elements to work in, 'tis no wonder if our estimates are loose and floating. We must work and affirm, but we have no guess of the value of what we say or do. The cloud is now as big as your hand, and now it covers a county. That story of Thor, who was set to drain the drinking-horn in Asgard, and to wrestle with the old woman, and to run with the runner Lok,[18] and presently found that he had been drinking up the sea, and wrestling with Time, and racing with Thought, describes us who are contending, amid these seeming trifles, with the supreme energies of Nature. We fancy we have fallen into bad company and squalid condition, low debts, shoe-bills, broken glass to pay for, pots to buy, butcher's meat, sugar, milk, and coal. 'Set me some great task, ye gods! and I will show my spirit.' 'Not so,' says the good Heaven; 'plod and plough, vamp[19] your old coats and hats, weave a shoestring; great affairs and the best wine by and by.' Well, 'tis all phantasm; and if we weave a yard of tape in all humility, and as well as we can, long hereafter we shall see it was no cotton tape at all, but some galaxy which we braided, and that the threads were Time and Nature.

We cannot write the order of the variable winds. How can we penetrate the law of our shifting moods and susceptibility? Yet they differ as all and nothing. Instead of the firmament of yesterday, which our eyes require, it is today an eggshell which coops us in; we cannot even see what or where our stars of destiny are. From day to day, the capital facts of human life are hidden from our eyes. Suddenly the mist rolls up, and reveals them, and we think how much good time is gone, that might have been saved, had any hint of these things been shown. A sudden rise in the road shows us the system of mountains, and all the summits, which have been just as near us all the year, but quite out of mind. But these alternations are not without their order, and we are parties to our various fortune. If life seem a succession of dreams, yet poetic justice is done in dreams also. The visions of good men are good; it is the undisciplined will that is whipped with bad thoughts and bad fortunes. When we break the laws, we lose our hold on the central reality. Like sick men in hospitals, we change only from bed to bed, from one folly to another; and it cannot signify much what becomes of such castaways,—wailing, stupid, comatose creatures,—lifted from bed to bed, from the nothing of life to the nothing of death.

In this kingdom of illusions we grope eagerly for stays and foundations. There is none but a strict and faithful dealing at home, and a severe barring out of all duplicity or illusion there. Whatever games are played with us, we must play no games with ourselves, but deal in our privacy with the last honesty and truth. I look upon the simple and childish virtues of veracity and honesty as the root of all that is sublime in character.[20] Speak as you think, be what you are, pay your debts of all kinds. I prefer to be owned as sound and solvent, and my word as good as my bond, and to be what cannot be skipped, or dissipated, or undermined, to all the *éclat*[21] in the universe. This reality is the foundation of friendship, religion, poetry, and art. At the top or at the bottom of all illusions, I set the cheat which still leads us to work and live for appearances, in spite of our conviction, in all sane hours, that it is what we really are that avails with friends, with strangers, and with fate or fortune.[22]

One would think from the talk of men, that riches and poverty were a great matter; and our civilization mainly respects it. But the Indians say, that they do not think the white man with his brow of care, always toiling, afraid of heat and cold, and keeping within doors, has any advantage of them. The permanent interest of every man is, never to be in a false position, but to have the weight of Nature to back him in all that he does. Riches and poverty are a thick or thin costume; and our life—the life of all of us—identical. For we transcend the circumstance continually, and taste the real quality of existence; as in our employments, which only differ in the manipulations, but express the same laws; or in our thoughts, which wear no silks, and taste no ice-creams. We see God face to face every hour, and know the savor of Nature.

The early Greek philosophers Heraclitus and Xenophanes measured their force on this problem of identity. Diogenes of Apollonia[23] said, that unless the atoms were made of one stuff, they could never blend and act with one another. But the Hindus, in their sacred writings, express the liveliest feeling, both of the essential identity, and of that illusion which they conceive variety to be. "The notions, '*I am*,' and '*This is mine*,' which influence mankind, are but delusions of the mother of the world. Dispel, O Lord of all creatures! the conceit of knowledge which proceeds from ignorance." And the beatitude of man they hold to lie in being freed from fascination.

The intellect is stimulated by the statement of truth in a trope, and the will by clothing the laws of life in illusions. But the unities of Truth and of Right are not broken by the disguise. There need never be any confusion in these. In a crowded life of many parts and performers, on a stage of nations, or in the obscurest hamlet in Maine or California, the same elements offer the same choices to each new comer, and, according to his election, he fixes his fortune in absolute Nature. It would be hard to put more mental and moral philosophy than the Persians have thrown into a sentence:—

> "Fooled thou must be, though wisest of the wise:
>   Then be the fool of virtue, not of vice."

There is no chance, and no anarchy, in the universe. All is system and gradation. Every god is there sitting in his sphere. The young mortal enters the hall of the firmament: there is he alone with them alone, they pouring on him benedictions and gifts, and beckoning him up to their thrones. On the instant, and incessantly, fall snow-storms of illusions. He fancies himself in a vast crowd which sways this way and that, and whose movement and doings he must obey: he fancies himself poor, orphaned, insignificant. The mad crowd drives hither and thither, now furiously commanding this thing to be done, now that. What is he that he should resist their will, and think or act for himself? Every moment, new changes, and new showers of deceptions, to baffle and distract him. And when, by and by, for an instant, the air clears, and the cloud lifts a little, there are the gods still sitting around him on their thrones,—they alone with him alone.

THE END

NOTES

Introduction

1. First published in Boston by Ticknor and Fields in 1860.

2. Misunderstandings of Emerson on this point are important in the relative neglect of his later work. See for instance, O.W. Holmes, *Ralph Waldo Emerson* (1885), p. 230, where begins a history of misunderstandings.

3. John Dewey 1903, "Emerson—The Philosopher of Democracy," reprinted in Dewey, *The Middle Works*, Vol. 3. See pp. 187 and 192.

4. William James 1903, "Address to the Emerson Centenary at Concord," published in James 1911, *Memories and Studies*, pp. 19-34. See the final page.

5. Samuel Taylor Coleridge (1772-1834), English poet, critic, and philosopher. Coleridge's books, *The Friend* and *Biographia Literaria* were important for Emerson. See the discussion in Flower and Murphey 1977, *A History of Philosophy in America*, Vol. 1, pp. 408f.

6. Emerson 1842, "The Transcendentalist," reprinted in Stroh and Callaway 2000, *American Ethics*, pp. 117-122. See pp. 117-118.

7. Emerson 1841, "Lecture on the Times," in *The Works of R. W. Emerson*, Vol. 1, *Miscellanies*, pp. 211-236. See p. 212.

8. See Emerson 1836, "Modern Aspects of Letters," where he says of Coleridge: "He has made admirable definitions, and drawn indelible lines between things heretofore confounded. He thought and thought truly that all confusion of thought tended to confusion in action; and said that he had never observed an abuse of terms obtain currency without being followed by some practical error. He has enriched the English language and the English mind with an explanation of the object of philosophy; of the all important distinction between Reason and Understanding; the distinction of an idea and a conception; between Genius and Talent; between Fancy and Imagination; of the nature and end of Poetry; of the Idea of a State."

9. Emerson 1841, "Lecture on the Times," pp. 212-213.

10. Emerson 1844, "Address on the Emancipation of the Negroes in the British West Indies," in Gougeon and Myerson eds., 1995, *Emerson's Antislavery Writings*, p. 13.

11. See "Behavior," in the present volume, p. 85.

12. Emerson 1842, "The Transcendentalist," reprinted in Emerson 1971, Alfred R. Ferguson, ed. *The Collected Works of Ralph Waldo Emerson*, Vol. I, p. 203.

13. See "Worship," in the present volume, p. 106.

14. "Worship," p. 107.

15. See "Fate," in the present volume, p. 5.

16. See "Worship," in the present volume, p. 101.

17. "*Éclat,*" French: Grand appearance, shattering affect, sparkle, or pomp.

18. See "Illusions," in the present volume, p. 161.

19. Compare Emerson on the creativity of the poet in his 1875 book, *Letters and Social Aims*, "Do they think there is chance or willfulness in what he sees and tells? To be sure, we demand of him what he demands of himself,—veracity, first of all. But with that he is the lawgiver, as being an exact reporter of the essential law. He knows that he did not make his thought,—no, his thought made him, and made the sun and the stars. Is the solar system good art and architecture? the same wise achievement is in the human brain also, can you only wile it from interference and marring." See the opening essay, "Poetry and Imagination."

20. Emerson 1842, "The Transcendentalist," p. 213.

21. See "Fate," in the present volume, p. 23.

22. See "Fate," p. 23.

23. See "Fate," p. 23.

24. See Emerson's letter to Carlyle of 11 March 1854, published in Joseph Slater, ed. *The Correspondence of Emerson and Carlyle*, pp. 497-499.

25. See "Culture," in the present volume, p. 69.

26. See "Culture," p. 65.

27. See "Culture," p. 65.

28. Emerson 1855, "Lecture on Slavery," in *Emerson's Antislavery Writings*, pp. 99-100.

29. *Ibid.*, p. 100.

30. Emerson 1844, "Address on the Emancipation," in *Emerson's Antislavery Writings*, p. 9.

I. Fate

1. Including just a pinch of ironic understatement, this is a brief summary statement of Emerson's view of the topic: It is fine to speculate and elect a view or choice—an assertion of freedom—, but only if we respect the demands of truthfulness and law. This is the "polarity" of the proper inquirer.

2. Equation of fate and unalterable law follows traditional definition: "Fate": a power superior to the human will and operating in accord with arcane laws knowable only to the initiate.

3. The New England Puritans were Calvinists emphasizing the inherent sinfulness of man and our predestination for salvation or damnation in view of the Divine foreknowledge. The dignity mentioned comes of accepting what cannot be changed.

4. Geoffrey Chaucer (*ca.* 1340-1400), author of the *Canterbury Tales*, from which the quoted poetry comes, is the most noted English writer prior to Shakespeare, and he counts among England's greatest poets. Emerson later wrote, on the Northern opposition to the Civil War: "It is wonderful to see the unseasonable senility of what is called the Peace party, through all its masks, blinding their eyes to the main feature of the war, namely, its inevitableness. ... It might have begun otherwise or elsewhere, but war was in the minds and bones of the combatants, it was written on the iron leaf, and you might as easily dodge gravitation." See "The President's Proclamation," in Gougeon and Myerson, p. 133.

5. Believing in predestination, the Calvinists held that those destined for salvation belong to "the elect" of God and that there was evidence of such status in a person's positive role in the congregation or in general prosperity and well-being.

6. Johann Heinrich Jung-Stilling (1740-1817) was a German writer and associate of Goethe, best known for his autobiography (1806), including an account of life in the eighteenth-century pietistic (German, Lutheran-puritan) family. Goethe said of him: "The basis of his energy was an indestructible faith in God and in help flowing immediately there from, which apparently confirmed itself in uninterrupted provisions and in an unfailing rescue from every emergency and every evil."

7. A "Pistareen" is an old Spanish silver coin which circulated at a debased rate. Rejecting a "pistareen-Providence," Emerson allows a foreground of accident in experience.

8. As happened to Emerson's friend and associate, Margaret Fuller (1810-1850). Returning home from Italy, she was drowned at sea together with her husband and son in a shipwreck off Fire Island, New York.

9. A famous example of Voltaire (1694-1778), who in *Candide* (1759) replied to the optimistic *Theodicy* (1710) of Leibniz and his claim that this is the "best of all possible worlds"—with the example of the great Lisbon earthquake, on All Saint's Day, 1755. Some 40,000 people died, often crushed in their churches. Emerson evokes here the classical "problem of evil" which reflects on the power (or goodness) of Divinity. In some contrast, William James wrote of Leibniz's teaching in the *Theodicy* that his "feeble grasp of reality is too obvious to need comment from me." See James 1907, *Pragmatism*, pp. 28-30. Compare Emerson, "Fate": "The day of days, the great day of the feast of life, is that in which the inward eye opens to the Unity in things, to the omnipresence of law;—sees that what is must be, and ought to be, or is the best." We might gain from criticism of Emerson (and Leibniz) a realistic meliorism: We need to recognize (not always accept) reality for what it is, given as Emerson puts the matter "the way of Providence is a little rude," in order to understand where to make reforms or improvements.

10. Cayenne is the capital and port-city of French Guiana on the northern coast of South America. It was notorious in the nineteenth-century for its prison.

11. "Ague": a fever involving a fit of shivering.

12. "Bombyx": silk worm.

13. "Labrus": species of carnivorous fish.

14. "Grampus": group of carnivorous seas mammals including the killer whale.

15. Johann Kaspar **Spurzheim** (1776-1832) was a famous nineteenth-century phrenologist, who, in the pseudo-scientific vogue of the times, studied the shape of the skull in the attempt to determine mental abilities and character traits. Lambert Adolphe Jacques **Quételet** (1796-1874) was a Belgian astronomer, statistician, and sociologist recognized for the early application of statistics and probability in social studies. His work, *A Treatise on Man and the Development of His Faculties*, which appeared in English in 1842, presented his conception of the "average man" as a statistical norm around which measurements of human traits are distributed in accord with the normal curve of probability. He was able to predict important social phenomena, for instance, the incidence of crime, thus disturbing confidence in human freedom.

16. "Huckaback": an absorbent, strong, cotton or linen fabric used for towels.

17. "Jobber": a wholesaler; one who works by the job or assignment: a day laborer.

18. Laws of physics as formulated by Sir Isaac Newton (1643-1727), English physicist and mathematician, whose *Mathematical Principles of Natural Philosophy* (1687) was the greatest work of classical (pre-Einstein) physics.

19. Matthew, 5: 28.

20. "*Camarilla*," Spanish: 'a small room,' suggesting a special tendency or ability.

21. Joseph von Fraunhofer (1787-1826) was a German physicist who studied the dark lines of the sun's spectrum, now known as Fraunhofer lines, and initiated modern spectroscopy.

22. The **Whigs** were a more conservative, business-oriented political party before the Civil War; the **Free Soil** Party campaigned before the Civil War against extending slavery into the territories. Invoking **Fraunhofer** and **Carpenter** suggests special, precise observation.

23. This is the Hindu notion of Karma.

24. F. W. J. Schelling, German philosopher (1775-1854). See, *Philosophical Inquiries into the Nature of Human Freedom*, 1807, from which the quotation is translated, and Gutmann's 1936 translation, p. 64. Self-identity is equated with origins, and freedom with expression of origins, thus deriving from an original state or condition of grace, in contrast with Emerson's emphasis on development and direction of development. Schelling viewed ultimate origin as defining both circumstance and freedom.

25. Edmund **Burke** (1729-1797) British statesman and philosopher who defended the motives of the American Revolution and criticized the French Revolution. Henry Peter **Brougham** (1778-1868) British Whig politician, reformer, and Lord Chancellor of Great Britain (1830-1834). Brougham was influential in the founding of the University of London. Daniel **Webster** (1782-1852), a native of New Hampshire, was a famous orator and politician, practicing law before the U.S. Supreme Court and serving as a Congressman, later Senator from Massachusetts and Secretary of State. He was an enthusiastic nationalist and an advocate of business interests. Emerson's mention of Webster is suggestive of the themes of "The Devil and Daniel Webster," a play written by the American novelist and poet Stephen Vincent Benét (1898-1943) and later used as the basis of a motion picture. In a famous speech of 7 March 1850, Webster supported the Fugitive Slave Act of 1850. Lajos **Kossuth** (1802-1894) was a Hungarian political reformer who led Hungary's struggle for independence from Austria. He briefly held power in 1848 and 1849.

26. A "vesicle," a small pocket or bud of embryonic tissue. "A vesicle in new circumstances," thus suggests a changed or modified potentiality.

27. Apparently a reference to the German romantic naturalist Lorenz Oken (1779-1851) who proposed a theory of organic origins out of vesicles or cells.

28. "**Zoophytes**": animals resembling plants; "**trilobium**": extinct triple-lobed sea animal.

29. Here "race" is equivalent to "biological species," though elsewhere Emerson uses the word to denote cultural-ethnic groups: English, French, Germans, the Jews, the Indians, the Negroes, etc. The concepts are not clearly distinguished. But "race" surely belongs to "circumstance," as contrasted with Emerson's concept of "positive power." Thus Robert Knox's account of the relation of race to habitat is, at most, part of the negative side of Emerson's story. Notice that Americans are predominantly both "transplanted" from the old world and mixed in their ethnic and/or racial background.

30. Dr. Robert Knox author of *The Races of Man, a fragment* (1850), argued that races are distinct, like biological species, and that hybrids degenerate.

31. "Crab": small, sour form, as in "crab apple."

32. "Guano": bird droppings used as fertilizer, newly discovered and valued at the time.

33. "Fagot": bundle.

34. "Adamantine": incapable of being broken, dissipated or penetrated.

35. The French Emperor, Napoleon Bonaparte (1769-1821).

36. Originally Johanna Maria Lind (1820-1887) a famous Swedish-born soprano.

37. Nathaniel Bowditch (1773-1838) was an American mathematician and astronomer. He authored a famous book on navigation, *The New American Practical Navigator*, 1802. Bowditch also translated Laplace from the French.

38. *Emerson's note*: "Everything which pertains to the human species, considered as a whole, belongs to the order of physical facts. The greater the number of individuals, the more does the influence of the individual will disappear, leaving predominance to a series of general facts dependent on causes by which society exists, and is preserved."-Quételet.

39. **Homer**: Greek epic poet (fl. 850 BC) author of the Iliad and the Odyssey. **Zoroaster**: from the old Iranian. Ancient Persian religious prophet (*ca.* 628-551 BC) and founder of Zoroastrianism. **Menu**: in Hindu mythology, the first man, and the legendary author of a Sanskrit code of law, the *Ordinances of Manu*.

40. **Tubal Cain** is the first worker in metals mentioned in the Old Testament. In Roman mythology, **Vulcan** is the god of fire and divine blacksmith. **Cadmus**, figure in Greek mythology. Cadmus was the brother of Europa, and sent to find her when she was carried off by Zeus, king of the gods. According to tradition he brought the alphabet to Greece. Nicolaus **Copernicus** (1473-1543) was a Polish astronomer who originated the heliocentric theory of the heavens which replaced the ancient earth-centered, Ptolemaic system. Johann **Fust** (1400-1466), German printer and financial backer of Johannes Gutenberg, inventor of printing in Europe. Fust was a founder of the first successful printing firm. Robert **Fulton** (1765-1815) was an American inventor and engineer who brought the steamboat from experimental to commercial success.

41. From Ellery Channing's 1843 poem "Death."

42. Jacques de **Vaucanson** (1709-1782) was a French inventor of devices imitating living things and of important industrial machines. Benjamin **Franklin** (1706-1790) is mentioned here in his role as inventor, e.g., of the Franklin stove, the lightning rod, and bifocal eyeglasses. James **Watt** (1736-1819) was a Scottish inventor. His steam engine was a key development of the Industrial Revolution.

43. Pierre-Simon, marquis de Laplace (1749-1827) was a French mathematician, astronomer, physicist, and philosopher, famous for his advocacy of physical determinism and for studies of the solar system.

44. **Aristarchus** of Samos (*ca.* 310-230 BC), Greek astronomer and the first to hold that the Earth rotates and revolves around the sun. He thus anticipated Copernicus. **Pythagoras** (*ca.* 580-500 BC) Greek philosopher and mathematician, who influenced the thought of Plato and Aristotle. According to Pythagoras the world is to be understood as a whole in terms of formal mathematical relations. **Thales, Anaximenes**, etc.: Pre-Socratic philosophers and thinkers of ancient Greece.

45. "Cowrie" or "cowry": South Pacific sea-shell prized for its beauty.

46. "*Orangia*," compare "orangy" or "orangey": similar to or suggesting an orange, e.g., in flavor or color.

47. "Punch," or The London Charivari, English illustrated periodical published 1841 to 1992 and more recently revived. The name is connected with the aggressive puppet figure from "Punch and Judy" shows, and the periodical is famous for its satire, humor, and caricatures.

48. Vishnu is a chief god of Hindu mythology, and "Maya" also means illusion.

49. "Ichor": an ethereal fluid serving as blood in the ancient Greek gods.

50. This is the strongly anti-nominalist theme in Emerson's thought—deriving, in part, from the distinction in Coleridge between "fancy" and "imagination."

51. A Welsh triad is an ancient form of poem.

52. Miguel de Cervantes (1547-1616) author of Don Quixote and one of the most celebrated of all Spanish writers.

53. Proper morality or "the world of morals," we must imagine, reflects the conditions of human existence. "Freedom is necessary," says Emerson directly below, but so is moral limitation. This implies that morally we must chose freedom and that it is possible not to do so. Generally, this paragraph is very close to the themes of Emerson's essay "Compensation."

54. The passage suggestions an ultimate rejection of a dualism of fate vs. power, consistent with Emerson's general rejection of dualism.

55. "Quadrumanous": relating to the primates, other than humans, distinguished by 4 hand-shaped feet. From the Latin, "manus": hand.

56. This is said to be one of the "Chaldaen oracles" ascribed to Zoroaster.

57. Cf. C. S. Peirce (Collected Papers, 8. 256), who says of consciousness, in a letter to William James, 25 November 1902, "But if it is to mean Thought it is more without us than within. It is we that are in it, rather than it in any of us." In context, this is an expression of Peirce's anti-nominalism, and this anti-nominalism is rooted or expressed in pantheistic or pan-psychic conceptions of the world.

58. Alaric (370-410 AD) chief of the Visigoths and leader of the army that sacked Rome in 410 AD, thus ending the Roman Empire in the West.

59. Hafiz: Mohammad Shams od-din Hafiz, fourteenth-century Persian lyric poet and theologian of Sufi mysticism. The concept of fate is transformed by Hafiz, if, as he suggests, we may rightly consider ourselves agents (passive or active) of our own fate.

60. Voltaire: pen name of François-Marie Arouet (1694-1778), French author and philosopher of the Enlightenment.

61. Can we believe in unity?—that is, reject an ultimate dualism?

62. "On change," that is, at the exchange.

63. "Reprobate": one who is morally corrupt: depraved.

64. Marquis of Worcester (1601-1667) was a supporter of Charles I. during the English Civil Wars, and he claimed to have invented an early steam engine.

65. Emerson here shows his commitment to democratic equality in contrast with rule of aristocratic elites.

66. Here Emerson both considers and resists "race" as associating historical ethnic groups with excesses or defects of culture. Notice that the Saxons and Celts come off better than "the Neapolitan"–which is even less plausibly a "race" biologically distinct.

67. Man, the human race, in contrast to earlier species, so that "race" again means "species"—the human race.

68. "Consentaneous": depends on connections, correspondences or agreements.

69. Christopher Wren (1632-1723) English classical architect and scientist famous for designing St. Paul's Cathedral and many other famous buildings in Britain.

70. "Inosculation": uniting or blending of parts.

71. **Dante** Alighieri (1265-1321) was an Italian poet and giant figure of Western literature. Christopher **Columbus** (1451-1506) was an Italian navigator who, in the service of Spain, opened the New World to exploration.

72. "Pericarp": the ripened, matured wall of a plant ovary or the seed case of the fruit.

73. Johann Wolfgang **Goethe** (1749-1832) German poet and writer. Emerson shared with Goethe a romantic quasi-pantheism and the idea of an upward striving of all forms. Georg Wilhelm Friedrich **Hegel** (1770-1831) German Idealist philosopher. Prince Klemens von **Metternich** (1773-1859) Austrian minister of foreign affairs (1809-1848), and a champion of conservatism who helped form the alliance against Napoleon. Metternich was a chief figure at the Congress of Vienna in 1814-1815. John Quincy **Adams** (1767-1848) sixth President of the U.S. and son of John Adams, the second President. Adams was also later U.S. Representative from Massachusetts. Senator John C. **Calhoun** (1782-1850) Vice President of the U.S. and then Senator from South Carolina. Calhoun was a leading Southern voice in national government before the Civil War. François Pierre Guillaume **Guizot** (1787-1874) was a French politician and historian. A leader of the constitutional monarchists under Louis-Philippe, Guizot became the dominant minister in France. He was forced to resign in February of 1848, and Emerson's praise of Guizot reflects his negative view of the events of Paris in 1848. Sir Robert **Peel** (1788-1850) was British prime minister (1834-35, 1841-1846) and a founder of the Conservative Party. He was also partly responsible for the repeal of the Corn Laws which had kept food prices high and power in the hands of the landed gentry. Richard **Cobden** (1804-1865) British politician best remembered for his successful fight to repeal the Corn Laws and his defense of free trade. Lajos **Kossuth**, the Hungarian political reformer. Famous European banking family, founded by Mayer Amschel **Rothschild** (1744-1812) and his sons. The banking business grew up during the Napoleonic wars and afterwards made the transition from banking and finance for princes and war to banking for the Industrial Revolution. John Jacob **Astor** (1763-1848) founded a wealthy American family. The family fortune originated in the fur trade and later became centered in New York real estate. Isambard Kingdom **Brunel** (1806-1859) was a British civil and mechanical engineer and designer of the Great Western railroad and of the first transatlantic steamer.

74. **Herodotus** (*ca.* 484-430 or 420 BC) Greek historian and first historian in the West. **Plutarch** (*ca.* 46-119 AD) Greek historian, philosopher, and biographer famous for his parallels between Greek and Roman lives.

75. Virgil, *Aeneid*, VI.743, "Whatever the spirits we suffer" (they are ourselves). Or, less literally, "We bear each one our own destiny."

76. "The races of men" are here distinguished culturally by "the quality of thought."

77. Greatness here depends on fine sensibility.

78. Georg Möller (1784-1852) was a German architect of the late Classicist school. Note the "functionalist" theme: beauty follows function.

79. "Bilious": having an excess of bile; having a peevish or ill-natured disposition.

80. "Truculent": feeling or displaying ferocity: cruel, savage.

81. "Curculio": any of various weevils; especially, those that injure fruit.

82. "Moloch": a deity to whom children were sacrificed in the ancient Middle East, a practice forbidden by the laws of Moses: "You shall not give any of your children to devote them by fire to Moloch, and so profane the name of your God" (Leviticus, 18:21).

83. From Chaucer's *The House of Fame*, lines 43-52, a work of the 1370s.

84. Cf. Luke, 11:9.

85. Goethe, in his autobiography, *Aus meinem Leben, Wahrheit und Dichtung* (1811).

86. "Double consciousness": In a sense, Emerson implies that if you can't beat them, then join them, and the doctrine expresses Emerson's anti-nominalism. So, in particular, if your private view fails you, admit your mistakes, and join the opposition. The idea is also suggestive of Emerson on society and solitude, the need for both: Perspective from outside and from inside a situation forms a creative tension. Compare W. E. B. Du Bois's early picture of the "double-consciousness" of African-Americans as both African and American, insiders and outsiders, in *The Souls of Black Folks,* 1903. Notice, too, that Emerson proposed a practical or methodological solution to the problem of "freedom and foreknowledge."

87. "Sciatica": pain along the sciatic nerve, in the lower back, buttocks, hips, or thigh.

88. This "Blessed Unity" is at least a rejection of mind-matter dualism, and suggests as well a reconciliation of the factual and the ethical; of circumstance and freedom.

89. Concluding the essay, Emerson returns to a quasi-Leibnizian conception of law, beauty, goodness, and ultimate improvement in the world, reaffirming his faith in the possibility of a better world. While we may doubt that melioration is inevitable, what is less doubtful is that our growing understanding of the world and of our place in it, sometimes yields the power to make improvements. Given our aims and their development, we must accept the objective conditions of improvements, if we are to establish improvements: Circumstance becomes a complex of law and facts to be mastered. Growing understanding makes a difference to what we can do, and though we are not *predestined* to grow in understanding in any way independent of our insight, inquiry, plans and action, growth remains possible; and the possibility may be cultivated, as long as distinctively human life persists: increasing harmony and joy are possible in nature.

90. "Beautiful Necessity": there are laws and conditions which we cannot change but which we can learn to recognize and use to achieve our ends—thus introducing new order into the world. In the absence of laws and conditions beyond our power to change, we could not act with any predictable effect. Compare the first paragraph: "'Tis fine for us to speculate and elect our course, if we must accept an irresistible dictation."

91. "No contingencies," that is, the accidents of experience are not of ultimate concern but are best viewed as conditions we must be prepared to master and use.

II. Power

1. A counter-thesis to Voltaire's epicurean "cultivate your own garden" and to the communalists among the New England Transcendentalists. See also "Wealth" below.

2. Emerson here connects universal causation with his principle of "compensation." The themes of the present and prior essay may be usefully viewed as developments of an earlier essay "Compensation" (1841). "The league between virtue and nature engages all things to assume a hostile front to vice," Emerson wrote, and "the beautiful laws and substances of the world persecute and whip the traitor . . . . things are arranged for truth and benefit. . . ." The compensation for good works is power.

3. "Intrepid": having resolute fearlessness, fortitude, and endurance.

4. In the Icelandic Sagas, **Bjarni** Herjulfsson first sighted Vinland (in North America) when blown off his course from Iceland to Greenland. **Thorfin** Karlsefni (980 to after 1007 AD), Icelandic-born leader of the early colony in North America. See the Saga of Erik and the Tale of the Greenlanders.

5. Commander Charles Wilkes (1798-1877) was an American naval officer who discovered a region of Antarctica subsequently called Wilkes Land.

6. Bertel Thorvaldsen (1770-1844), a Danish neoclassical artist of the early nineteenth-century who experimented with revival of low relief sculpture.

7. Alexandre Dumas (1802-1870), the elder, author of *The Count of Monte Cristo* and *The Three Musketeers*, was known to have worked with literary collaborators.

8. "Aplomb": complete and confident composure or self-assurance: poise.

9. "Peccant": guilty: sinning; violating a principle or rule: faulty.

10. *"Demos,"* Greek: the people.

11. "Pernicious": destructive.

12. The point reflects an early nineteenth century debate concerning the use of English common law in American courts, a policy favored by the Federalists and conservatives.

13. The broader meaning of "commerce" is social interaction, interchange of ideas, opinions, or sentiments.

14. "Exigency": what is required in a particular situation.

15. **"Hooser"**: nickname for natives of Indiana, perhaps from English dialect "hoozer" meaning big of its kind; "**Sucker, Wolverine, Badger**," names for other Westerners.

16. "Cupidity": lust after wealth: avarice; greed.

17. Thomas **Jefferson** (1743-1826) was the third President of the United States, author of the Declaration of Independence, a leader of the American Revolution, and political philosopher. As American representative in Paris, Jefferson also took part in the early stages of the French Revolution, but he was recalled from Paris in 1789. Andrew **Jackson** (1767-1845) was a U.S. General, victor over the British at New Orleans, and seventh President of the United States (1829-1837). Jackson was the first President from the West, and he gained office by appeal to the mass of voters. While in office, he vetoed the bill to renew the charter of the second Bank of the United States.

18. President James K. **Polk**, slaveholder and Tennessee Democrat, conducted the Mexican-American War (1846-1847) in the face of anti-slavery, Northern-Whig opposition, though Senator John C. **Calhoun** of South Carolina briefly joined the opposition because he thought Polk high-handed. Thomas Hart **Benton** was a power-

ful Senator from Missouri, and Daniel **Webster** the (silent) anti-slavery Whig from Massachusetts.

19. "Red republicanism," here, is that of Jefferson and the Republican party of the early republic. It is worth reflecting that the post-Civil War Republicans, starting as the party of Lincoln and freedom later supported big business and the Gilded Age.

20. Emerson's argument that positive power is based in energy and vitality extends a critical tolerance to American economic growth, and this set him in some opposition to the doubts of his friend Henry David Thoreau. The argument is that, even in the commune, "Judas," a traitor, is wanted as steward. Emerson also says that culture is wanted as the judge of success and the regulator of power.

21. Several of Emerson's close literary associates were involved in projects for communal living, at Brook Farm, though Emerson, much the family man, always resisted. He wrote of the project in summary that "It was a perpetual picnic, a French Revolution in small, an Age of Reason in a patty-pan."

22. "Burgesses": citizens of a borough.

23. "Shakers": United Society of Believers in Christ's Second Appearing, a celibate, pacifist, communalist sect which established settlements in the U. S. starting in the eighteenth century. Shaker communities flourished early on and created an austere, characteristic style of architecture, furniture and handicrafts, but the sect inevitably faded away.

24. "Coney": rabbit; (archaic:) dupe.

25. "Malignant": malcontent, the rebellious; actively evil in nature, or effect.

26. Suggests a comparison to Pope Boniface VIII. (1235/40-1303), famous for his extreme defense of the spiritual authority of the Roman church and of the Bishop of Rome. This emphasis evoked serious conflict with secular authorities. Dante, his contemporary, placed him in eternal damnation in the *Inferno*.

27. "Horse-rake": horse-drawn hay rake.

28. "Baby-jumper": a suspended seat for a child.

29. "Elegy": a pensive or reflective poem, usually nostalgic or melancholy.

30. Pike's peak is a mountain in Colorado, 10 miles west of present-day Colorado Springs. In 1859, it became the focus of a gold rush with the slogan "Pike's Peak or bust."

31. "Roister": a rude or uncultured person; one who engages in loud revelry.

32. "Maelstrom": a powerful whirlpool which sucks in surrounding objects.

33. The Hellespont is a narrow waterway in Istanbul between Europe and Asia.

34. George **Borrow** (1803-1881) was an English traveler and linguist who famously wrote of his contacts with the gypsies in the English countryside, in Spain, and elsewhere. Sir Charles **Waterton** (1782-1865), English naturalist and explorer.

35. "**Bedouin**": nomadic Arabs of the Arabian, Syrian, or African deserts. "**Sheik**": an Arab chief. "**Pacha**": also written "pasha;" Turkish: a man of high rank or office.

36. Sir Austen Henry Layard (1817-1894) was an English archaeologist. His excavations expanded knowledge of the civilizations of ancient Mesopotamia.

37. In mid-century France, the **Orleanists** were partisans of Louis-Philippe, the **Bourbonists** were monarchist favoring the old ruling house, and Charles-Forbes-René, Count de **Montalembert** (1810-1870) was an orator, politician, and liberal

Catholic leader in the struggle against absolutism in church and state. Nevertheless, he supported Louis-Napoleon. Emerson, who visited Paris in 1848, suggests that party politics easily escapes any connection to genuine issues.

38. "Solfatara": natural volcanic vent in which sulfur gases escape with steam.

39. "Pelegasi," ancient Greek: the non-Greek inhabitants of the Aegean area.

40. "Pericles and Phidias": paradigmatic figures of classical Greek civilization and of Greek statesmanship and sculpture respectively.

41. "Corinthian civility": suggests overly refined or decadent life.

42. "Astringency": suggestive of an astringent effect upon tissue, capable of drawing tissues together: rigidly severe: austere; pungent, harsh.

43. Battle of Eylau (7-8 February 1807). A battle in East Prussia during the Napoleonic Wars, against the Russians and Prussians, where Napoleon suffered a major deadlock.

44. Michelangelo Buonarroti (1475-1564) was an Italian sculptor and painter, widely held to be one of the greatest artists of all times.

45 ."Sibyl": a woman prophet.

46. "*Succedanea*": replacement, that is, the next best thing.

47. Benvenuto Cellini (1500-1571) was a Florentine sculptor, goldsmith, and the author of a famous autobiography.

48. First Cause: the Creator.

49. Thomas Campbell (1777-1844) was a Scottish poet, remembered for his sentimental and martial lyrics. He helped initiate a plan to found the University of London.

50. Pericles (*ca.* 495-429 BC) Athenian statesman closely connected with the development of democracy and empire. He was also responsible for the construction of the Acropolis. Plutarch wrote his biography.

51. Edward Buxton was the son of the famous Sir Thomas Buxton, who was important in the emancipation of the slaves of the British West Indies.

52. Samuel Johnson (1709-1784) was an English critic, biographer, essayist, novelist, poet, and lexicographer.

53. "Hack," Roadster, "Arab barb," types of domesticated horse. The last is more spirited or temperamental.

54. "Trunnions": the pivots on which a cannon swings up or down.

55. John Kemble (1757-1823) was a popular English Shakespearean actor and manager of London theaters.

56. Basil Hall (1788-1844), British naval officer and traveler who wrote accounts of his travels in the Orient, Latin America, and the U. S.

57. "Stumping it": speaking from tree stumps; speaking to the popular mind.

58. Wendell Phillips (1811-1884), eloquent American abolitionist crusader who helped inspired the anti-slavery movement.

59. "Exercitation": exercise, or practice, especially devotional.

60. Democritus (460-*ca.* 370 BC) was a Greek philosopher and central figure in the development of the ancient atomic theory. His ethical system makes *ataraxia* ("cheerfulness") an ultimate value—a state of untroubled pleasure or tranquility, undisturbed by fear or superstition.

61. "Bookmakers": here, writers and publishers of books.

62. At the end of the essay, and before taking up the topic of "wealth" in the next, Emerson signals the need of moral constraint in the accumulation of wealth.

III. Wealth

1. The steam engines of James Watt were used in mining, and George Stephenson (1781-1848), English engineer, was the chief inventor of the steam locomotive and railroad.
2. "Fulsomely": copiously; excessively complimentary or flatteringly effusive.
3. Implicitly, Emerson offers a criticism of Thoreau's project of subsistence-living as described in *Walden*.
4. "Bread and Games": phrase from the Latin, often translated "bread and circuses."
5. "Pay his scot": compare the British phrase "scot and lot": a parish tax formerly paid by the British, according to wealth; thus obligations of all kinds taken as a whole. A related idiom is "scot free": completely free from obligation, harm, or penalty.
6. See Burke (1780) "Oeconomical Reformation of the Civil and Other Establishments."
7. "Fop": a man vain about his appearance or dress: a dandy.
8. "Ostentatious": marked by conspicuous or pretentious display: showy.
9. "Importunity": troublesome urgency.
10. Contrary to the suggestion that "party" enthusiasm only benefits the few, Emerson suggests that "speculative" organizational genius may bring long-term benefit to the world.
11. The Grand Junction Railway opened its Liverpool-to-Birmingham line in England in 1837.
12. Alexander von Humboldt (1769-1859) was a German naturalist and explorer. His book *Cosmos* made important contributions to the popularization of science. It aims for a generally comprehensible account of the universe as it was then known.
13. Dominique Vivant **Denon** (1747-1825) was a French artist, archaeologist, and museum official. He traveled with Napoleon and was instrumental in the development of the Louvre collection. William **Beckford** (1760-1844), wealthy English writer, collector, and traveler, known as author of *Vathek* (1786) and for building Fonthill Abbey and its art collection. Giovanni Battista **Belzoni** (1778-1823), an Italian engineer, was an early excavator of Egyptian archaeological sites. John Gardner **Wilkinson** was an English Egyptologist who spent 12 years (1821-1833) copying and collecting material in Egypt. He published his *Popular Account of the Ancient Egyptians* in 1854. After his famous archeological work in the near East, Austen Henry **Layard** was a member of the British Parliament (1852-1857) and (1860-1869), under secretary of foreign affairs (1861-1866), and was appointed chief commissioner of works and privy councilor (1868) and later ambassador to Turkey (1877-1880). Elisha Kent **Kane** (1820-1857) was an American physician and Arctic explorer. Kane led an expedition to Greenland in search of the missing explorer Sir John Franklin. Karl Richard **Lepsius** (1810-1884), German Egyptologist and a founder of modern archaeology. David **Livingstone** (1813-1873) was a Scottish missionary and explorer who influenced early Western attitudes regarding Africa. In 1857, he published his account of the discovery of Victoria Falls in his *Missionary Travels in South Africa*.

14. Saadi or Sa'di, Musharrif od-Din Muslih od-Din (1213-1291), one of Emerson's favorite poets and one of the great figures of classical Persian literature. For the quote see Saadi, *Gulistan* (English: *The Rosegarden*).

15. Pope **Leo X.** (1475-1521) was one of the most extravagant popes. He made Rome a center of European culture and increased the power of the papacy. He also depleted the papal treasury. During the Reformation, he excommunicated Martin Luther. Charles **Townley** was a collector of Roman art and antiquities for the British Museum. The Dukes of **Devonshire** and the **Vernon** family had famous art collections at their palatial homes. **Peel**, see "Fate," above note 73.

16. The *Jardin des Plantes* in Paris, is one of the world's greatest botanical gardens. It was founded as a Royal garden in 1626. The **Philadelphia Academy** of Natural Sciences, founded 1812, is the oldest natural history museum in the United States and supported the early work of Joseph Leidy (1823-1891) in zoology and paleontology. **Bodleian** library: chief library of Oxford University. The great **Ambrosian** library in Milan dates from 1609.

17. James **Cook** (1728-1779), renowned British naval captain and navigator, who explored the seaways and coasts of Canada and conducted expeditions through the Pacific, charting New Zealand and Australia. Sir James Clark **Ross** (1800-1862), British naval officer. Ross carried out magnetic surveys in the Arctic and Antarctic, and he discovered the Ross Sea. Sir John **Franklin** (1786-1847) was an English rear admiral and explorer whose ill-fated expedition is credited with proving the existence of the Northwest Passage, the Canadian Arctic waterway between the Atlantic and the Pacific. Sir John **Richardson** (1787-1865) was a Scottish naval surgeon, explorer, and naturalist who made accurate surveys of the coast of the Canadian Arctic. **Kane**, see note 13, above.

18. "Ablution": the washing of a person's body, or part of it, as in a religious rite.

19. "Inundation": to cover, as with a flood; an overflow; something that overwhelms.

20. "Waif": a foundling; a stray animal; a homeless child.

21. "Skit": a provocative or satirical remark; a satirical or humorous story.

22. "Faro": a betting game based on cards drawn from a dealing box.

23. A Bank-note detector was an early nineteenth-century periodical listing the value of paper notes issued by various American banks.

24. Paisley is a burgh and industrial area in Scotland just west of Glasgow.

25. "Sumptuary laws": Laws designed on moral, religious, or political grounds to regulate extravagant expenditures or habits.

26. "Chaffering": haggling, intensive bargaining.

27. "Ostler": from "hostler;" a worker who takes care of horses or mules.

28. Benjamin **Franklin** was famous for his published advice on how to acquire wealth. Thomas Robert **Malthus** (1766-1834), English economist and demographer, was best known for his theory that population always tends to outrun food supply.

29. The following paragraph was added at this point in the later editions appearing during Emerson's life-time, though it was removed from the posthumous editions:

These were the prevalent opinions in 1850. Yet this result is no more final than the last. We have hardly time to study this adjustment and deplore these disadvantages, before the scale rights itself again, this time disclosing new and immense benefits. For this countless host of immigrants are now seen to be adding by their labor to the wealth of the country. They plant the wilderness with wheat and corn, work the mines for coal and lead and copper and gold, build roads and towns and states, create a market for the manufacturers and commerce of either sea-coast, and swell by their taxes the national treasury.

30. Washington Allston (1779-1843), painter and author, usually regarded as the first important American Romantic painter.

31. Michel de Montaigne (1533-1592), French writer whose *Essays* helped establish the literary form. Emerson's fullest account of Montaigne appeared in his *Representative Men* (1849).

32. "**Purslane**": A family of common, usually succulent herbs, sometimes considered weeds but also eaten as a potherb or in salads. "**Lyed corn**": Hominy.

33. "Arcadian": idyllically pastoral. Emerson explains why he did not join his Transcendentalist colleagues in plans for rural agricultural communes.

34. "Dock": plant of the buckwheat family of coarse weedy plants with long taproots, sometimes used as potherbs; any of several usually broad-leaved weedy plants.

35. "Dun": one who duns; an urgent request or demand for payment.

36. Emerson's philosophy is like Aristotle's, "peripatetic," as is suggested here. He walked for inspiration, and he implicitly rejects the contrary suggestion of Voltaire that one should literally (or figuratively) "cultivate one's own garden." Emerson's more stoic ethics contrast with Voltaire's tendency to the social-epicurean.

37. "Catalepsy": literally, loss of voluntary motion in which the limbs remain rigid.

38. Sir David Brewster (1781-1868) was a Scottish physicist famous for his experiments in optics and polarized light.

39. Not by "sallies and saltations," that is, not by leaps or jumps, as in supposed discontinuous change of one form into another in the course of biological evolution.

40. "Cholera in the potato": potato blight?

41. "To get blown": said of an ox or cow, to become swollen or affected with bloat.

42. "*Impera parendo*," Latin: govern or manage by obeying.

43. The reference is to the building of the British Great Western railroad.

44. Stephenson surveyed and constructed the Liverpool-Manchester line in 1829 and many other railroads in England and elsewhere.

45. Dock-square and Milk-street are locations in old central Boston.

46. The Blue Hills are near Milton and the Atlantic coast, south of Boston, Massachusetts. Wachusett is a mountain peak about thirty miles west of Emerson's home in Concord, near Clinton, Massachusetts. Mt. Monadnock is a solitary mass of rock (3,165 ft.) in Monadnock State Park, southeast of Keene, in Cheshire County, southwestern New Hampshire, and Uncanoonuc is also in southwestern New Hampshire.

47. "To cavil": to make trivial or frivolous objections.

IV. Culture

1. "**Dropsy**": a medical symptom characterized by swelling with water; edema. "**Tympany**": a large orchestral drum; bombast, pomposity; turgidity; swollenness.

2. Joseph **Fouché**, Duke of Ortrant (1758?-1820), French statesman and organizer of the police. With efficiency and opportunism, he served every French government through

the Revolution and under Napoleon. "**Poniards**": daggers. Santorio **Santorio** (1561-1636), Italian physician who first employed precision instruments in medical practice. He studied basal metabolism, in particular, by quantitative and experimental methods. Sir Edward **Coke** (1552-1634) was a British jurist and politician. He defended the common law against the King's powers and influenced the English law and constitution, and he is known for his dictum that "A man's home is his castle."

3. Chorea is a symptom of several diseases, though it is likely Huntington's Chorea in question here. Chorea means brief, variable, and involuntary dance-like movements.

4. "Goiter": enlargement of the thyroid gland visible as a swelling of the front of the neck; here used metaphorically.

5. Emerson met the painter Washington **Allston** in Florence in 1833, during his first trip to Europe, as reported in Emerson's *English Traits* (1856). William Ellery **Channing** (1780-1842) was an American author, moralist, and Unitarian clergyman. He was a leading light for the New England Transcendentalists and in organizing opposition to slavery, poverty, and war. John Quincy **Adams**, sixth President of the U.S. (1825-1829) and eldest son of President John Adams. In his later career as U.S. Congressman from Massachusetts (1831-1848), he fought the expansion of slavery. Horatio **Greenough** (1805-1852), neoclassical sculptor and writer on art. His writings on architecture are closely associated with functionalism. See his essays in Greenough 1947, *Form and Function.*

6. Edward **Everett** (1794-1865) was Professor of Greek Literature at Harvard University. He served in the U.S. House of Representatives (1825-1835), as Governor of Massachusetts (1835-1839), and as American ambassador to England (1841-1845). After becoming President of Harvard in 1846, he withdrew from politics for several years, but returned in 1852 as Secretary of State. In 1853 he entered the U.S. Senate. Everett was a teacher to Emerson and helped bring higher-biblical criticism to America. William Lloyd **Garrison** (1805-1879), American journalist, radical champion of the abolition of slavery, and publisher of *The Liberator* (1831-1865). "Father" Edward **Taylor**, Methodist clergyman, Pastor of the Seamen's Bethel Chapel (immortalized by Melville in *Moby Dick*), and friend of Emerson's. Charles Dickens described Taylor and his mission in his *American Notes* (1842), ch. 3, "The only preacher I heard in Boston was Mr. Taylor, who addresses himself peculiarly to seamen, and who was once a mariner himself. I found his chapel down among the shipping, in one of the narrow, old, water-side streets, with a gay blue flag waving freely from its roof. In the gallery opposite to the pulpit were a little choir of male and female singers, a violoncello, and a violin. The preacher already sat in the pulpit; which was raised on pillars, and ornamented behind him with painted drapery of a lively and somewhat theatrical appearance. He looked a weather-beaten, hard-featured man, of about six or eight and fifty; with deep lines graven as it were into his face, dark hair, and a stern, keen eye. Yet the general character of his countenance was pleasant and agreeable."

7. Theodore Parker (1810-1860) Unitarian theologian, pastor, scholar, and social reformer who was long active in the anti-slavery movement.

8. "Bantling": literally, a very young child .

9. "Dominie": minister or schoolmaster.

10. Plato (428/427-348/347 BC), Greek philosopher. Plato was the greatest student of Socrates and teacher to Aristotle. See Plato, *Laws* VII, 808d.

11. George Gascoigne (1525-1577), English poet and Renaissance literary innovator.

12. Marshal Jean Lannes, Duke of Montebello (1769-1809) was a General under Napoleon during the First Empire.

13. "Poltroon": person lacking in spirit; cowardly.

14. Robert Owen (1771-1858), Welsh manufacturer who became a reformer and utopian socialist. He sponsored several experimental communities including New Harmony, Indiana.

15. "Poltroonery": mean, pusillanimity; cowardice.

16. "Trope": the use of a word or expression in a figurative sense.

17. John Milton (1608-1674), English poet. Milton is best known for Paradise Lost, one of the greatest epic poems in the English language.

18. *Gradus*: steps (of learning).

19. Walter Savage Landor (1775-1864), English writer best remembered for *Imaginary Conversations*, prose dialogues between historical personages.

20. Baron Herbert of Cherbury (1583-1648) was an English soldier, diplomat, historian, poet, and philosopher, said to be the father of English Deism.

21. "Captious": often ill-natured tendency to stress faults and objections.

22. "Sedulously": involving careful perseverance; diligent in application or pursuit

23. Cf. Emerson 1841, "Self-Reliance" in *Essays, First Series*, "Traveling is a fool's paradise," a statement for which he was much criticized. Here we find a reply to his critics.

24. "Solstice": here metaphorically, a high or low point.

25. Charles Thomas Jackson (1805-1880), American physician and chemist who worked in the early application of ether as an anesthetic.

26. John **Aubrey** (1626-1697), English writer, known for his intimate and sometimes very critical biographical sketches of his contemporaries. Thomas **Hobbes** (1588-1679), English philosopher and political thinker, famous for his emphasis on the need of individual security and on the idea of the social contract, important in the background of liberalism and for political absolutism in his times.

27. "Paling": a fence of pales or pickets.

28. Quoted from John Aubrey's *Brief Lives*, p. 153 in Barber's 1982 edition.

29. Thomas **Fuller** (1608-1661), British scholar, preacher, and a witty and prolific biographic author of the seventeenth century. **William I.**, called, the Silent, was the prince of Orange and led the revolt of the Netherlands against Philip II. and Spain from 1568 to his death in 1584.

30. Madame de Staël (1766-1817) was a French-Swiss literary figure, conversationalist, and theorist of Romanticism. She exemplified the European culture of her time, gaining considerable fame with her intellectual salons. Her writings include novels, plays, moral and political essays, literary criticism, history, autobiographical memoirs, and poems.

31. "Levee": a reception usually in honor of a particular person.

32. Robert **Burns** (1759-1796), national poet of Scotland, who wrote in the Scottish dialect of English. Sir Walter **Scott** (1771-1832), Scottish novelist, poet, historian, and biographer, author of *Waverly* and *Rob Roy* among many other historical novels. Ludwig van **Beethoven** (1770-1827), German composer. The Duke of **Wellington** (1769-1852), victor over Napoleon at Waterloo and later Prime Minister of Britain.

Epaminondas (410-362 BC), Theban statesman and military leader who was responsible for breaking the military dominance of Sparta.

33. "Box coat": a heavy nineteenth-century overcoat worn for driving.

34. *Emerson's note*: Beaumont and Fletcher: *The Tamer Tamed*. [John Fletcher (1579-1625) and Francis Beaumont (1584-1616) were English dramatists. This is likely a reference to the selections from these two authors in the 1855 London edition of their works with an Introduction by Leigh Hunt.]

35. Richard Monckton Milnes (1809-1885), English Victorian poet and writer, influential on public literary taste. Milnes helped establish Emerson's reputation in Great Britain.

36. William **Pitt** (1708-1778), the elder, called "the Great Commoner," was a British statesman, twice chief minister, and he transformed Britain into an imperial power. John **Pym** (1583-1643) was an powerful member of Parliament and formative in Parliament's victory over King Charles I. in the early phase of the English Civil Wars.

37. *Emerson's note*: Béranger. [Pierre-Jean de Béranger (1780-1857) was a French poet and writer of popular songs, who was celebrated for his liberal and humanitarian views.]

38. "Myrmidons": ant-men, according to a Greek myth; minions: subordinates who relentlessly carry out orders.

39. William Wordsworth (1770-1850), English poet and Poet Laureate of England (1843-1850). Along with Samuel Taylor Coleridge, he helped start English Romanticism. Emerson visited Wordsworth 28 August 1833, at Rydal Mount, Westmoreland, England.

40. **Plotinus** (205-270 AD), ancient Hellenistic philosopher, regarded as the founder of the neo-Platonic philosophy. **Archimedes** (*ca.* 290-280 to 212 or 211 BC), Greek mathematician and inventor. **Hermes** Trismegistos, ancient mythical author (identified with an Egyptian god) of religious and philosophical texts.

41. Probably the influential, Jewish-born, Lutheran church historian Johann **Neander** (1789-1850) who followed theologian Friedrich Schleiermacher from Halle and also became Professor in Berlin. **Halle** is a university town in eastern Germany and a home of the Martin Luther University "*Civitas Dei*," Latin: City of God.

42. An alternative account of "double consciousness."

43. "*à l'outrance*," French: In excessive degree or manner.

44. Thomas **Fairfax** (1612-1671) was commander of the Parliamentary army during the English Civil Wars. Lazare **Carnot** (1753-1823), called "Organizer of the victory": French statesman, general, and official of the French Revolution. See the biographies by Duprè 1975 and Gillispie 1971 which include an account of Carnot's political and scientific work.

45. Horace, Quintus **Horatius** Flaccus (65-8 BC), Latin lyric poet and satirist under the emperor Augustus. His most frequent themes are love, friendship, philosophy, and poetry. Marcus Valerius Martialis **Martial** (38-41-*ca.* 103 AD), Roman poet famous for his Latin epigrams and who provides a picture of Roman society during the early empire, complete with multiple human foibles. Pedro **Calderón** de la Barca (1600-1681), Spanish dramatist and poet.

46. Saint John the Evangelist or Saint John the Divine (fl. first century AD), the author, according to Christian tradition, of three letters, one of the Gospels, and Revelations in the New Testament.

47. Anaxagoras (*ca.* 500-428 BC), ancient Greek philosopher of nature known for his cosmology and his conception of "*nous*" or mind. He was allied with the Athenian statesman Pericles.

48. John Adams (1735-1826) second President of the United States.

49. Ben Jonson (1572-1637), English playwright, lyric poet, and critic. He is often regarded as the second most important English playwright, after Shakespeare. See Jonson's *Epigrammes*.

50. Coventry, English town. To be "sent to Coventry" means to enter a state of ostracism or exclusion.

51. Porphyry (*ca.* 234-305, AD) was a Neoplatonist philosopher. He is known as an editor and biographer of Plotinus and for his commentary on Aristotle's *Categories*.

52. Marcus Aurelius Antoninus Augustus (121-180 AD) was Roman Emperor (161-180 AD) and a Stoic philosopher famous for his *Meditations*. Marcus Aurelius symbolizes for many the cultural and ethical high point of the Roman Empire.

53. Bettine von Arnim (1785-1859) was a foremost women writer of modern German literature. Bettine idolized Goethe; and she visited and corresponded with Goethe's mother to recorded stories from the poet's childhood. She professed her chief maxim of action was to be independent: "*Eigenmächtig sein.*"

54. "Secular": lacking monastic vows; pertaining to clergy not belonging to a religious order or community; happening once in an age or a century, or lasting over ages; pertaining to a long term or indefinite duration. Thus "secular melioration" means improvement over the long-term by a slow cumulative process, as in the growth of knowledge or wisdom—as contrasted with plans and aims based on binding organizational forms and orthodoxy.

55. "Chrysalis": a pupa of a butterfly; a protecting covering; a sheltered stage of growth.

56. Also called *Gehinnom*, dwelling place of the damned in the afterlife in Jewish and Christian eschatology (the doctrine of last things).

V. Behavior

1. "Tableaux": a graphic description or representation; picture.

2. "Mien:" manner or bearing, often expressing attitude or personality; demeanor.

3. "Consuelo": 1842 novel, and character of the novel, by the French woman George Sand (pen name of Amandine-Aurore-Lucile Dudevant).

4. François-Joseph Talma (1763-1826) was a French actor and theatrical manager who won the patronage of Napoleon.

5. "Abstergent": cleansing, detergent.

6. Asmodeus, Hebrew: *Ashmedai*. In Jewish legend, Asmodeus was king of demons. In the non-canonical book of Tobit, Asmodeus was in love with Sarah, and he killed Sarah's seven successive husbands each on their wedding night. In the Talmud, Solomon captures the demon and enslaved him for the building of the Temple at Jerusalem.

7. See Dickens 1842, *American Notes*, which tells of meeting Emerson. Received with honor as a literary celebrity, in 1842, Dickens also offended American sensibilities with his protests. Dickens says, of Emerson "This gentleman has written a volume of Essays, in which, among much that is dreamy and fanciful (if he will pardon me for

saying so), there is much more that is true and manly, honest and bold. Transcendentalism has its occasional vagaries (what school has not?), but it has good healthful qualities in spite of them; not least among the number a hearty disgust of Cant, and an aptitude to detect her in all the million varieties of her everlasting wardrobe. And therefore, if I were a Bostonian, I think I would be a Transcendentalist." See ch. 3, "Boston."

8. "Factitious": formed by special efforts or adapted to artificial or conventional standard.

9. Matthew Calbraith Perry (1794-1858) was an American naval officer. His expedition in 1853-1854 forced Japan to open itself to trade and diplomatic relations with the West.

10. "Fop": a fool or dandy.

11. "Puissant": powerful.

12. Abdel-Kader, also written Abdul-Qadir (1808-1883) military and religious leader of nineteenth-century Algeria who led the country in its struggle against France.

13. "Furtive": done by stealth: surreptitious.

14. "Lacedaemon ": Sparta.

15. Johann **Winckelmann** (1717-1768) was a German archaeologist and art historian whose writings directed taste toward classical art and ancient Greece. Johann Kaspar **Lavater** (1741-1801), Swiss writer, Protestant pastor, an associate of Goethe, and founder of an anti-rational, religious, and literary movement.

16. Honoré de Balzac (1799-1850) was a French writer. He helped establish the classical novel and is considered one of the greatest writers of fiction.

17. "*Théorie de la démarche*," French: Theory of the walk or posture.

18. Louis de Rouvroy Duke of **Saint-Simon** (1675-1755), French soldier and writer. His *Mémoires* are an insightful historic document of the court of Louis XIV. and of the following period. Jean-François-Paul de Gondi, **Cardinal de Retz** (1613-1679) was a leader of the aristocratic rebellion known as the Fronde (1648-1653). His memoirs are a classic of seventeenth-century French literature. Comte Pierre Louis **Roederer**, politician of the French Revolution and of the Napoleonic era who later wrote history.

19. Henry Richard Vassall Fox, third Baron of Holland (1773-1840), British Whig politician, an associate of the party leader, and nephew and follower of Charles James Fox. As Minister, he helped to secure the abolition of the slave trade in the British colonies.

20. James **Northcote** (1746-1831), English portraitist, painter, and a rival of Fuseli. Henry **Fuseli** (1741-1825), Swiss-born painter who made his career in England. Fuseli's works are among the most original and romantic pieces of his time.

21. "Pariah": a member of a low caste of southern India; an outcast.

22. **Euripides** (*ca.* 484-406 BC) Greek writer of tragedy in classical Athens. **Aspasia** (fl. fifth century BC) was the mistress of the Athenian statesman Pericles and a lively figure in Athenian society, continually subject to public attack. **Sophocles** (*ca.* 496-406 BC) Athenian writer of tragedy and older contemporary of Euripides.

23. *Emerson's note*: Landor: Pericles and Aspasia.

24. Cassandra, in Greek mythology, is daughter of Priam, the last king of Troy. She was given the power of prophecy but cursed that no one would believe her.

25. The royal colossi of ancient Egypt were ritual sculptures which expressed the grandeur and power of the king.

26. **Aristotle** (384-322 BC), Plato's student and his chief rival in terms of influence on the development of Western philosophy. Gottfried Wilhelm **Leibniz** (1646-1716) was a German philosopher and mathematician. Noted for his work in logic, he set himself the goal of creating a universal language. He also wrote metaphysics, including the *Theodicy*, mentioned above, "Fate," note 9. Along with his contemporary, Newton, he is credited with inventing the calculus. The connection to "grammar," suggests that this is Franz **Junius** the younger (1589-1677), librarian to Thomas Howard, Earl of Arundel. Junius contributed much to the study of Anglo-Saxon (Old English) and related Germanic languages. Jean-François **Champollion** (1790-1832), French historian and linguist who played the chief role in deciphering ancient Egyptian hieroglyphics.

27. Sanskrit is the ancient Indo-European language of the Hindu scriptures.

28. Friedrich Heinrich Jacobi (1743-1819), German philosopher and advocate of a philosophy of feeling and belief. Jacobi was a critic of rationalism, especially that of Spinoza, professing the superiority of immediate feeling as contrasted with reason.

29. "Phlegethon," from Greek legend: a river of fire in the underworld of Hades.

30. "Elysian Fields": ancient conception of paradise, where the dead would enjoy an ideal agricultural life in a marshy land of abundance.

31. Marcus Aemilius Scaurus (*ca.* 162-89 BC) was an influential Senator in the Roman Republic about 100 BC. At the outbreak of the Social War in 90 BC, his enemies charged him with intriguing with the allies. He was acquitted.

VI. Worship

1. "Cerebus": a three-headed dog in Greek mythology, requiring to be placated, because guarding the entrance to the underworld of Hades.

2. Ralph Cudworth (1617-1688) was a non-conformist English theologian and philosopher and the leading exponent of Cambridge Platonism. John Dryden said that Cudworth's defense of theism "has raised such strong objections against the being of a God and Providence that many think he has not answered them," though this was Cudworth's aim.

3. "**Behmenism**": A reference to the doctrines and influence of Jakob Böhme (1575-1624), German philosophical mystic, who had a deep influence on various intellectual and religious movements including idealism and romanticism. "**Romanism**": the doctrines or traditions of the Roman Catholic church. "**Mormonism**": the doctrines of the (originally American) Church of the Latter Day Saints.

4. "Azote": French for nitrogen, which does not alone support fire or life.

5. John **Calvin** (1509-1564), French-Swiss leader of early Protestantism and an important influence on English and Scottish Protestants–eventually including the New England Puritans, the Presbyterians, Baptists, etc. His influence is directly represented in America by the philosopher and theologian Jonathan Edwards. François de Salignac de La Mothe **Fénelon** (1651-1715) was a French archbishop, theologian, and writer whose liberal views on politics and education brought him opposition from both church and state. Following Louis XIV.'s revocation of the Edict of Nantes, and toleration of Protestants, in 1685, Fénelon rejected forced conversions. John **Wesley**

(1703-1791), clergyman, evangelist, and co-founder of the Methodist movement within the Church of England.

6. Cf. Revelations, 4 and 5.

7. "Votary": staunch believer or advocate.

8. "Petulant": insolent or rude; peevish.

9. Laomedon is the legendary King of Troy and father of King Priam.

10. *Emerson's note*: Homer, *Iliad*, Book xxi. l. 455.

11. Olaf, King of Sweden (990-1022) who, according to the Icelandic Sagas, attempted to impose Christianity but was blocked by the Swedish chieftains.

12. "Fere," from Old English: companion, comrade.

13. *Emerson's note*: "Mathen": Moths or worms.

14. King Richard I. is Richard the Lion-hearted, known from the story of Robin Hood.

15. "Womanhede": womanhood.

16. "Scortatory": pertaining to lewdness.

17. "To maunder": to wander slowly and idly; to speak indistinctly or disconnectedly.

18. "Mesmerism": Originally popular pseudo-scientific doctrines of Franz Anton Mesmer (1734-1815); more generally, hypnotic induction held to involve animal magnetism; hypnotism and hypnotic power.

19. "Mummery": ridiculous, hypocritical, or pretentious ceremony.

20. The point here is closely related to Emerson's themes in his "Divinity School Address" (1838).

21. "The question of God lacks for contemporary interest."

22. William Ewart Gladstone (1809-1898), British statesman and four-time Liberal Prime Minister of Great Britain.

23. See Gladstone's *Gleamings of Past Years*.

24. Senator William Henry Seward of New York (later Lincoln's Secretary of State) used the phrase "higher law" in a famous 1850 speech against compromise with slavery; the high rhetoric was equated with subversion of the constitutional status of slavery. Emerson equates rejection of higher law with stupidity and lack of faith.

25. Death by "sea-storm" again evokes the memory of Emerson's friend Margaret Fuller; the reader might be invited to doubt that America is "the best of all possible worlds" in view of skepticism and prevalent anti-intellectualism.

26. "Enginery": instruments of war.

27. Paraphrase of Blaise Pascal from the *Pensées*.

28. Notice the implied contrast between "common sense" and higher moral sensibility, which suggests a similar contrast between accepted moral sentiment and higher sensibility. Emerson gives a taste of his critical perspective on the "common sense" school of philosophy in the American universities of his day.

29. Emerson returns to his theme of compensation. Good deeds, will be and are to be rewarded, and the opposite are ultimately punished.

30. Not only the moral sentiment of the present but also that which we may come to have.

31. Paraphrase from the *Vishnu Purana*. Cf. H.H. Wilson, 1979.

32. The point compares to Einstein's dictum that God does not play dice with the universe. In contrast, Emerson allows a foreground of chance, rejecting a "pistareen-

Providence" (see above, "Fate," note 7), but he holds that the dice of chance are loaded.

33. "Muniment": the evidence (such as documents) needed to defend the title to an estate or a claim to rights and privileges.

34. Thomas à Kempis: attributed author of *The Imitation of Christ*, a classic expression of Catholic devotion written between 1390 and 1440.

35. Crystal Palace: giant glass-and-iron exhibition hall in Hyde Park, London, used for the Great Exhibition of 1851.

36. Notice here the influence of the ancient Stoics. It is not distant consequences of work which chiefly count toward success, but the work itself.

37. San Filippo Neri (1515-1595), canonized 1622; Italian priest and a preeminent mystic of the Counter-Reformation.

38. "Arnica": a European plant, once used in treatment bruises and sprains.

39. Cf. Peter Eckermann, *Gespräche mit Goethe*, 1998, p. 316.

40. William of Orange (1650-1702), Stadholder of the Netherlands as William III. (1672-1702) and King of Great Britain (1689-1702). William organized the European opposition to Louis XIV. of France and in Britain represented the triumph of Protestantism and Parliament following the Glorious Revolution of 1688.

41. Vishnu Sarma: Sanskrit sage and attributed author of the *Hitopadesha* or "Friendly Instruction."

42. "Pusillanimity": cowardliness or lack of resolution.

43. Marcus Aurelius, *Meditations*, Book 2. In an alternative translation, the statement is: "But to go away from among men, if there are gods, is not a thing to be afraid of, for the gods will not involve thee in evil; but if indeed they do not exist, . . . , what is it to me to live in a universe devoid of gods or devoid of Providence?" Marcus then continues: "But in truth they do exist, and they do care for human things, and they have put all the means in man's power to enable him not to fall into real evils."

44. Freedom here requires obedience to the moral law, though we are obligated, too, sometimes, to first discover it. Emerson's conception of freedom involves an evolving moral realism, expressed in his religious language.

45. "**Shawm**": an early double-reed woodwind instrument. "**Psaltery**": an ancient musical instrument resembling the zither. "**Sackbut**": hooked lance or the medieval and Renaissance trombone.

VII. Considerations by the Way

1. "Garrulity": talkativeness; tendency to senseless or annoying talk.

2. Emerson records medical advice in his journals of 1859: "On Wachusett, I sprained my foot. It was slow to heal and I went to the doctors. Dr. Henry Bigelow said, 'Splint and absolute rest.' Dr. Russell said, 'Rest, yes; but splint no.' Dr. Bartlett said, 'Neither splint nor rest, but go and walk.' Dr. Russell said, 'Pour water on the foot, but it must be warm.' Dr. Jackson said 'Stand in a trout brook all day'. "

3. Cf. Psalms, 115: 1.

4. Sydney Smith (1771-1845) was an English preacher, an advocate of parliamentary reform, and one of the founders of *The Edinburgh Review*. His writings deeply influenced public opinion toward Roman Catholic emancipation.

5. Honoré-Gabriel Riqueti, comte de Mirabeau (1749-1791) was a French politician and orator and a figure in the National Assembly that governed France during the early years of the Revolution. He was a moderate advocate of constitutional monarchy.

6. "Torpid": dormant, benumbed; lacking in vigor; apathetic, dull.

7. "Fribble": a frivolous person, thing, or idea; a person lacking serious commitment.

8. "Pedantry": characterized by narrow, dull or old-fashioned, or ostentatious learning.

9. "Prating": idle chatter.

10. Emerson comments on the plight of mill workers in *English Traits* (1856): "The incessant repetition of the same hand-work dwarfs the man, robs him of his strength, wit, and versatility, to make a pin-polisher, a buckle-maker, or any other specialty; . . . , in a change of industry, whole towns are sacrificed like ant-hills, when the fashion of shoe-strings supersedes buckles, when cotton takes the place of linen, . . . or when commons are enclosed by landlords. Then society is admonished of the mischief of the division of labor, and that the best political economy is care and culture of men; for, in these crises, all are ruined except such as are proper individuals, capable of thought, and of new choice and the application of their talent to new labor."

11. "*Lazzaroni*," Italian: the (monarchist) Neapolitan poor.

12. In 480 BC 300 Spartan heroes under King Leonidas fought a famous battle on behalf of the Greeks against an enormous invading Persian army at the narrow pass of Thermopylae.

13. "*Cent mille*," French: Hundred thousand.

14. "Coxcomb": (from a word for the jester's hat) a fool; a person conceited and foolish.

15. "Acridity": irritating sharpness of taste or odor; bitterness, acrimoniousness.

16. "Pupilage": The state or time of being a pupil.

17. **Socrates**: Greek philosopher and teacher to Plato, who flourished in the last half of the fifth century BC. Francis **Bacon** (1561-1626) was an English lawyer, statesman, and philosopher; among many other works, he is the author of the *Novum Organum* (1620), on the advancement of knowledge. He famously held that "knowledge is power" and "Nature to be commanded must first be obeyed." For a critical discussion of Bacon see Emerson's early lecture "English Literature," in Whicher and Spiller eds. *The Early Lectures of Ralph Waldo Emerson*, Vol. 1, pp. 320-336. **Erasmus** of Rotterdam (1469-1536), great European scholar of the sixteenth century. He criticized abuses in the church and pointed to a better age in the ancient world, thus encouraged reform, both the Reformation and the Catholic Counter-Reformation. He was a man of independent conviction in a time of dangerous controversy, disputing both predestination and the power of the Papacy. He was a target for partisans on both sides. François **Rabelais** (1494-1553), French writer and priest who was an eminent physician and humanist and the author of the comic masterpiece *Gargantua and Pantagruel*, a work ranging from bawdy humor to profound satire. Chevalier de **Boufflers** (1738-1815), French writer, soldier, and academician. He left France for Germany during the French Revolution.

18. William I., or William the Conqueror (1028-1087), King of England and Duke of Normandy, who lead the Norman invasion of England in 1066. *Magna Charta*: the Great Charter of English liberties, granted by King John in 1215 under threat of civil war. Edward I. (1239-1307), son of Henry III., was king of England from 1272 to 1307.

19. Friedrich Schiller (1759-1805), German playwright, poet, historian, and literary theorist. Emerson's point here relates to Schiller's *History of the Thirty Years' War*, and his portrait of the power-seeking imperial commander in the *Wallenstein* cycle.

20. Oliver Cromwell (1599-1658), English soldier, statesman and devout Calvinist, was Lord Protector of the republican Commonwealth of England, Scotland, and Ireland from 1653 to 1658.

21. "Insipid": dull, flat, uninteresting.

22. "Not Antoninus": that is, not Marcus Aurelius, from whom we might expect a Stoic doctrine.

23. "Sabine": member of an ancient Italic tribe long in conflict with the Romans. There is a legend, recounted by Plutarch, that Romulus, the founder of Rome, invited the Sabines to a feast and then carried off (and raped) their women.

24. **Alfred** the Great (849-899), king of Wessex, a Saxon kingdom in southwestern England. He prevented England from falling to the Danes and promoted learning and literacy. John **Howard** (1726-1790), English philanthropist and reformer of prisons and public health. Johann Heinrich **Pestalozzi** (1746-1827), Swiss educator and reformer, who advocated education of the poor and aimed to strengthen the student's own abilities. Elizabeth **Fry** (1780-1845), British Quaker philanthropist and one of the chief promoters of prison reform in Europe. Florence **Nightingale** (1820-1910) was an English nurse and a founder of professional nursing. She is famous for her work in a military hospital during the Crimean War.

25. "Believe me, error also has its merit."

26. Cf. Psalms, 76:10.

27. Cf. Shakespeare, *Measure for Measure*, V. i., ". . . And, for the most, become much more the better . . . "

28. Marcus Cornelius Fronto (100-166 AD) was a Roman orator, rhetorician, and grammarian whose high reputation was based chiefly on his (lost) orations.

29. Charles James Fox (1749-1806) was the first Foreign Secretary of Great Britain and an advocate of liberty, famous for his opposition to King George III. and for his support for American independence. He brought through Parliament a resolution pledging it to abolish the slave trade and also the 1792 Libel Act, which strengthen the role of juries.

30. **Aesop** is the legendary author of a collection of Greek fables, important for the morals drawn. He is said to have once been a slave and later advisor to a King. **Socrates** claimed to know nothing except his own ignorance. Cicero said that Socrates "brought down philosophy from heaven to earth,"—from cosmological speculation to morals. Miguel de **Cervantes** lived as a soldier, was wounded in battle, and was later captured by privateers of the Barbary Coast and sold into slavery in Algiers. There are stories, current long after **Shakespeare**'s death, of his poaching deer and getting into trouble with the local gentry; working as a country school teacher; going to London and associating with the theater by taking care of the horses of theatergoers; it has also been claimed that he was once a soldier, perhaps in the Low Countries. The story of Benjamin **Franklin**'s rise from poverty to wealth, influence, and wisdom is supplied by his *Autobiography*.

31. "Cockered": indulged, pampered.

32. In "Bleeding Kansas," before the Civil War, civil strife between the contending parties defeated a proposed political compromise of "popular (local) sovereignty" on slavery in the territories.

33. **Saadi** is said to have been captured by crusaders and taken as a prisoner to the West, returning home after many adventures. See Goethe's *Divan* (1819), 1998, p. 159. Jean-François **Regnard** (1655-1709) was one of the most successful French dramatist after Molière. He traveled extensively, and when captured by Algerian pirates, was imprisoned for seven months until ransomed by his family.

34. Faneuil Hall, Boston. The victims of the Boston massacre at the start of the American Revolution were carried to Faneuil Hall, and it has remained ever since a scene of patriotic devotions in public address.

35. "Ennui": weariness and dissatisfaction; boredom.

36. "Turkish cadi": a minor judge or administrator.

37. The Berkshire Hills are a segment of the Appalachian Mountains, mainly in Berkshire County, western Massachusetts.

38. Charles-Maurice de Talleyrand (1754-1838) was a French statesman and diplomat noted for political survival. He held high office during the French Revolution, under Napoleon, under the restored Bourbon monarchy, and under King Louis-Philippe.

39. Ali Ibn Abu Talib (*ca.* 600-661), son-in-law of Mohammad, and fourth Caliph, reigning from 656 to 661 AD. Ali is revered by the Shiites as the true successor of the Prophet.

40. "Pudency": modesty, freedom from conceit or vanity.

41. "Hussy": a shameless, immodest, or mischievous woman or girl.

42. "Tutelar": concerning or performing the office of a guardian.

43. "Harridan": a shrew; an ill-tempered, difficult, or harshly critical woman.

44. John Horne Tooke (1736-1812), radical politician and supporter of the American Revolution. Tooke was one of the most effective English advocates of parliamentary reform and freedom of dissent in the late eighteenth century.

45. Jeremiah, 45:5.

VIII. Beauty

1. "Marl": loose earthy deposits containing calcium carbonate and useful as fertilizer.

2. "Alluvium": clay, silt, sand, gravel, or similar materials.

3. William Charles Macready (1793-1873) was an English actor and theater manager.

4. "Chicane": to use chicanery: to trick, cheat.

5. "To rive": to tear or split with force or violence.

6. Cf. Goethe, *Maximen und Reflexionen.* This is substantially the neo-classical conception of the educational role of aesthetics in moral development.

7. Cupid: Roman god of love corresponding to the Greek Eros and to Amour in Latin poetry. According to myth, Cupid was son of Mercury, the messenger of the gods, and Venus, the goddess of love; he is represented as a winged infant carrying a bow and arrows. The wounds of his arrows inspired love or passion in his victims.

8. The Pre-Raphaelite painters sought to express moral seriousness and sincerity in their works and were inspired by Italian art of the fourteenth and fifteenth centuries— before Raphael.

9. "Imperious": commanding, overbearing, extremely compelling.

10. From the name of Amelia Bloomer, an American feminist reformer who campaigned for temperance and women's rights: a nineteenth-century woman's costume consisting of a skirt over long loose trousers gathered closely around the ankles.

11. Note the aesthetic constraint on feminist reforms: an elegant gradualism.

12. "Alar strength": strength of wing.

13. This passage expresses the functionalist conception of art and beauty which brought Emerson to his admiration for Horatio Greenough and especially his writings on architecture. Beauty is conceived as a functional elegance, the economy of means effectively serving an end. See Emerson's comments on Greenough in *English Traits*.

14. "Nothing so beautiful as the truth."

15. "Spermaceti": a waxy solid from whales used in ointments, cosmetics, and candles.

16. The **Belvedere Apollo** (Roman copy, Vatican Museum). The original is attributed to the Greek sculptor Leochares (mid-fourth century BC). The **Venus** de Milo, ancient statue of Aphrodite, Greek goddess of love, now at the Louvre Museum. Carved by a sculptor of Antioch about 150 BC, it was found on the Aegean island of Melos in 1820. **Parthenon**, chief temple of the Greek goddess Athena at the Acropolis in Athens. The name refers to the cult of Athena Parthenos (Athena the Virgin). The Temple of **Vesta** in the Roman Forum was of great antiquity and maintained through republican and imperial times. There burned the perpetual fire of the public hearth attended by the Vestal Virgins.

17. Horatio Walpole (1717-1797), English writer, connoisseur, and collector. The youngest son of the prime minister Sir Robert Walpole, he is now famous chiefly for his correspondence, recounting the manners and taste of his times. Elizabeth and Maria Gunning were famous beauties in the court of George II.

18. "Post chaise": a type of horse carriage.

19. "Contumely": harsh language or treatment arising from haughtiness and contempt.

20. Gilles **Ménage** (1613-1692) was a French scholar and man of letters who worked in philology and conducted weekly literary meetings for some 30 years. Louis **Le Bailleul** , high official of the Royal French government.

21. Robert Hooke (1635-1703), English physicist who discovered the law of elasticity, "Hooke's law," and who entered into a great debate with Newton.

22. Bertrand du Guesclin (1320-1380), French national hero of the Hundred Years' War.

23. Sir Philip Sidney (1554-1586), courtier, statesman, soldier, poet, and patron of letters and poetry in the day of Elizabeth I. He was widely considered the ideal gentleman.

24. "Lineaments": outline, features, or contours of the body, figure or the face; distinguishing or characteristic features.

25. Proclus (*ca.* 410-485 AD), the last major Greek Neoplatonist philosopher.

26. From William Wordsworth, "Elegiac Stanzas Suggested by a Picture of Peele Castle in a Storm by Sir George Beaumont" (1805).

27. The most famous of the secret religious rites of ancient Greece. The rites, performed in the Hall of Initiation at Eleusis, were and remain a secret.

28. Or, the "splendid power of form."

IX. Illusions

1. Mammoth Cave is now part of a National Park in west-central Kentucky.
2. "Acanthus": an ornamentation (as in a Corinthian capital) representing or suggesting the leaves of the Mediterranean acanthus plant.
3. **"Lethe"**: a river in the Greek underworld whose waters cause drinkers to forget their past; thus, forgetfulness, oblivion. **"Styx"**: the principal river of the Greek underworld. **"Acanthus"**: Motif in architecture and decoration, starting from the Greeks, which resembles the Mediterranean plant *Acanthus spinosus*. **"Bengal lights"**: a kind of flare.
4. "Domino": long hooded cloak or also the half mask worn as a masquerade costume.
5. Jean le Rond d'Alembert (1717-1783) was a French mathematician and Enlightenment philosopher. "An attack of the vapors [depression] was very distressing, since it made us see things as they are."
6. **"Yoganidra"**: another name for the Hindu god Maya, personification of illusion. In Greek mythology, **Proteus**, who knew all, assumed various shapes to escape questions. He is often taken as a symbol of the original matter entering into all creation. **"Momus"**: Greek god of censure and mockery. **"Gylfi"**: Swedish king of Icelandic mythology. In answer to his questions, the gods tell Gylfi the Norse myths about the beginning of the world, the adventures of the gods, and the fate of all in the twilight of the gods. **"Titans"**: powerful and dreadful progenitors of the ancient Greeks' Olympian gods. **"Apollo"**: Greek god symbolizing reason and rational order.
7. "Charivari": a noisy serenade suggestive of satire.
8. "Risibility": the ability or inclination to laugh.
9. "Hist a boy": Sic 'em!
10. "Comity": friendly social atmosphere: social harmony; a loose widespread community based on common social institutions.
11. "Chaff": seed coverings and debris separated from the seed; thing of little value.
12. "Frippery": showy, frivolous; ostentatious, foolish, or affected elegance.
13. **Claude Lorraine**, artistic name of Claude Gellée (1600-1682), French artist known for ideal-landscape painting—which seeks to present a view of nature more beautiful and harmonious than nature itself. "To pluck away the *coulisses*": to see behind the stage settings.
14. A Pandora's box: from Greek mythology, a prolific source of troubles.
15. **Teague** is an Irish footman, in Sir Robert Howard's (1626-1698) popular play, "The Committee," a comedy satirizing the Puritan Commonwealth. **"Jade"**: disreputable or flirtatious woman.
16. "Jackstraws": somewhat like "Pick-up-sticks," a game in which a set of straws falls in a pile and each player tries to remove one at a time without disturbing the others.
17. Mizar and Alcor are stars in the Orion nebula. The ability to distinguish Alcor ("the dim one") may have been used by the Arabs as a test of good vision. Alcor makes a visual double with Mizar in the middle of the handle of the Big Dipper.
18. In Norse mythology, **Thor** is the god of thunder. **"Asgard"**: The home of the Norse gods. **"Lok"**: also Loki, a cunning trickster among the Norse gods.

19. "To vamp": nineteenth-century usage, to patch.

20. Emerson's "transcendentalist" theme survives, at least in this derivative form, by keeping intellectual integrity and virtue at the center of his method. Emphasis on Colridgean unity, comprehension, and organization of inquiries resembles the emphasis on self-control among the Stoics and in the Reformation. This is no mere subjectivism.

21. *Éclat*, French: Grandeur of appearance, shattering affect, sparkle, or pomp. Compare Emerson "Self-Reliance" (1841), "As soon as he has once acted or spoken with *éclat* he is a committed person, watched by the sympathy or the hatred of hundreds, whose affections must now enter into his account."

22. Here, and in the following paragraph, we find the book's final statement on the theme of fate and freedom.

23. **Heraclitus**, Greek philosopher (fl. 500 BC), native of Ephesus. He argued that we cannot step in the same river twice, since new waters are always flowing by. **Xenophanes** (*ca.* 560-*ca.*478 BC), Greek poet, rhapsodist, and religious thinker, is the reputed precursor of Parmenides and the Eleatic school—which stressed unity over diversity and viewed the separate existences of material things as mere appearance. **Diogenes** of Apollonia (fl. fifth century BC) was a Greek philosopher remembered for his cosmology and his efforts to synthesize details of observation.

A BRIEF EMERSON CHRONOLOGY

1796
October 25. Marriage of Reverend William Emerson (1769-1811), a Unitarian Minister, and Ruth Haskins (1768-1853), future parents of Ralph Waldo Emerson.

John Adams (1735-1826) is elected second President of the United States.

1800
Thomas Jefferson (1743-1826) is elected third President of the United States.

1803
May 2. Treaty between the U.S. and France signed for the purchase of the Louisiana Territory. The physical size of the United States is doubled.

May 25. Ralph Waldo Emerson born in Boston, Massachusetts.

1808
James Madison (1751-1836) elected fourth President of the United States.

1811
May 12. Death of Rev. William Emerson, Emerson's father.

1812
Emerson starts at the Boston Public Latin School.

June. War of 1812 begins between the United States and Great Britain.

1815
January 8. General Andrew Jackson (1767-1845) victorious over the British at the Battle of New Orleans.

1816
James Monroe (1758-1831) elected fifth President of the United States.

1817
July. 12. Henry David Thoreau (1817-1862) born in Concord.

Emerson enters Harvard College and begins his journals.

1820
Missouri Compromise forbids expansion of slavery in the Northern territories formed from the Louisiana Purchase. Maine admitted as a free state and Missouri as a slave state.

1821
August 29. Emerson graduates from Harvard College.

1824

June. Start of Thomas Carlyle's (1795-1881) correspondence with Johann Wolfgang von Goethe (1749-1832).

John Quincy Adams (1767-1848) elected sixth President of the United States.

1825

Emerson registers as student at Harvard Divinity School.

1826

July 4. Death of Thomas Jefferson and John Adams.

October 10. Emerson approved to preach by the American Unitarian Association.

1828

Andrew Jackson elected seventh President of the United States.

1829

March 11. Emerson ordained as a Unitarian ministry at the Second Church, Boston.

1829

September 30. Emerson marries Ellen Louisa Tucker (1811-1831).

1831

February 8. Ellen Louisa Emerson dies of tuberculosis.

1832

March 22. Death of Goethe.

October 28. Emerson resigns from the Unitarian ministry, on the grounds that he cannot in good conscience deliver the Lord's Supper; his resignation is accepted.

December 25. Emerson sails for Europe, to travel through Malta, Sicily, Italy, France and Britain.

1833

Emerson meets in Britain with Samuel Taylor Coleridge (1772-1834), William Wordsworth (1770-1850), and Thomas Carlyle.

1834

May. Emerson's 40-year Correspondence with Thomas Carlyle begins.

July 25. Death of Coleridge, near London.

October 9. Emerson moves to Concord, Massachusetts.

1835

September 14. Emerson marries his second wife, Lydia Jackson (1802-1892).

1836

August 31. "The American Scholar," Emerson's Phi Beta Kappa oration, delivered in Cambridge, Massachusetts.

September 9. Emerson's *Nature* published. The first printing of 500 copies is sold out within a month.

October 31. Birth of Emerson's first child, Waldo.

Martin Van Buren elected eighth President of the United States

1838

April 23. Emerson writes to President Van Buren to protest the expulsion and exile of the Cherokees from their home territories in the East.

July 15. "Divinity School Address" delivered to the graduating class of Harvard Divinity School.

1839

Birth of Emerson's daughter Ellen Tucker Emerson (1839-1909).

1840-1844

Emerson and Margaret Fuller (1810-1850) edit *The Dial* and publish works of the New England Transcendentalists.

1841

Emerson's *Essays* published, including "History," "Self-Reliance," "Compensation," "Spiritual Laws," "The Over-Soul," and "Circles."

1842

January 27. Death of Emerson's 5-year old son, Waldo.

October 2. Death of Dr. William Ellery Channing (1780-1842).

1844

July 10. Birth of Edward Waldo Emerson (1844-1930), Emerson's eldest surviving son.

August 1. Emerson delivers his "Address on the Emancipation of the Negroes of the West Indies."

October 19. *Essays, Second Series* published, including "Experience," "Character," "Nominalist and Realist."

James K. Polk (1795-1849) of Tennessee elected eleventh President of the United States.

1845

Annexation of Texas to the United States approved by the Texas and the U.S. congresses.

Thoreau takes up residence at Walden Pond.

1846

Texas becomes a U.S. state with a slave-state constitution.

May 13. Congress declares war on Mexico.

July. Thoreau refuses to pay his poll tax and spends a night in jail.

Emerson's *Poems* published.

1847

October 14. Emerson sails for Liverpool and his second trip to Europe.

1848

February 2. Treaty of Guadalupe Hidalgo signed with Mexico and the territory of the states of New Mexico, Utah, Nevada, Arizona, California, Texas, and western Colorado are ceded to the United States. This vast new territory represents the potentiality of the further expansion of slavery.

May. Emerson visits Paris following the revolution of 1848.

1849

Emerson's *Miscellanies* [Nature, Lectures, and Addresses] published.

May. Thoreau's "Civil Disobedience" published.

Emerson's *Representative Men* published.

1850

July 19. Death of Margaret Fuller.

September. Fugitive Slave Act passed by Congress, with the support of Daniel Webster (1782-1852), and signed into law by President Millard Fillmore. California enters the Union as a free state.

1851

Memoirs of Margaret Fuller Ossoli edited by Emerson (with W.H. Channing and J.F. Clarke) published.

1852

Death of Daniel Webster.

Publication of *Uncle Tom's Cabin* by Harriet Beecher Stowe (1811-1896).

1853

Death of Emerson's mother, Ruth Haskins Emerson, at Concord.

1854

March 7. Emerson delivers his address on "The Fugitive Slave Law."

1855

Publication of Walt Whitman's (1819-1892) *Leaves of Grass*.

Emerson delivers his "Lecture on Slavery."

1856

Emerson's *English Traits* published.

1857

March 6. The Supreme Court announces its decision in the Dred Scott case, declaring the Missouri Compromise of 1820 unconstitutional and that Congress cannot forbid slavery in the territories.

November. The essay "Illusions," later to appear as the last chapter of *The Conduct of Life*, first published in *The Atlantic Monthly*.

1858

John Brown's (1800-1859) raid on Harper's Ferry, Virginia, his capture and eventual death sentence.

1860

Abraham Lincoln (1809-1865) elected sixteenth President of the United States.
December 8. *The Conduct Of Life* is published in Boston by Ticknor and Fields.

1861

April 12. Civil War begins with the Confederate attack on Union forces at Fort
Sumter in Charleston harbor, South Carolina.

1862

May 6. Death of Thoreau.
Emerson meets President Lincoln in Washington, D.C.

1863

Lincoln's Emancipation Proclamation.

1865

April 15. Death, by assassination, of President Lincoln.
Adoption of the thirteenth Amendment to the U.S. constitution abolishes slavery
and involuntary servitude.

1867

Emerson's *May-Day and Other Pieces* published.
Appointment as Overseer of Harvard University.

1870

Emerson's *Society and Solitude* published.

1872-1873

Emerson's house in Concord burns, and his neighbors raise the money for repairs.
Third trip to Europe. Emerson sails up the Nile. Last visit with Carlyle.

1875

Emerson's *Letters And Social Aims* published.

1876

Emerson's *Selected Poems* published.
Election of Rutherford B. Hayes (1822-1893) as the nineteenth President of the
United States marks the end of Reconstruction in the American South.

1878

Emerson delivers address on "Fortune of the Republic" at Boston.

1881

February 5. Death of Thomas Carlyle.

1882

April 27. Emerson dies at Concord.

1893

Emerson's *Natural History of Intellect And Other Papers* published.

1903

William James (1842-1910) speaks at the Emerson Centenary Ceremony in
   Concord.

1903-1904

Emerson's *Complete Works*, Centenary Edition published.

BIBLIOGRAPHY

Selected Writings of and about Emerson

Emerson, Ralph Waldo (1836) "Modern Aspects of Letters," in Whicher, Stephen E. and Robert E. Spiller eds. (1966) *The Early Lectures of Ralph Waldo Emerson*, vol. I., 1833-1836. Cambridge, MA: Harvard University Press, pp. 371-385.

— (1836) "English Literature," in Whicher and Spiller eds. (1966) *The Early Lectures of Ralph Waldo Emerson*, vol. 1, pp. 205-388.

— (1838) "Divinity School Address." Reprinted in Bode and Cowley, *The Portable Emerson*, pp. 72-91.

— (1841) "Self-Reliance," in *Essays, First Series*. Reprinted in Bode and Cowley, *The Portable Emerson*, pp. 138-164.

— (1841) "Compensation," in *Essays, First Series*. Reprinted in Bode and Cowley, *The Portable Emerson*, pp. 165-186.

— (1841) "Lecture on the Times," in *The Collected Works of R. W. Emerson*, vol. 1. Cambridge: Harvard University Press, pp. 211-236.

— (1842) "The Transcendentalist," reprinted in Stroh and Callaway (2000) *American Ethics*, pp. 117-122; reprinted in Emerson (1971) Alfred R. Ferguson ed., *The Collected Works of Ralph Waldo Emerson*, vol. I, Cambridge, MA: Harvard University Press, pp. 201-216.

— (1844) "Address on the Emancipation of the Negroes in the British West Indies," in Gougeon and Myerson eds., (1995) *Emerson's Antislavery Writings*, pp. 7-38.

— (1860) *The Conduct of Life*. Boston: Ticknor and Fields; (2003) *The Collected Works of Ralph Waldo Emerson*, vol. VI. Slater, J. and E.W. Douglas, eds. Cambridge: Harvard University Press.

— (1862) "The President's Proclamation," in Gougeon and Myerson (1995) *Emerson's Antislavery Writings*, pp. 129-136.

— (1875) *Letters and Social Aims*. Boston: James R. Osgood & Co.

— (1903-04) *The Complete Works of Ralph Waldo Emerson*. Centenary Edition. Emerson, Edward W. ed. 12 vols. Boston and New York: Houghton Mifflin.

— (1971-) *The Collected Works of Ralph Waldo Emerson*. Spiller, Robert E. *et al.* eds. 6 vols. to date. Cambridge: Harvard University Press.

— (1981) *The Portable Emerson*. Bode, Carl and Malcolm Cowley eds., new ed. New York: Penguin.

— (1995) *Emerson's Literary Criticism*. Carlson, Eric W. ed. Lincoln: University of Nebraska Press.

— (1995) *Emerson's Antislavery Writings*. Gougeon, L. and Joel Myerson eds. New Haven and London: Yale University Press.

— (1997) *The Selected Letters of Ralph Waldo Emerson*. Myerson, Joel ed. New York: Columbia University Press.

— and Thomas Carlyle (1964) *The Correspondence of Emerson and Carlyle*. Slater, Joseph ed. New York: Columbia University Press.

Arnold, Matthew (1885) *Discourses in America*. London: Macmillan.

Baker, Carlos (1996) *Emerson Among the Eccentrics*. New York: Viking.

Buell, Lawrence (2003) *Emerson*. Cambridge, MA: Harvard University Press.

Callaway, H.G. and Guy W. Stroh (2000) *American Ethics: A Sourcebook from Edwards to Dewey*. Lanham, MD: University Press of America.

Dewey, John (1903) "Emerson—The Philosopher of Democracy," *International Journal of Ethics*, vol. 13, pp. 405-413. Reprinted in *John Dewey, The Middle Works*. Carbondale, IL: Southern Illinois University Press, vol. 3. pp. 184-192.

Flower, Elizabeth and Murray P. Murphey (1977) *A History of Philosophy in America*. 2 vols. New York: G. P. Putnam.

Gougeon, Len (1990) *Virtue's Hero, Emerson, Antislavery, and Reform*. Athens, GA and London: University of Georgia Press.

Holmes, Oliver Wendell (1885) *Ralph Waldo Emerson*. Second ed. London: Kegan Paul, Trench.

James, William (1903) "Address to the Emerson Centenary at Concord," in James (1911) *Memories and Studies*, pp. 19-34.

— (1907) *Pragmatism*. New York: Longmans, Green; (1955) reprinted with four essays from *The Meaning of Truth*. New York: New American Library.

— (1911) *Memories and Studies*. New York: Longmans, Green.

Mott, Wesley T and Robert E. Burkholder eds. (1997) *Emersonian Circles, Essays in Honor of Joel Myerson*. Rochester, NY: University of Rochester Press.

Peirce, Charles S. (1931-1958) *Collected Papers*. 8 vols. Cambridge: Harvard University Press.

Richardson, Robert (1995) *Emerson, The Mind on Fire*. Berkeley and London: University of California Press.

Robinson, David M. (1993) *Emerson and the Conduct of Life, Pragmatism and Ethical Purpose in the Later Work*. Cambridge and New York: Cambridge University Press.

Selected editions of Emerson's authors and references

Aesop (2002) *Aesop's Fables*. Gibbs, Laura trans. and ed. Oxford: Oxford University Press.

Ali Ben Abu Taleb (1978) *Nahj al-balaghah, Peak of eloquence: sermons, letters and sayings of Imam Ali.* Jafery, Askari trans. fifth ed. Bombay: Islamic Seminary for World Shia Muslim Organization.

Armin, Bettine von (1835) *Goethes Briefwechsel mit einem Kinde.* Berlin: Ferdinand Dümmler; (1986) Berlin: Aufbau-Verlag; (1839) Eng. trans. *Goethe's Correspondence with a Child.* London: Longman, Orme, Brown, Green, and Longmans; (1868) Boston: Ticknor and Fields.

— (1840) *Die Günderode.* Grünberg/Leipzig: Levysohn; (1989) Berlin: Aufbau-Verlag.

— (1844) *Clemens Brentanos Frühlingskranz.* Charlottenburg: Egbert Bauer; (1989) Berlin: Aufbau-Verlag.

— (1959-63) *Werke und Briefe.* 5 vols. Konrad, Gustav ed. Fechen: Bartmann.

Aubrey, John (1812) *Lives of Eminent Men.* Philadelphia: Benjamin Johnson; (1982) *John Aubrey, Brief Lives, a modern English version.* Barber, Richard ed. Totowa, NJ: Barnes and Noble; (1999) Lawson, Oliver ed., and with a *Life of John Aubrey.* Boston: D. R. Godine.

Bacon, Francis (1605) *Advancement of Learning*; (1955) *Advancement of learning; Novum Organum. New Atlantis.* Chicago: Encyclopedia Britannica.

— (1620) *Novum Organum*; (1955) in *Advancement of learning; Novum Organum; New Atlantis.* Chicago: Encyclopedia Britannica.

— (1625) *The Essays*; (1985) *The Essays.* Pitcher, John ed. London: Penguin Books.

Beckford, William (1786) *Vathek: an Arabian Tale*; (1993) *Vathek and other stories: a William Beckford Reader.* Jack, Malcolm ed. London: Pickering.

— (1957) *Life at Fonthill, 1807-22.* Alexander, Boyd ed. London: R. Hart-Davis.

Belzoni, Giovanni Battista (1821) *Narrative of the Operations and Recent Discoveries Within the Pyramids, Temples, Tombs and Excavations, in Egypt and Nubia.* 2 vols. London: J. Murray.

Béranger, Pierre-jean de (1850) *Béranger: two hundred of his lyrical poems, done into English verse.* Young, William trans. New York: G. P. Putnam.

Böhme, Jakob (1989) *Jacob Boehme: Essential Readings.* Edited and introduced by Waterfield, Robin. New York: Sterling Publishing.

Borrow, George (1851) *Lavengro, the Scholar, the Gypsy, the Priest.* 3 vols. London: J. Murray; (1970) London: Heron Books.

— (1857) *The Romany Rye.* New York: Harper and Bros; (1984) Quennell, Peter Intro. Oxford: Oxford University Press.

Boswell, James (1791) *The Life of Samuel Johnson.* London: C. Dilly; (1994) Edinburgh: Edinburgh University Press; New Haven: Yale University Press.

Boufflers, Chevalier de (1792,1828) *Oeuvres du chevalier de Boufflers.* New ed., 2 vols. Paris: J.N. Barba.

— (1977) *Aline, reine de Golconde.* Exeter: University of Exeter; (1926) *Queen of Golconda, and other tales, by Stanislas Jean de Boufflers.* Sutton, Eric trans. London: Chapman and Hall; New York: R. M. McBride.

Bowditch, Nathaniel (1802) *The New American Practical Navigator*. Newbury-port, MA: Printed by Edmund M. Blunt for Brown and Stansbury, New York; (1966) Washington: U.S. Govt. Print. Office.

Brewster, Sir David (1831) *Treatise on Optics*; (1849) London: Longman, Brown, Green and Longmans.

— (1855) *Memoirs of the Life, Writings and Discoveries of Sir Isaac Newton*. 2 vols. Edinburgh: T. Constable.

Brougham, Baron Henry Peter (1803) *An Inquiry into the Colonial Policy of the European Powers*. 2 vols. Edinburgh: E. Balfour, Manners and Miller; (1970) reprinted, New York: A. M. Kelley.

— (1804) *A Concise Statement of the Question Regarding the Abolition of the Slave Trade*. third ed. London: J. Hatchard by M. and S. Brooke.

Buonarroti, Michelangelo (1989) *The Sonnets of Michelangelo Buonarroti*. Italian text with trans and Intro by Symonds, J. A. London: Vision.

Burke, Edmund (1757) *A Philosophical Enquiry into the Origin of our Ideas of the Sublime and Beautiful*; (1990) reprinted, Oxford: Oxford University Press.

— (1780) "Oeconomical Reformation of the Civil and Other Establishments." In (1826) *The Works of the Right Honorable Edmund Burke*. London: R. Gilbert.

— (1790) *Reflections on the Revolution in France*. London: J. Dodsley; (1986) reprinted, Harmondsworth: Penguin.

— (1844) *Correspondence of the Right Honourable Edmund Burke*. William, Charles, Earl Fitzwilliam and Richard Bourke eds. London: F.& J. Rivington.

— (1938) *Speeches and Letters on American Affairs*. London: J.M. Dent.

— (1975) *Edmund Burke on Government, Politics, and Society*. Hill, B.W. ed. London: Fantana.

— (1999) *The Portable Edmund Burke*. Kramnick, Isaac ed. New York: Penguin Books.

— (1999) *Selected Works of Edmund Burke*. Indianapolis: Liberty Fund.

— (2000) *On Empire, Liberty and Reform*. Bromwick, D. ed. New Haven and London: Yale University Press.

Burns, Robert (1786) *Poems, Chiefly in the Scottish Dialect*. Kilmarnock: Wilson; (1987) reprinted, Paisley: Gleniffer.

Calhoun, John C. (1851-56) *The Works of John C. Calhoun*. Crallé, Richard K. ed. 6 vols. New York: D. Appleton; Reissued (1968).

— (1953) *A Disquisition on Government and Selections from the Discourse*. Post, C. Gordon ed. Indianapolis: Hackett.

Calvin, John (1536) *Institutio Christianae religionis, cum brevi annotatione atque indicibus locupletissimis ad editionem Amstelo-damensem accuratissime exscribi curavit*. Tholuck, A. ed. 2 vols. Berolini: G. Eichler; (1845-46) *Institutes of the Christian religion. A new trans. by Henry Beveridge*. 3 vols. Edinburgh: Calvin Translation Society; (1983) reprinted, 2 vols. Grand Rapids, Michigan: Wm. B. Eerdmans.

— (1578) *A Commentarie of John Calvine, upon the first Booke of Moses called Genesis*. Tymme, Thomas trans. London: J. Harison and G. Bishop.

— (1961) *A Calvin treasury, selections from the Institutes of the Christian Religion*. Keesecker, William F. ed. New York: Harper.

Cellini, Benvenuto (1728) *Vita di Benvenuto Cellini*; (1961) Symonds, John A. ed. 2 vols. *The Life of Benvenuto Cellini Written by Himself*. Garden City, NY: Doubleday.

— (1803) *Leben des Benvenuto Cellini, florentinischen Goldschmieds und Bildhauers, von ihm selbst geschrieben*. Goethe, J. W. ed. and trans. 2 vols. Tübingen: J.G. Cotta.

Cervantes, Miguel de (1636) *Primera y segvnda parte del ingenioso hidalgo Don Qvixote de la Mancha*. Madrid: D. Gonzalez.

— (1951) *The Portable Cervantes*. Putnam, Samuel ed. and trans. New York: Viking; reprinted (1976) Harmondsworth: Penguin. (Includes *Don Quixote*.)

Champollion, Jean-François (1823-25) *Panthéon égyptien: collection des personnages mythologiques de l'ancienne Égypte, d'après les monuments, avec un texte explicatif*. Paris: Firmin Didot.

— (1841-43) *Dictionnaire égyptien*; (2000) reprinted, Arles: Solin-Actes Sud.

Channing, William Ellery (1836) *Slavery*. Second revised ed. Boston: J. Munroe.

— (1842) *Self-culture*, An address introductory to the Franklin lectures, delivered at Boston, September, 1838. Boston, MA: J. Munroe.

— (1841-43) *The works of William E. Channing*. First complete American ed. Boston: J. Munroe.

— (1985) *William Ellery Channing: Selected Writings*. Robinson, David ed. New York: Paulist Press.

Chaucer, Godfrey (1989) *The Complete Poetry and Prose of Godfrey Chaucer*. Fisher, J.H. ed. New York: Holt Rinehard & Winston.

Cherbury, (Baron) Herbert (1624) *De Veritate*. Paris; (1937) *On Truth*. trans. and Intro. by Carré, Meyrick H. Bristol: for the University of Bristol by J. W. Arrowsmith.

— (1645) *De Causis Errorum una cum tractatu de religione laici, et appendice ad sacerdotes, nec non quibusdam poematibus*. London: Typis Joannia Raworth.

— (1645) *De Religione Laici*; (1944) *Lord Herbert of Cherbury's De religione laici*. ed. and trans. Hutcheson, Harold R. New Haven and London: Yale University Press and Oxford University Press.

— (1649) *The Life and Raigne of King Henry the Eighth*. London: Thomas Whitaker.

— (1663) *De Religione Gentilium. Errorumque apud eos causis*. Amsterdam; (1967) Gawlick, Günter ed. Stuttgart: Frommann-Holzboog; (1996) *Pagan Religion: a translation of De religione gentilium*, Butler, John Anthony ed. Ottawa: Dovehouse Editions.

— (1656) *Expeditio in Ream insulam.* London: Prostant apud Humphredum Moseley; (1860) *The Expedition to the Isle of Rhé.* London: Whittingham & Wilkins.

— (1923) *The poems, English and Latin, of Edward Lord Herbert of Cherbury.* Moore Smith, G. C. ed. Oxford: Clarendon Press.

— (1997) *Poems of Lord Herbert of Cherbury*, selected by Astbury, Anthony. Warwick: Greville Press Pamphlets.

Coleridge, Samuel Taylor (1812) *The Friend*; (1831) First American ed. from the second London ed. Burlington VT: C. Goodrich.

— (1817) *Biographia Literaria or, Biographical Sketches of my Literary Life and Opinions.* New York: Kirk and Merein; (1834) New York; (1997) reprinted, Leask, Nigel ed. London: J.M. Dent.

— (1825) *Aids to Reflection, in the Formation of a Manly Character.* London: Taylor and Hessey; (1993) Beer, John ed. London and Princeton: Routledge; Princeton University Press.

— (1990) *Table Talk, Recorded by Henry Nelson Coleridge.* Princeton: Princeton University Press.

Copernicus, Nicholaus (1543) *De revolutionibus orbium coelestium*; (1972) reprinted, with German trans. Berlin: De Gruyter; (1992) Rosen, Edward trans. *On the Revolutions of the Celestial Spheres.* London: Johns Hopkins University Press.

Cromwell, Oliver (1937-47) *The Writings and Speeches of Oliver Cromwell.* Abbott, Wilbur C. ed. 4 vols. Cambridge: Harvard University Press.

Cudworth, Ralph (1642) *A discourse concerning the true notion of the Lord's supper.* London: Printed for R. Royston.

— (1678) *The True Intellectual System of the Universe: The First Part: Wherein All the Reason and Philosophy of Atheism Is Confuted and its Impossibility Demonstrated*; (1964) Stuttgart: Frommann Verlag.

— (1731) *A Treatise Concerning Eternal and Immutable Morality.* London: J. and J. Knapton; (1996) Hutton, Sarah ed. Cambridge and New York: Cambridge University Press.

— (1829) *The works of Ralph Cudworth.* New ed., 4 vols., with a life of the author by T. Birch. Oxford: Oxford University Press.

— (1838) *A Treatise of Freewill.* Allen J. ed. London: John W. Parker.

D'Alembert, Jean le Rond (1764-1767) *Mélanges de littérature, d'histoire et de philosophie.* 5 vols. Amsterdam: Zacharie Chatelain.

— (1775-77) *Histoire des membres de l'Académie française morts depuis 1700 jusqu'en 1771.* 6 vols. Paris: Moutard.

— (1821-22) *Oeuvres complètes de d'Alembert.* Bossange and Belin eds. 5 vols. Paris: A. Belin etc.

Dante Alighieri (1321) *La Divina commedia*; (1987) *The Divine Comedy.* Kirkpatrick, Robin ed. Cambridge: Cambridge University Press.

— (ca. 1293) *La vita nuova*; (1903) *The New Life.* Ricci, Luigi trans. London: Kegan Paul, Trench and Truber.

Denon, Dominique Vivant (1802) *Voyage dans la basse et la haute Égypte.* Paris: P. Didot l'aîné; (1803) *Travels in Upper and Lower Egypt during the campaigns of General Bonaparte.* Aikin, Arthur trans. New York: S. Campbell.

— (1829) *Monuments des Arts du Dessin chez les Peuples tant Anciens que Modernes.* 4 vols. Paris.

Dickens, Charles (1842) *American Notes.* New York: Harper and Brothers; (2000) reprinted, Cologne: Könemann.

Du Bois, W. E. B. (1903) *The Souls of Black Folks.* A. C. McClurg Co.: Chicago; (1994) reprinted, New York: Dover.

Dumont, Étienne (1832) *Souvenirs sur Mirabeau*; (1951) new ed.; Eng. trans. (1835) *Recollections of Mirabeau and of the two first legislative assemblies of France.* London: E. Churton.

Eckermann, Peter (1836-48) *Gespräche mit Goethe in den letzten Jahren seines Lebens, 1823-32.* 3 vols.; (1981) Bergmann, F. ed. Frankfurt am Main: Insel Verlag; (1839) *Conversations with Goethe in the Last Years of his Life.* Margaret Fuller trans. Boston; (1998) John Oxenford trans. New York: Da Capo Press. Reprint of the 1930, London edition; (1964) *Selected Conversations with Goethe.* O'Brien, G. trans. New York: Unger.

Erasmus, Desiderius. (1511) *In of Praise of Folly;* (2003) *The Praise of Folly.* New Haven CT: Yale University Press.

Fénelon, François de Salignac de La Mothe (1699) *Les Aventures de Télémaque*; (1993) reprinted, Paris: Nizet; (1794-1801) *The Adventures of Telemachus: the Son of Ulysses*, trans. Hawkesworth, John. London: C. Cooke.

— (1697) *Explication des maximes des saints sur la vie intérieure.* Paris: Chez Pierre Aubouin; (1911) reprinted Paris: Bloud.

— (1845) *Oeuvres de Fénelon, archevêque de Cambrai* / précédées d'Etudes sur sa vie, par m. Aimé Martin. 3 vols. Paris: Firmin Didot Frères.

Franklin, Benjamin (1981) *The Autobiography of Benjamin Franklin: A Genetic Text.* Knoxville: University of Tennessee Press.

Franklin, Sir John (1824) *Narrative of a Journey to the Shores of the Polar Sea, in the Years 1819, 20, 21 and 22.* Philadelphia: H.C. Carey and I. Lea.

— (1828) *Narrative of a Second Expedition to the Shores of the Polar Sea, in the Years 1825, 1826, and 1827.* London: J. Murray.

Fuller, Margaret (1845) *Woman in the Nineteenth Century.* New York: Greeley and McElrath; (1994) *Woman in the Nineteenth Century and Other Writings.* Dickenson, Donna ed. Oxford and New York: Oxford University Press.

— (1992) *The Essential Margaret Fuller.* Steele, Jeffrey ed. New Brunswick, NJ: Rutgers University Press.

Fuller, Thomas (1642) *The Holy State, the Profane State*; (1841) new ed. London: T. Tegg.

— (1646) *Andronicus, or the Unfortunate Politician.* Second edition. London: Printed by W.W. for John Williams.

— (1655) *The Church-History of Britain*. London: John Williams; (1837) new ed. London: T. Tegg.

— (1662) *History of the Worthies of England*; (1811) Nichols, John ed. 2 vols. London: F.C. and J. Rivington.

Garrison, Wendell P. and Francis J. (1885-89) *William Lloyd Garrison, 1805-1879: The Story of His Life Told by His Children*. 4 vols. New York: Century Co.

Gascoigne, George (1573) *A Hundreth sundrie Flowres*; (2000) new ed. with intro. by Pigman, G.W. Oxford: Oxford University Press.

Gladstone, William Ewart (1879) *Gleanings of Past Years, 1843-78*. 7 vols. New York: C. Scribner's sons; Reissued (1976) in 8 vols.

Goethe, Johann Wolfgang (1811) *Aus meinem Leben, Wahrheit und Dichtung*; (1998) reprinted, Stuttgart: Reclam; (1848) *Autobiography*. Oxenford, John trans.; Reprinted (1971) London: Sedgwick & Jackson.

— (1819) *West-Östlicher Divan*; (1998) reprinted, Frankfurt: Insel Verlag.

— (1833) *Maximen und Reflexionen*, Vol. IX of Goethe's *Nachgelassene Werke*. Stuttgart: Cotta.

— (1887) *Correspondence between Goethe and Carlyle*. Norton, Charles Eliot ed.; (1970) reprinted, New York: Cooper Square.

Greenough, Horatio (1852) *The Travels, Observations, and Experience of a Yankee Stonecutter*. New York: G.P. Putnam; (1958) Intro. by Wright, Nathalia. Gainesville, FL: Scholars' Facsimiles and Reprints.

— (1947) *Form and Function*. Berkeley: University of California Press.

Guizot, François Pierre Guillaume (1828) *History of Civilization in Europe, from the Fall of the Roman Empire to the French Revolution*. New York: John B. Allen.

—(1852) *History of the Origin of Representative Government in Europe*. Scoble, Andrew R. trans. London: Henry G. Bohn.

— (1854) *Life of Oliver Cromwell*; (1860) reissued; (1874) new ed. London: Bentley.

Hafiz, Mohammad Shams od-din (1891, 1971) *Divan*; Clarke, H. Wilberforce eng. prose trans., *Hafiz Shirazi. The Divan* (1947) Arberry, A.J. ed., *Fifty Poems of Hafiz*. Cambridge: Cambridge University Press.

Hall, Basil (1818) *Account of a Voyage of Discovery to the West Coast of Corea, and the Great Loo-Choo Island*. Philadelphia: Abraham Small.

— (1824) *Extracts from a Journal Written on the Coasts of Chili, Peru and Mexico, in the Years 1820, 1821, 1822*. 2 vols. Philadelphia: E. Littell.

— (1829) *Travels in North America in the Years 1827 and 1828*. 3 vols. Philadelphia: Carey, Lea and Carey.

Homer (1987) *The Iliad*. Hammond, Martin intro. and trans. Harmondsworth: Penguin.

Hooke, Robert (1665) *Micrographia or, Some physiological descriptions of minute bodies made by magnifying glasses: With observations and inquiries thereupon*. London: Martyn and Allestry; (1961) reprinted, New York: Dover.

Horace, Quintus Horatius Flaccus (1963) *The Odes of Horace*. Michie, James trans. London: R. Hart-Davis.

Humboldt, Alexander v. (1847) *Kosmos*. Copenhagen: F. H. Eibe; (2004) Frankfurt am Main: Eichborn Verlag.

Hunt, Leigh (1855) *Beaumont and Fletcher* or, The finest scenes, lyrics, and other beauties of those two poets, now first selected from the whole of their works, to the exclusion of whatever is morally objectionable: with opinions of distinguished critics, notes explanatory and otherwise. London: H. G. Bohn.

—(2003) *The Selected Writings of Leigh Hunt*. Morrison, R. and M. Eberle-Sinatra eds. 6 vols. London: Pickering and Chatto.

Jacobi, Friedrich Heinrich (1792) *Eduard Allwills Briefsammlung*. Königsberg; (1962) reprinted, Stuttgart: J.B. Metzler.

— (1779) *Woldemar: ein Seltenheit aus der Naturgeschichte*. Flensburg and Leipzig; (1969) reprinted, Stuttgart: J. B. Metzler.

— (1786) *Über die Lehre des Spinoza, in Briefen an den Herrn Moses Mendelssohn*. Leipzig: Georg Joachim Goeschen.

— (1787) *David Hume über den Glauben, oder Idealismus und Realismus*; (1983) reprinted, Beck, Hamilton Intro. New York: Garland.

— (1799) *Jacobi an Fichte*. Hamburg: F. Perthes.

— (1812-25) *Werke*. Roth, R. F. Koppens et al. eds. 6 vols. Leipzig: G. Fleischer; (1998-) *Werke, Friedrich Heinrich Jacobi*. Hammacher, Klaus and Walter Jaeschke eds. Hamburg: Meiner.

Johnson, Samuel (1755) *Dictionary of the English Language*. 2 vols.; (1979) reprinted, London: Times Books.

— (1798) *Dr. Johnson's Table Talk*. London: C. Dilly.

— (1806) *Works*. 12 vols. London: J. Johnson.

— (1905) *Lives of the English Poets*. Birkbeck, George ed. 3 vols.; (1967) reprinted. New York: Octagon.

— (1958-) *The Yale Edition of the Works of Samuel Johnson*. 16 vols. to date. New Haven: Yale University Press.

Jonson, Benjamin (1616) *Epigrammes*. London: William Stansby; (1984) *Epigrams and the Forest*. Dutton, Richard ed. Manchester: Carcanet Press.

Jung-Stilling, Johann Heinrich (1806) *Heinrich Stillings Leben*. 5 vols.; (1831) Eng. trans. by Hazelius, E. L. *The life of John Henry Stilling*. Gettysburg, PA: The Theological Seminary, H. C. Neinstedt.

Kane, Elisha Kent (1856) *Arctic Explorations: The Second Grinnell Expedition in Search of Sir John Franklin, in the Years 1853, '54, '55*. London: T. Nelson

Knox, Robert (1850) *The Races of Man, A fragment*. Philadelphia: Lea and Blanchard.

La Barca, Pedro Calderón de (1853-73) McCarthy, D.F. eng. trans., 10 plays and autos; (1960) rev. by Wells, H.W.; (1906) *Eight Dramas of Calderón*. Fitzgerald, E.E. trans. London: Macmillan.

— (1966-) *Obras Completas*, new ed. Vol. 1, *Dramas*, Vol. 2, *Comedias*, Vol. 3, *Autos sacramentales*. Valbuena, Briones A. ed. Madrid: Aguilar.

Landor, Walter Savage (1824) *Imaginary Conversations*. 2 vols.; (1882) 5 vols. Boston: Roberts Brothers.

— (1836) *Pericles and Aspasia*. C.G. Crump ed.; (1890) 2 vols. London: J. M. Dent, Saunders and Otley.

— (1846) *The Works of Walter Savage Landor*. 2 vols. London: E. Moxon.

Laplace, Pierre-Simon (1796) *Exposition du système du monde*; (1809) *The System of the World*. Pond, J. trans. London: Phillips.

— (1798-1827) *Traité de mécanique céleste*. 5 vols.; (1829-39) Bowditch, Nathaniel, trans. *Celestial Mechanics*. 4 vols. Boston: Hillard, Gray, Little and Wilkins.

— (1814) *Essai philosophique sur les probabilités*. Fifth ed.; (1825) Paris: Mme. Ve Courcier. (1995) *A Philosophical Essay on Probability*. trans. of the fifth ed. New York: Springer.

— (1878-1912) *Oeuvres complètes de Laplace*. 14 vols. Paris: Gauthier-Villars.

Layard, Austen Henry (1851) *A popular Account of Discoveries at Nineveh*. London: J. Murray.

— (1853) *Discoveries in the Ruins of Nineveh and Babylon*. London: J. Murray; New York: G.P. Putnam.

Lavater, Johann Kaspar (1782) *Aussichten in die Ewigkeit*. Zurich: Orell, Gesznee and Füeszli.

— (1775) *Nachdenken über mich selbst*. Offenbach: Weiß; (1795) *Secret Journal of a Self-Observer*. Will, Peter trans. London: T. Cadell.

— (1826) *Physiognomy*; (1853) *Essays on Physiognomy*. Holcroft, Thomas trans. London: William Tagg.

— (1859-1860) *Ausgewählte Schriften*. 4 vols. Orelli, Johann Kasper ed. Zurich: F. Schulthess.

— (1901) *Goethe und Lavater, Briefe und Tagebücher*. Funck, Heinrich ed. Weimar: Goethe-Gesellschaft.

Leibniz, G.W.F. (1710) *Theodicy*. In George R. Montgomery (1924) *Leibniz: Discourse on Metaphysics, Correspondence with Arnauld, and Mondadology*. trans. revised by Chandler Albert R. La Salle IL: Open Court.

Lepsius, Richard (1852) *Briefe aus Ägypten, Äthiopien und der Halbinsel des Sinai*; (1975) Osnabrück: Zeller; (1853) *Discoveries in Egypt, Ethiopia and the Peninsula of Sinai*. second ed. London: R. Bentley.

— (1858) *Königsbuch der Alten Ägypter*. Berlin: W. Hertz.

Livingstone, David (1857) *Missionary Travels in South Africa*. London: John Murray; (1858) Philadelphia: J.W. Bradley.

Malthus, Thomas Robert (1798) *An Essay on the Principle of Population*. London: J. Johnson; (1970) reprinted, Flew, A. ed. Harmondsworth: Penguin.

Manu (1991) *The Laws of Manu.* trans by Doniger, W. and Smith, B.K. London: Penguin.

Marcus Aurelius, *Meditations.* Farquharson, A.S.L. trans. Oxford: Oxford University Press.

Martial, Marcus Valerius Martialis (1919-20) *Martial.* Latin with eng. trans. by Ker, W. C. A. 2 vols. Cambridge, MA: Loeb Classical Library.

— (1987) *Martial, Selected Epigrammata.* Sullivan, J.P. and P. Whigham eds. Berkeley: University of California Press.

Milnes, Richard Monckton (1844) *Palm Leaves.* London: E. Moxon.

— (1848) *Life, Letters, and Literary Remains of John Keats*, with a memoir by Richard Monckton Milnes. London: E. Moxon.

Milton, John. (1924) *The Complete Works of John Milton.* Boston and New York: Houghton Mifflin.

— (1998) *The Riverside Milton.* Flannagan, R. ed. Boston: Houghton Mifflin.

— (2005) *Paradise Lost.* Teskey, G. ed. New York: W.W. Norton.

Mirabeau, Honoré-Gabriel Riqueti, comte de. (1776) *Essai sur le despotisme.* London; (1821) Paris: A. Brailleul.

— (1832) *Mirabeau's Letters during his residence in England.* 2 vols. London: E. Wilson.

Möller, Georg (1824) *An Essay on the Origin and Progress of Gothic Architecture.* London: Priestley and Weale.

Montalembert, Charles-Forbes-René, Count de (1868-82) *Les Moines d'Occident.* Paris: Lecoffre; (1966) *Monks of the West, a study of the growth of Western monasticism.* Gasquet, F.A. Intro. New York: AMS Press.

— (1852) *Des Intérêts Catholiques au XIXe siècle.* Paris: J. Lecoffre; (1852) *The Catholic Interest in the Nineteenth Century.* London: C. Dolman.

— (1856) *De L'Avenir politique de l'Angleterre.* Paris: Didie.

— (1970) *Catholicisme et liberté.* Paris: Editions du Cerf.

Montaigne, Michel de. (1877) *Essays of Montaigne.* Cotton, Charles trans. Hazlitt, William Carew ed. 3 vols. London; (1991) *Michel de Montaigne, The Complete Essays.* Screech, M.A. trans. London: Penguin.

Newton, Sir Isaac (1687) *Philosophiae Naturalis Principia Mathematica.* Amsterdam; (1848) *Mathematical Principles of Natural Philosophy.* New York: D. Adee; (1947) Berkeley, CA: University of California Press.

—(2004) *Newton: Philosophical Writings.* Janikak, Andrew ed. Cambridge: Cambridge University Press.

Northcote, James (1817) *Memoirs of Sir Joshua Reynolds.* Philadelphia: M. Carey & Son.

Owen, Robert (1813) *New View of Society*; (1966) *New View of Society and Other Essays.* Intro. by Cole, G.D.H. London and New York: Dent; Dutton.

— (1857-58) *The life of Robert Owen, with selections from his writings and correspondence.* 2 vols.; (1967) reprinted, London: Cass.

Parker, Theodore (1863-71) *The collected works of Theodore Parker.* 14 vols. Cobbe, F.P. ed. London. Trubner.

Pascal, Blaise (1671) *Pensées*. Paris: Chez Guillaume Disprez; (1950) *Pascal's Pensées*, with an English trans. New York: Pantheon.

— (1963) *Oeuvres complètes Pascal*. Paris: Editions du Seuil.

Pestalozzi, Johann Heinrich *(1797) Meine Nachforschungen über den Gang der Natur in der Entwicklung des Menschengeschlechts*; (1993) Bad Heilbrunn: J. Klinkhart.

— (1801) *Lienard und Gertrude*. (1977) reprinted, Munich: Winkler.

— (1801) *Wie Gertrud ihre Kinder lehrt;* (1982) Bad Heilbrunn: J. Klinkhardt; (1973) *How Gertrude Teaches her Children*. New York: Gordon Press.

—(1991) *Politische Schriften*. Graf, R. ed. Basel: Birkhäuser.

Plato (1875) *Dialogues*. Jowett, Benjamin trans. 5 vols. Oxford; (1961) *The Collected Dialogues of Plato*. Hamilton, E. and Cairns, H. eds. Princeton: Princeton University Press.

Plotinus (1994) *Collected Writings of Plotinus*. Taylor, Thomas trans. Frome, Somerset, U.K.: Prometheus Trust.

Plutarch (1870) *Plutarch's Morals, Translated from the Greek by Several Hands*. corrected and revised by William W. Goodwin. 5 vols. Boston; (1927-1976) *Moralia*. 15 vols. Cambridge, MA and London: Harvard University Press.

— (1963) *Parallel Lives*. Fontwell: Centaur Press.

Proclus (1816) *The Six Books of Proclus*. trans. and ed. by Taylor, Thomas; (1985-1986) *The Platonic Theology in Six Books*. Kew Gardens, NY: Selene Books.

Quételet, Lambert Adolphe Jacques (1842) *A Treatise on Man and the Development of His Faculties*. Edinburgh: W. and R. Chambers.

Rabelais, François. (1532, 1534) and *Gargantua and Pantagruel*; (1955) Cohen, J. M. trans. London and New York: Penguin.

Retz, Jean-François Paul Cardinal de (1655) *Mémoires*; (1935) Paris: Garrier Frères.

Saadi or Sa'di, Musharrif od-Din Muslih od-Din (1257) *Bustan*; (1891) London: W.H. Allen.; (1911) *Bustan of Sa'di*. Hart, A. trans. and Intro. London: J. Murray.

— (1258) *Gulistan;* (1808) *The Rose Garden*. Gladwin, Francis trans. London: J. Murray; (1865) *Gulistan, or Rose Garden by Sheik Saadi*. Preface by R. W. Emerson. Boston: Ticknor and Fields.

Saint-Simon, Louis de Rouvroy Duke of (1965-) *Mémoires Complets et authentiques*. Paris: J. de Bonnot.

Sand, George (1842) *Consuelo*; (1897) *Consuelo by George Sand*. Potter, Frank H. trans. Boston: Estes and Lauriat; (1979) New York: Da Capo Press.

Schelling, F. W. J. (1807) *Über das Wesen der menschlichen Freiheit;* (1834) Reutlingen: J. N. Enklinschen Buchhandlung; (1936) *Philosophical Inquiries into the Nature of Human Freedom*. Gutmann, James trans. La Salle IL: Open Court.

Schiller, Friedrich (1791-93) *Geschichte des dreißigjährigen Krieges*. 3 vols. Frankenthal: Im Verlag der Gegelischen Buchdruckerey und Buchhandlung;

(1846) *History of the Thirty Years' War*. Morrison, A.J.W. trans. New York: Harper.

— (1794-95) *Briefe über die ästhetische Erziehung des Menschen*; (1967) *Letters on the Aesthetic Education of Man*. Wilkinson, Elizabeth M. and L.A. Willoughby trans. and eds. Oxford: Clarendon Press.

— (1800, 1869) *Wallenstein: ein dramatisches Gedicht*. Berlin; (1805) *Wallenstein: a drama in two parts*. Coleridge, S.T. trans. New York: David Longworth.

Scott, Walter (1819) *The Bride of Lammermoor*; (2000) Alexander, J. H. ed. New York and London: Penguin.

Sidney, Sir Philip (1591) *Astrophel and Stella*; (1931) reprinted, London: Nonesuch Press.

— (1595) *The Defence of Poesie*. London: William Ponsonby.

— (1912-26) *The Complete Works of Sir Philip Sidney*. Feuillerat, A. ed. 4 vols.

Smith, Sydney (1808) *Letters of Peter Plymley to My Brother Abraham Who Lives in the Country*. London: J. Budd; (1929) New York: Dutton.

Staël, Anne Louise Germaine (Madame) de. (1794) *De l'influence des passions sur le bonheur des individus et des nations*; (1813) *A Treatise on the Influence of the Passions upon the Happiness of Individuals and of Nations*. Boston: W. Wells and T.B. Wait.

— (1800) *De la Littérature Considérée dans ses Rapports avec les Institutions Sociales*; (1845) *A Treatise of Ancient and Modern Literature and The Influence of Literature upon Society*. Hartford, CT: S. Andrus

— (1810, 1813) *De l'Allemagne*. London: R. Minder; (1847) *De l'Allemagne, par Madame de Staël*. Paris: F. Didot frères. (1814) *Germany*. New York: Eastburn, Kirk; (1985) *Madame de Staël Über Deutschland*. Frankfurt: Insel Verlag.

— (1818) *Considérations sur la Révolution française*; (2000) Paris: Tallandier; (1818) *Considerations on the principal events of the French revolution*. Posthumous work of the Baroness de Staël. Edited by the Duke de Broglie and the Baron de Staël. New York: J. Eastburn.

— (1821) *Dix Années d'exil*; (1821) *Ten Years' Exile*. New York: Collins.

— (1820-21) *Oeuvres complètes de Mme. la baronne de Staël*. pub. par son fils; précédées d'une notice sur le caractère et les écrits de Mme. de Staël, par Madame Necker de Saussure. 17 vols. Paris: Treuttel et Würtz.

—(1964) *Madame de Staël on Politics Literature, and National Character*. Berger, Morroe trans. and ed. Garden City, NY: Doubleday.

Vaucanson, Jacques de (1738) *Le mécanisme du fluteur automate, présenté a messieurs de l'Académie royale des sciences*. Paris: Chez J. Guerin; (1979) reprinted, Buren: F. Knuf; (1742) *An account of the mechanism of an automaton, or, Image playing on the German-flute: as was presented in a memoire to the gentlemen of the Royal-Academy of Sciences at Paris*. London: Stephen Varillon.

Virgil (Publius Vergilius Maro) (1697) *Aeneid.* Dryden, John eng. trans.; (1997) *Virgil's Aeneid*, Dryden translation, Keener, Frederick M. ed. London: Penguin.

Vishnu Purana, a System of Hindu Mythology and Tradition. (1840) Wilson, H. H. eng. trans. London: J. Murray; (1961) third edition. Calcutta: Punthi Pustak.

Voltaire (Arouet, François-marie) (1759) *Candide, ou L'optimisme.* Genève: Cramer; (1843) *The history of Candid.* New York: Holland and Glover; (2003) *Candide.* New York, NY: Fine Communications Inc.

Walpole, Horace (1822-59) *Memoirs;* (2000) *Memoirs of the reign of King George III. by Horace Walpole.* Jarrett, Derek ed. New Haven, CT and London: Yale University Press.

— (1857-59) *Letters of Horace Walpole.* Cunningham, Peter ed. 8 vols. London: R. Bentley.

Waterton, Charles (1828) *Wanderings in South America and the Antilles*; (1900) London: T. Nelson & Sons.

Wesley, John (1955) *Selections from the Journal of John Wesley.* Martin, Hugh ed. London: SCM Press.

Wilkinson, John Gardner (1847) *Handbook for Travelers in Egypt.* London: J. Murray.

— (1854) *Popular Account of the Ancient Egyptians.* New York: Harper & Bros.

Winckelmann, Johann (1764) *Geschichte der Kunst des Altertums;* (2002-) reprinted, Mainz: Verlag Phillip von Zabern; (1849-73) *History of the Art of Antiquity.* Boston: J. R. Osgood.

Wordsworth, William (1984) *William Wordsworth.* Gill, Stephen ed. Oxford and New York: Oxford University Press.

Selected Works Secondary to Emerson's Sources, Authors, and References

Bach, Adolf (1923) *Goethes Rheinreise mit Lavater und Basedow im Summer 1774.* Zurich: Seldwyla.

Beattie, William (1850) *Life and Letters of Thomas Campbell.* Second ed. London: Hall & Virtue.

Benét, Stephen Vincent (1937) *The Devil and Daniel Webster.* Denison, Harold Illustr. New York and Toronto: Rinehart.

— (1999) *The Devil and Daniel Webster and other Writings.* Ludington, Townsend ed. New York: Penguin Books.

Bloom, Harold (1986) *Samuel Taylor Coleridge, Modern Critical Views.* New York and Philadelphia: Chelsea House Publishers.

Boyer, Allen D. (2003) *Sir Edward Coke and the Elizabethan Age.* Stanford, California: Stanford University Press.

Brett, S. Reed (1940) *John Pym, 1583-1643: The Statesman of the Puritan Revolution.* London: J. Murray.

Butler, E.M (1926) *The Saint-Simonian Religion in Germany: A Study of the Young German Movement*; (1968) reprinted, New York: H. Fertig; Cambridge: Cambridge University Press.

Condivi, Ascanio (1553) *Vita di Michelangelo Buonarroti*; (1746) second ed. Florence; (1999) *The Life of Michelangelo*. Sedgwick, A. trans. University Park: Pennsylvania State University Press.

Carlyle, Thomas (1825) *Life of Friedrich Schiller: Comprehending an examination of his works*. London: Taylor and Hessey; (1833) Boston: Carter, Hendee; (1992) *Thomas Carlyle's life of Friedrich Schiller*. Columbia, SC: Camden House.

— (1837) *The French Revolution*. (1989) Fielding, K.J. and David Sorensen eds. Oxford and New York: Oxford University Press.

— (1837) *Memoirs of Mirabeau*. London: London and Westminster Review, January issue.

— (1901) *Complete Works of Thomas Carlyle*. 20 vols. Illustrated. New York: P. F. Collier.

Churchill, Charles Henry (1867) *The Life of Abdel Kader, Ex-Sultan of the Arabs of Algeria*; (1971) *La vie d'Abdel Kader*. Alger: SWED.

Davis, Sarah Matilda Henry (1859) *The Life and Times of Sir Philip Sidney*. Boston: Ticknor and Fields.

Dupre, Huntley (1940, 1975) *Lazare Carnot, Republican Patriot*. Oxford, OH: The Mississippi Valley Press.

Feuchtwanger, E. J (1975) *Gladstone*. London: Allen Lane.

Gill, Stephen (1989) *William Wordsworth: A Life*. Oxford and New York: Oxford University Press.

Gillespie, Charles C. (1971) *Lazare Carnot Savant*. Princeton: Princeton University Press.

Greville, Fulke Baron (1816) *Lord Brook's Life of Sir Philip Sidney*. Brydges, Sir Egerton ed. 2 vols. Kent: Lee Priory.

Grimsley, Ronald (1963) *Jean d'Alembert, 1717-83*. Oxford: Clarendon Press.

Hammacher, K. (1969) *Philosophie Friedrich Heinrich Jacobis*. Munich: W. Fink.

Holland, Saba (1855) *A Memoir of the Reverend Sydney Smith*. 2 vols. New York: Harper & Bros.

Hornberger, Theodore (1962) *Benjamin Franklin*. Minneapolis: University of Minnesota Press.

Hostettler, John (1997) *Sir Edward Coke: a force for freedom*. Chichester: Barry Rose Law Publishers.

Jouhandean, Marcel (1960) *St. Philip Neri*. Lamb, G. trans. London: Longmans.

Mendelsohn, Jack (1971) *Channing, the Reluctant Radical, a Biography*. Boston: Little, Brown.

Neal, Daniel (1732-38) *The History of the Puritans or Protestant Non-Conformists*. 4 vols. London: R. Hett.

Passmore, John (1951) *Ralph Cudworth: an interpretation*. Cambridge: Cambridge University Press; (1990) reprinted, Bristol: Thoemmes.

Ponnelle, Louis (1932) *St. Philip Neri and the Roman Society of his Times*. Kerr, R.F. trans. London: Sheed & Ward.

Preyss, C.R (1989) *Joseph von Fraunhofer, Optiker, Erfundner, Pionier*. Weilheim: OB.

Salmon, J.H.M. (1969) *Cardinal de Retz*. London: Weidenfeld and Nicholson.

Silber, Kate (1976) *Pestalozzi: The Man and His Work*. fourth ed. New York: Schocken Books.

Sullivan, J.P. (1991) *Martial, the Unexpected Classic: A Literary and Historical Study*. Cambridge and New York: Cambridge University Press.

Trevelyan, George Otto (1880) *The Early History of Charles James Fox*. Second ed. London: Longmans, Green.

— (1905) *The American Revolution*. 3 vols. London: Longmans, Green; (1965) with an intro. and notes by Morris, Richard B. London: Longmans.

Varey, J.E. (1973) *Critical Studies of Calderón's Comedias*. Franborough: Gregg International.

Vasari, Giorgio (1550, 1568) *Le vite de più eccellenti pittori*; (1850-1907) *Lives of the Most Eminent Painters, Sculptors and Architects*. 6 vols. London: H. G. Bohn; (1976) reprinted, 10 vols. New York: AMS Press.

Woodham-Smith, Cecil (1951, 1983) *Florence Nightingale, 1820-1910*. New York: Atheneum.

Weiss, John (1864) *Life and Correspondence of Theodore Parker*. 2 vols. New York: D. Appleton.

Wilson, John (1985) *Fairfax: a life of Thomas, Lord Fairfax, Captain-General of all the Parliament's forces in the English Civil War, creator and commander of the new model army*. New York: Franklin Watts.

Wehr, Gerhard (1971) *Jakob Böhme*. Hamburg: Rowohlt Taschenbuch Verlag.

Yarborough, M. C (1926) *John Horne Tooke*. New York, Columbia University Press.

INDEX